014433569 Liverpool Univ

KT-388-033

CUSTOM TEXTBOOK
MANAGING KNOWLEDGE
ULMS352

Renew Online at:
http://www.liv.ac.uk/library/patroninfo
For further assistance please ring:
Harold Cohen Library - 0151 794 5412
Sydney Jones Library - 0151 794 2678

Withdrawn from stock

University of Liverpool

MANAGING KNOWLEDGE

ULMS352

Compiled for

JASON FERDINAND

palgrave
macmillan

Selection, introduction, and editorial matter © Jason Ferdinand 2013

The Sources list on page viii constitutes a continuation of this page.

All rights reserved. No reproduction, copy or transmission of this publication may be made without written permission.

No portion of this publication may be reproduced, copied or transmitted save with written permission or in accordance with the provisions of the Copyright, Designs and Patents Act 1988, or under the terms of any licence permitting limited copying issued by the Copyright Licensing Agency, Saffron House, 6–10 Kirby Street, London EC1N 8TS.

Any person who does any unauthorized act in relation to this publication may be liable to criminal prosecution and civil claims for damages.

The authors have asserted their rights to be identified as the authors of this work in accordance with the Copyright, Designs and Patents Act 1988.

First published 2013 by
PALGRAVE MACMILLAN

Palgrave Macmillan in the UK is an imprint of Macmillan Publishers Limited, registered in England, company number 785998, of Houndmills, Basingstoke, Hampshire RG21 6XS.

Palgrave Macmillan in the US is a division of St Martin's Press LLC, 175 Fifth Avenue, New York, NY 10010.

Palgrave Macmillan is the global academic imprint of the above companies and has companies and representatives throughout the world.

Palgrave® and Macmillan® are registered trademarks in the United States, the United Kingdom, Europe and other countries.

ISBN 978–1–137–33857–0

This book is printed on paper suitable for recycling and made from fully managed and sustained forest sources. Logging, pulping and manufacturing processes are expected to conform to the environmental regulations of the country of origin.

A catalogue record for this book is available from the British Library.

A catalog record for this book is available from the Library of Congress.

10 9 8 7 6 5 4 3 2 1
22 21 20 19 18 17 16 15 14 13

Printed and bound in Great Britain by
CPI Antony Rowe, Chippenham and Eastbourne.

CONTENTS

LIST OF FIGURES

LIST OF TABLES

SOURCES

This custom publication has been compiled for use in the University of Liverpool. The chapters included are reproduced from the following works:

Chapter 1 from **MERIC S. GERTLER AND DAVID A. WOLFE: *INNOVATION AND SOCIAL LEARNING* © MICHAEL STORPER** 2002

Chapter 2 from **PHOEBE MOORE: *THE INTERNATIONAL POLITICAL ECONOMY OF WORK AND EMPLOYABILITY* © PHOEBE MOORE** 2010

Chapter 3 from **SUE NEWELL, MAXINE ROBERTSON, HARRY SCARBOROUGH AND JACKY SWAN: *MANAGING KNOWLEDGE WORK AND INNOVATION 2ND EDITION* © SUE NEWELL, MAXINE ROBERTSON, HARRY SCARBOROUGH AND JACKY SWAN** 2002, 2009

Chapter 4 from **SUE NEWELL, MAXINE ROBERTSON, HARRY SCARBOROUGH AND JACKY SWAN: *MANAGING KNOWLEDGE WORK AND INNOVATION 2ND EDITION* © SUE NEWELL, MAXINE ROBERTSON, HARRY SCARBOROUGH AND JACKY SWAN** 2002, 2009

Chapter 5 from **JOURNAL OF DATABASE MARKETING (8) 49–52© R. G. TIAN AND B. G. TOBAR** 2000

Chapter 6 from **KNOWLEDGE MANAGEMENT RESEARCH AND PRACTICE (10) 141–152 © CHRISTIAN GANZERT, DANTE P. MARTINELLI AND IVETE DELAI** 2012

Chapter 7 from **KEVIN DESOUZA: *NEW FRONTIERS OF KNOWLEDGE MANAGEMENT* © KEVIN DESOUZA AND GANESH VANAPALLI** 2005

Chapter 8 from **KNOWLEDGE MANAGEMENT RESEARCH AND PRACTICE (8) 173–188 © ZHICHANG ZHU** 2010

Chapter 9 from **HARIDIMOS TSOUKAS AND NIKOLAOS MYLONOPOULOS: *ORGANIZATIONS AS KNOWLEDGE SYSTEMS* © MARLEEN HUYSMAN** 2004

Chapter 10 from **PAUL THOMPSON AND DAVID MCHUGH: *WORK ORGANISATIONS 4TH EDITION* © PAUL THOMPSON AND DAVID MCHUGH** 1990, 1995, 2002, 2009

Every effort has been made to trace all copyright holders, but if any have been inadvertently overlooked the publishers will be pleased to make the necessary arrangements at the first opportunity.

LETTER TO THE STUDENT

DEAR ULMS 352 STUDENT:

Welcome to the customised textbook for the course! I have compiled this book to give you additional support to the weekly lecture notes and slides that are available via the module website. I have scoured the literature to find the best material that closely aligns to the ULMS 352 syllabus, giving you a bespoke text for this module. Each chapter in the book should be read in addition to my lecture notes, giving you further information of the topics discussed in lectures, as well as different perspectives on the material presented. This is NOT a textbook, but rather a reader that will provide invaluable information for you to develop your own critical appreciation of the subject matter introduced in lectures.

With so many books on 'Knowledge Management' available I put this book together to assist you in getting to grips with the subject material. As the module leader, it is very difficult for me to find a "one text fits all" book; sometimes, a textbook will include some very good chapters about one part of the module, but might not cover other areas of the syllabus at all! This is partly a result of the design of this module where I teach material that is usually only presented to postgraduate students. Even where a topic *is* included in textbooks, it might not be covered from the 'angle' I would like it to be, or might use notation that is at odds with that used in lectures. I strongly urge you to read the chapters after the lectures as the intention is to 'flesh out' what I cover in the limited time available in lectures.

I hope you will find the customised book useful. Please don't see it as a replacement for the materials I provide you with in class; rather, the book is here to *supplement* the resources that I offer, and to *enhance* your overall experience of the module.

Dr. Jason Ferdinand

INSTITUTIONS OF THE LEARNING ECONOMY[1]

COMPETITIVENESS AND THE LEARNING ECONOMY

Theories of competitiveness abound today, as do descriptive monikers for the new economy: post-industrialism, the informational economy, the knowledge-based economy, flexible specialization, post-Fordism. Though each of these labels helps in understanding some dimensions of contemporary economic activity, the logic of the most advanced forms of economic competition – those capable of generating high-wage employment – can best be described as that of learning. Those firms, sectors, regions and nations that can learn faster or better (higher quality or cheaper for a given quality) become competitive because their knowledge is scarce and therefore cannot be immediately imitated by new entrants or transferred, via codified and formal channels, to competitor firms, regions, or nations. The price-cost margin of such activities can rise, while market shares increase; the resulting rents can alleviate downward wage pressure. In this respect, such activities are promising for high wage areas. But the key defining condition of this happy picture is that these activities are only temporarily immune to relocation or to substitution by competitors. Economies must therefore be equipped to keep outrunning the powerful forces of standardization and imitation in the world economy. Once they are imitated or their outputs standardized, then there are downward wage and employment pressures. They must become moving targets by continuing to learn. Learning may enhance product differentiation at any given moment, or it may take the principal form of constantly adapting the configuration of products and processes so as to anticipate the competition.

The appellation 'learning economy' has considerable and important differences with other concepts applied to the 'new economy' of the post-1970 period. Its central emphasis is on *time* in sustaining a desirable form of imperfect competition, characterized by ongoing product-based learning. It generates temporary non-substitutability (scarcity) of key inputs, especially labor and human relations. It should be stressed that the term learning as used henceforth refers specifically to product-based technological learning (PBTL). This definition stresses the usefulness of technological change in adapting the product, which is the principal vector of competition. Learning may enhance product differentiation at any given moment, or it may take the principal form of constantly adapting the configuration of products and processes so as to *anticipate* the competition. Such product adaptation may involve many upstream forms of technological change, but in and of themselves, unsystematic forms of technological change will not be adequate to generate competitiveness. PBTL is quite different – analytically speaking – from technological imitation in production processes (such modernization being the main subject of management literatures, even those that now use fashionable terms such as 'learning', 'knowledge', or 'innovation').

The notion of a PBTL economy differs from a number of other current concepts as well. 'Informational' economy analyses suggest the existence of a new form of competition based on the collection and transmission of information, but they suffer from imprecision. Standardized and codified information and the high-tech processes and technologies used to transmit and analyze it are not the essence of contemporary economic competition: true knowledge of intellectual skill is at the heart of this process. The notion of a 'knowledge-based' economy comes closer to the target, but it also has a certain analytical imprecision, in that it fails to distinguish between knowledge as a stock – a factor of production – and as a flow – a subject of competition, which is the center of the creative and allocative dynamics of capitalism. Learning is the center of this knowledge-based competitive process and it includes not only intellectual (technical and scientific) knowledge, but also manual and implicit knowledge, and tools and organizations that accompany both of them.

'Learning' is also a more effective theoretical notion than the label 'post-Fordist', in that it affirms what is central to contemporary economic competition: not simply that it comes after the complete stability allegedly associated with mass production. It is, rather, that the nature of economic fluctuations has changed, from predictable risks to true uncertainty, and the latter is not amenable to the forms of production smoothing which were described by Galbraith and Chandler in their analyses of postwar mass production. It is thus more general than any single 'best practice' image of the contemporary economy; the particular practices that facilitate learning for competitiveness vary widely according to sector, country, and institutional context.

Finally, the notion of a learning economy rejects the central arguments of post-industrialism: learning concerns manufacturing, which continues to matter, as well as services. Learning can concern low-technology industries, which can generate high-wage jobs, as well as high-technology sectors. Moreover, all are organized in fundamentally 'industrial' ways (wage labor, capital, produced inputs, search for efficiency through divisions of labor, and so on). The industrial way of doing things, however, has entered a new phase where its content is being reshaped by the advent of learning-based competition.

PBTL activities, while central to the direct objective of generating high-wage, high-skill 'knowledge-intensive' employment, are never going to account for the majority of output or employment in any given economy. Other kinds of activities (locally serving activities, scale-based production, and so on) will continue to embody high proportions of employment. But PBTL has propulsive effects on economies in a number of ways: technological spillover effects can widen and lengthen the wealth-producing properties of learning (both upstream and downstream, and horizontally into technologically complementary activities), while the quasi-rents earned from imperfect competition can be channelled through the producing economy in the form of wages, investment and cumulative advantage.

To say that the learning economy is necessary to high-wage employment generation is not to claim that it represents a complete economic strategy. All the traditional tasks also remain necessary: balancing production and consumption; finding the right mix between export-oriented and locally serving activity; ongoing productivity improvements; and balanced reallocation of labor. But these traditional tasks of long-term economic management are by themselves no longer sufficient to generate adequate quantities of high-quality employment. That is the role of the learning economy.

THE ORGANIZATION OF THE LEARNING ECONOMY: CONVENTIONS

Coordination as the key problem of economic life and convention as a key form of coordination

Coordination among persons is the central problem of economic life. All productive activity depends on reciprocal, coherently matched actions by others which, if not forthcoming, will render our own actions inefficient or unproductive. Yet virtually all such situations of action are beset by uncertainty – each of us faces uncertainty in deciding what we should do with respect to a given set of circumstances. Part of this uncertainty is 'secondary', that is, it comes from the fact that others upon whom we depend also face uncertainty on their side, so they do not know, with assurance, what they will do; part of it comes from imperfect knowledge or communication of their intentions. All this is another way of saying that productive activity is, of necessity, a form of collective action founded on the paradox of individual actions. The question is how actors manage to get themselves into successfully coordinated forms of collective action.

The perspective which has been developed over recent years known as the 'social science of conventions' holds that coordination is achieved when actors develop appropriate conventions for doing so. The latter may be defined to include taken-for-granted mutually coherent expectations and practices, which are sometimes manifested as formal institutions and rules, often not. There are many different conventions in productive activity, for two principal reasons: because uncertainty, though pervasive, takes different forms according to the many and varied products of the economy, in light of the production technologies, markets, and resources associated with different kinds of products; and because historically constituted and geographically differentiated groups of actors bring to bear different rationalities to the uncertain situations of action they encounter.

Learning-based production systems are particular cases of conventional economies. They tend to involve particularly intense conventional underpinnings owing to the existence of rather 'non cosmopolitan' forms of knowledge. These are the cognitive foundations of learning and their effects on economic transactions. In addition, high rates of learning occur only when there are high levels of overall coherence of the many and varied conventions involved in a production system. Each of these will now be discussed in turn.

Transactions and cognition, relations and conventions

Transactions between firms and the external environment – labor markets and information-rich institutions, such as universities, trade associations and other institutions – are particularly important to learning. It is to the substantive content of transactions and their 'governance' or 'regulation' that we must look in order to penetrate deeper into the learning process itself. Yet transactions inherently involve uncertainty. Market systems are said to compensate uncertainty via the law of large numbers (with highly substitutable products or factors),[2] but this only really works when competition is perfect. In the case of learning-oriented production systems, the relations which compose the system cannot be of such large numbers and so substitutable that they function like true markets. Unlike transactions of standardized and substitutable goods, factor inputs, and information, transactions associated with the kind of learning analyzed here involve the development and – perhaps even more important – the mutually consistent interpretation of information which is not fully codified, hence not fully capable of being transmitted, understood, and utilized independently of the actual agents who are developing and using it. Stated another way, when the knowledge or skills involved have cognitive dimensions which are non-cosmopolitan (that is, non-universalist, particularistic), the transaction becomes a concrete, real *relation* and has dimensions which cannot be abstracted and thus divorced from its existence as a relation.

Moreover, beyond such tension between non-cosmopolitan technical models and meta-modeling, every kind of production system has to cope with some form of fluctuations in markets, product design, available technology and prices, which make difficult the full cognitive routinization of relations between firms, their environments and employees. Many such fluctuations, if they are to be dealt with in such a way that efficiency losses or conflicts are to be avoided, involve less than bureaucratic procedures and adjustment mechanisms, which are highly embedded in informal or partially formal rules and practices.

There are two levels of this relational quality of transactions. In the first, personal contacts, knowledge of the other, and reputation are the basis of the relation (Asanuma, 1989). In many other cases, however, transactions are not so completely idiosyncratic; they do have dimensions which can be reproduced or imitated by other agents. Most conventions are a kind of half-way house between fully personalized and idiosyncratic relations and fully depersonalized, easy to imitate relations (although even the latter do have conventional foundations, not natural or behaviorally universal foundations).

Conventional or relational transactions (henceforth C-R) affect many dimensions of production systems, but the nature and functions of such conventions differ from industry to industry, according to the nature of the product, the economic fluctuations associated with its markets and production processes, and the type of learning which is possible.[3] C-R transactions may be found in at least five principal domains: (a) interfirm 'hard' transactions, as in buyer–seller relations that involve market imperfections; (b) interfirm 'soft' transactions, as in the diffusion of non-traded information about the environment or about learning, for example through circulation of personnel through the same external labor market or through contact between producers; (c) in hard and soft intrafirm relations, as the bases for the functioning of large firms which are 'internally externalized' in the way we noted above; (d) in factor markets, especially labor markets, which involve skills that are not entirely substitutable on an interindustry or inter-regional basis, i.e., where there are industry- or region-specific dimensions to workers' skills; and (e) in economy-formal institution relationships, where universities, governments, industry associations and firms are only able to communicate and coordinate their interactions by using channels with a strong relational-conventional content.

Note that in this analysis, the learning economy and its conventional-relational foundations is not based on a stark contrast between internal ownership and externalization of production systems, or on hierarchies versus markets or external-embedded networks, but rather on the notion that all advanced, learning-based forms of economic activity involve complex transactional structures which in turn have a high conventional-relational content. Indeed, in many respects,[4] the big firm *is* a set of relations and it is such relations, as much as the physical or financial capital the firm commands, which allow it to compete and survive.

BUILDING RELATIONS: PRECEDENT, TALK AND CONFIDENCE

Relations and conventions are recursive outcomes of precedents which act as guides on action, and are reinterpreted and re-evaluated for their efficacy, and reproduced as conventions when they work to coordinate action under conditions of uncertainty. The problem is that if such precedents do not exist or are not adequate to the kind of learning system which is to be created, deliberate institutions to create them suffer from the circularity identified above. And a learning system is a complex organizational structure with many different actors and transactions between them, hence many different conventions and types of relations, built on precedents which are effectively indivisible, if the learning system is to work. It is probably no accident that considerable recent research reveals the cardinal importance of 'soft' factors such as 'civic culture' (Putnam, 1992; Doeringer and Terkla, 1990) in the performance of democratic institutions, but that few venture any policy-oriented recommendations on how the lack of such a culture could be redressed. Very unorthodox policy strategies are needed in order to break out of these labyrinthine prisons. Two of these may be labeled, respectively, 'talk' and 'confidence'.

The circular relation between public institutions and the institutionalized learning economy requires that the parties to public institutions somehow be convinced of the utility of having a public institution help in supporting the conventions and relations which make up the institutionalized learning economy. That is, they must share a convention of the utility of the public institution in some specific domain, before it can even get started. *Talk* between the parties may be one approach. Much has been said about the difference between institutions that function via a combination of loyalty and voice, versus those that rely on exit for adjustment and structure (Hirschman, 1970). Talk is upstream of voice, in that there is no institution yet existing in which the channels for voice among loyal parties are already established.

Talk refers to communicative interaction, designed not simply to transmit information and relay preferences, but to achieve mutual understanding.[5] In the case of prospective learning, information from other experiences where learning has worked (on evolutions in product markets, on suggested potentials for the parties at hand, given their current resources and skills) can be valuable as a stimulus, even though it cannot be represented as 'experimental', that is, as automatically useful or valid in other circumstances. Such information can, however, be used as the valid pretext for talk.

It can immediately be objected that if there is no tradition of communication or, worse, if there is distrust or antipathy, what is the possible basis for talk? The objection is important: it is probably difficult to stimulate talk, precisely because talk is not free; it takes time and effort, and payoffs are not evident, especially if the history of relations is bad, or relations are satisfactory for those already in them (Hirschmann, 1970). On the other hand, talk is cheap; it is not that costly and the risks are relatively low. Public institutions thus certainly have a possibility of getting low-cost talk going. Talk alone, however, is unlikely to be sufficient if such fears exist; but rather than bribing the parties with incentives (or at least doing so in more than a temporary way), it would be better to offer them some sort of reinsurance (Sabel, 1993), a safety net (at least partial) for failure, forcing them to reveal the efficacy of talk and their propensity to have confidence. Finally, talk of the sort referred to here means intensive communicative interaction. Shallow contact will not do. Thus, such talk is more likely to get going if carried out in low-cost ways where *depth* is also possible (more on this shortly).

Precedents which underpin conventions or relations inherently involve confidence, without which single events would be just that, and would have no impact on future expectations. Insofar as conventions and relations involve expectations about how others will interact with you in situations which involve some uncertainty, such confidence involves a measure of vulnerability: it is necessary for interacting agents to place themselves in a position where, should the other not follow precedent, they will suffer a real loss (Lorenz, 1992). To have confidence in what others will do is, in this sense, to trust them, not in the metaphysical sense, but in the analytical sense of making oneself vulnerable, on the basis of confidence in the precedent. But how to establish such confidence so as to bring into being precedent, relation and convention, where it does not exist or worse, where there are histories of mistrust, broken promises, antagonisms?

Talk may involve the parties in getting the ball rolling on a learning project, but it does not establish confidence in the specific sense that generates precedent and convention. Bribery through special material incentives (subsidies, and so on) provided by a public institution to private actors is likely to work only as long as the incentives last; if all actors calculate that the other actors only do what they do because of special incentives, then a convention based on incentives is established and with it, the possibility of lock-in to subsidy. Therefore, if the intention of a policy is to establish learning conventions that are not dependent on permanent subsidies, other approaches will have to be tried, or early incentives will have to be slowly replaced with precedents in other, non-subsidized forms of making oneself vulnerable.

One method of creating confidence in a sea of non-confidence is, of course, bureaucracy (hierarchy).[6] It has been found, in economic policy-making, that certain projects are amenable to isolation from the overall economic culture, by internalizing them within hierarchical bureaucracies. The military is the model. Defense procurement in the USA, or major indivisible high-technology projects such as the French TGV, are carried out by quasi-military bureaucracies with strong financial incentives and command-and-control authority. But internalization is not a solution for much of the learning economy, precisely because of the open-endedness and high degree of risk of much learning, which nobody in society wants to pay to internalize, and where the technological character of the product does not permit near-monopoly (scale economies, extreme indivisibilities, as in the case of the TGV).[7] Some other method of building confidence must be used.

Small, repeated, experimental interactions may be useful for this purpose. Experiments, as a policy device, means actually setting the parties to work in limited relations which facilitate learning and attempting to build up in complexity. It does not mean trying to prove the utility of any general, abstract solution. Most importantly, such experiments must proceed 'as if confidence existed. Small experiments build on the communicative understanding that comes from talk, asking the parties to interact by suspending their fears and doubts. The likelihood of getting the parties to act *as if* confidence existed, as the first step toward establishing real precedents, should logically rise with the degree of knowledge they have about each other. Depth is one dimension: the more I know about you in a specific domain; but breadth is another: the more I know about you in general, through collateral forms of information, the more I will be willing to enter into deep contact. These include risks of collective sanctions for violating the terms of a relation; reputation effects due to rich information flows; cultural proximity, behavioral norms which shape the anticipations of agents; and frequency of contacts in and outside of the particular business context (Haas-Lorenz, 1994). Attention has also been called to 'institutional thickness' – multiple, partially overlapping and partially redundant institutions – as a basis for breadth (Amin and Thrift, 1993).

Depth has a complicated geography, in that professional interactions, in some cases, have channels involving strong specific long-distance relations and weak local ones, above all in specialized or highly formalized (cosmopolitan) professions. Still, even in such circles, local relations often involve forms of depth not achieved in long-distance, infrequent contacts. Breadth has a more uniformly localist dimension: we are more likely to have information on someone's reputation, and to be able to validate it by interpreting it against a context with which we are intimately familiar, in a local context.[8] There is thus some relationship between localness and the mutual knowledge that should allow parties to act as if confidence existed, as a first step toward generating precedent. Talk and confidence – depth aided by confidence due to breadth – while not the province of the locality, are in some cases (certain products, certain worlds of production) more likely to succeed when they are geographically localized. This is not a hard-and-fast rule, of course, and much more theory and evidence, is needed before these relationships can be understood in a policy-relevant fashion.

THE NEW HETERODOX POLICY FRAMEWORK

There are many intricate dimensions of talk and confidence-building as the vehicles for creating precedent, relation, and convention. Who should talk? What should they talk about? What techniques should be used to facilitate such talk? What small relations should be attempted first? What kind of encouragement should be offered to get the parties to suspend skepticism? The answers will vary not only according to the kind of world which talk is intended to get started, but also according to the starting point of the parties. Some very modest beginnings will be attempted in this section.

Starting points: strategic assessment

It has long been standard practice in industrial policies to carry out strategic assessments of local, regional or national possibilities (depending on the policy's target). The idea is to eliminate unreasonable goals by assessing the existing state of such factors as technological level, the labor market, infrastructure, market structure, and so on. Such analyses, in practice, vary greatly in quality, and unfortunately there is a high propensity for error, especially excessive optimism (since the assessments are usually paid for by agencies with a vested interest in being in the policy business). Critics of industrial policy claim that this is inherent to such policies, but such skepticism is unwarranted, since there are also examples of excellent strategic assessments having led to wise decisions (examples include French high-speed trains; numerical controls developed by the US Army; the Japanese semiconductor industry as guided by MITI's strategic plan) (Ergas, 1992).

Simplifying, we can say that in the 1960s, it was possible for many European countries to carry out strategic assessment based on a standard factor input-cost method. The question to be answered was: what factor inputs do we need to create so as to be combined into an industry at something close to world best practice; and how much will it cost in the national context? In the context of rapid world, and especially European, economic expansion, the main consideration for efficiency was simply to assess whether the industry could find a market enabling it to enjoy optimal scale economies, and in that context, to implement state-of-the-art production technology. Oftentimes, *filière* (commodity chain) analysis was applied to maximize the 'local content' of the target industry in the national or regional space (Salomon, 1985).

The demands placed on strategic assessment in the context of the learning economy have become vastly more complex than in the 1960s, but the techniques of assessment have not caught up. It would no longer be possible, for example, to use the same method the French employed to plan Fos-sur-Mer today, because world capacity in virtually every major sector is much closer to saturation, and there is no comfortable time lag during which policy can simply copy the best of what is being done elsewhere. The Brazilians learned this with their market protection law for computers; though it has had some considerable positive effects, it has absolutely failed to encourage competitive computer-making in that country, leaving them generations behind the state of the art (Schmitz and Cassiolato, 1992). Any strategic assessment carried out today must use the existing starting point for the economy in question, but the goal of the policy has to be to catch up somehow to a moving target, a target which will move during the period in which the policy is getting started.

The product as the central unit of reasoning

Strategic assessment has characteristically been organized around the concept of sector: can we build a computer *industry* or a shipbuilding *industry*? The advent of the learning economy means that standard sectoral-filière assessments are no longer adequate to the task. Competition via learning takes place around real products and products do not correspond necessarily to industries-filières. The majority of output of our economies is intermediate goods, and social and spatial divisions of labor create all manner of organizational clusters in the economy which do not correspond to final output sectors, or even to the grand (and now crude) distinctions between consumer and producer goods. Some of the most significant such clusters have to do with cognate intermediate products that go to very different final output sectors; they also have to do with products which have little concrete resemblance but have parallel or convergent technological trajectories, or technological complementarities.

The upshot is that the principal unit of assessment has to be the product or a technological space of products (the latter defined by spillovers, complementarities and evolutionary dynamics). This does not mean that traditional sectoral analysis is ignored. Success in a given product generally depends on the existence of a production system which extends upstream and downstream of that product in a filière, or spills over to complementary technological spaces; but this is, from an industrial policy perspective, a tactic appropriate in some cases, not a universal goal.[9]

Developmental starting points

Countries and regions have different starting points: the size of the market; the current technological, infrastructural and knowledge endowments of the society and economy; the generic image of the country or region; underlying relationships between groups and especially between organized interests; the existing stock of firms and interlinkages between them; and the nature and effectiveness of public administration. Three standard approaches to starting points can be viewed with extreme caution in light of the analysis advanced here.

The first is to reason in terms of grand categories of starting points, the principal ones of which are: big wealthy technologically endowed regions/countries; small, wealthy, technologically endowed places; big less developed or latecomer countries; small, less developed or latecomer ('less favored' in the current EU jargon) countries; and, underdeveloped/poor countries/regions. These categories have some descriptive utility, but they do not lead anywhere in particular with respect to strategies for product-based technological learning. Their principal categories – size and technology endowments – are most relevant to big, capital- and technology-intensive industries, but even there, many small, rich countries have apparently broken the size rule (Holland with Philips, Sweden with Ericsson) and many big countries have failed in spite of it (France with Thomson and Bull). They are instructive, but only up to a point.

The second, and preferable, approach is to reason in terms of broad categories of products. For products with low barriers to entry, the experiences of Italy and Germany may be guides. In the Italian cases, traditional skills were deployed in inter-personal industries, to serve a national market in the 1950s and early 1960s. That market was big and relatively fragmented (Becattini, 1975 and Nuti, 1989). Smaller countries do not have such big markets, however, and virtually all countries are more open to import competition today than was Italy in the early 1950s. The lesson is that such industries are likely to flourish only where (a) skills are good enough or highly focused enough that they can contribute something unique to the world market; (b) they can serve a local or national market which is unsatisfied by imports or can do so in a way which passes the indifference test: higher local prices are compensated by better tailoring to local demand (but with open markets and media, the knife-edge problem is sharper and sharper); or (c) where innovative institutional arrangements, such as specification subcontracting (Gereffi and Fonda, 1992), are used to link local producers to order-givers in a way that builds their skills and responsibilities.

For industries with high barriers to entry, whether because of traditional scale concerns or because of high investment in technology, the choice is a very stark one: either go all the way with a major technology policy designed to cover a tech-nological space (for example, Airbus, the Japanese semiconductor policy, US military procurement), or target particular subsectors but still with potential for developing spillovers. It is likely that, in any country, big multinational partners will be necessary and substantial commitments of local resources over long time periods be required. The only strategies likely to succeed in the latter case are those where technological branching points (for example, which model of high-definition television? which system for transmitting mobile telephone calls?) are at hand, and where the risk is taken to develop along one branch rather than another. The optimistic note for this strategic assessment process is that there is rarely a single best world practice for any group of products.[10] Entrants can define products and practices, and they can trace out developmental pathways that continue to redefine such products and practices.

The third approach to strategic assessment is to reason in terms of norms for countries, points toward which we want to move, away from the starting point. This leads to a developmental recipe, in terms of such things as capital institutions, tech-nological infrastructure, political and administrative institutions, entrepreneurship, and so on, which – it is said – will bring about developmental results. This is quite wrong in two respects. One is that among the successful, rich countries and regions, a great diversity of products, and hence worlds of production and accompanying economic practices and institutions, exists. They do not all follow the same rules with respect to the provision of capital, skilling of the workforce, public administration, entrepreneurship, and so on (as in Nelson, 1993). Even within given sectors, there is a plurality of successful but different models. It is a gross oversimplification, except at the most abstract level (for example, honest versus corrupt public administra-tion; schooling versus no schooling) to try to reduce the development process to a single set of general goals with respect to different starting points. The ending points will be different, too, according to the specialization of the learning economy to be created, and the worlds of production they embody (Zysman, 1994). Those ending points are defined by assessing what kind of worlds are to be created, that is, the identities and capacities for action and coordination among the participants in the production system. A critical part of the strategic assessment of what is possible in a given time and place is, of course, talk. Technocrats may be able to offer the talking parties suggestions based on the entry conditions we mentioned above, but they cannot substitute for talk among the parties who ultimately will have to 'become' the collective actor of the world of production to be developed.

The new heterodox policy framework

In recent years, the analysis of the economic performance of certain successful industrial systems has prompted inquiry into policies and institutions that could be used to institute such systems. A new heterodox policy framework has emerged. This framework, while having many branches, shares a number of features, favoring policies that are context sensitive, that is, interested in the embeddedness of industrial practices in specific contexts and regions, hence 'bottom-up' (Thrift and Amin, 1994). It is production systems-oriented rather than firm-oriented in its focus. It has a non-Cartesian element, one that accepts the diversity of underlying technological and institutional situations of different economies. In many ways, it appears well positioned with respect to the foregoing analysis. Key words include: networks, flexibility, decentralization, cooperation, research and development, human capital, technopoles, training.

The policies are heterodox because of the kinds of public goods they would provide. In standard public goods theory, 'market failures' sometimes occur and when they do, public goods can be provided to rectify them. Such public goods must have economy-wide application, that is, they must be as *generic* as possible. The new theory also calls for policy to produce public goods, but allows that these goods may be *specific* to technological spaces: it is their developmental properties (evolution along trajectories through learning) that ultimately generalize (via spillovers and complementarities) their benefits to the wider economy and society.[11] We may now summarize the varying ingredients of this cocktail in more detail.[12]

Networking
The most widely shared element of new deal economic policies is to promote networking among firms. It is held that new forms of economic competition involve high levels of vertical disintegration and that there are extensive market failures in information exchange between firms. It follows that inter-establishment and interfirm relations and networks need to be supported to enhance their efficiency. Networking concerns both big and small firms and relations between them.

Promoting technology transfer
It is widely accepted that the rates at which technologies are absorbed by firms vary widely from place to place, especially when the economic base is composed mostly of small- and medium-sized firms. As a result, publicly funded innovation and technology transfer centers are becoming favored as means to enhance the uptake of new technologies, as well as to stimulate convergence in user–producer relations, so that incremental innovation can proceed more rapidly.

Local labor markets: training and focusing institutions
In industries with high levels of industry- or region-specific skills, but also with high levels of local labor market flexibility, there can be strong negative externalities: producers will not want to invest in adequate levels of labor training for fear of losing workers once they are trained. Moreover, in the face of rapid change in labor skills, no single employer will have the wherewithal to effect the change in skill supply and lack of coordination may lead to a downward competitive spiral. Under these conditions,

public institutions that provide for industry- or region-specific labor training, for strategic changes in the direction of training, and that help workers to secure jobs in the face of flexibility in specific, regionally concentrated sectors, can attenuate the effects of market failure.

Infant industry and getting a start: pre-competitive R&D and stimulating markets

Infant industries are based on new and experimental kinds of products. The probability of generating new products is high, but product configurations have not yet settled onto an identifiable technological trajectory. High levels of risk and uncertainty exist for producers in these nascent sectors. The collective effect of waiting, however, may create a vicious circle, where everyone waits for everyone else, and the overall rate of development is thereby retarded. By the same token, nations or regions that could successfully develop a new industry may find that a delayed start (especially when another region has moved ahead of them) locks them permanently out of a promising niche in the new industry. There are potential benefits to getting an early start, in contrast to this common free rider problem. Industries, firms, regions and nations that get ahead early often retain a leading position for quite some time, and in the early years there can be significant superprofits to new products. As a result, industry-specific pre-competitive R&D policies, and other policies to stimulate regional or national (often public) markets for risky new technology products, may be called for, in addition to networking and technology transfer centers.

Entrepreneurship, especially for small firms

Another element of the emerging consensus in the heterodox framework is that good ideas only become reality when potential entrepreneurs enjoy the conditions that permit them to start up firms and survive. The conditions favoring firm formation include traditional hard factors such as access to capital markets and some soft factors such as cultural images of the entrepreneur and sanctions to failure. They also include conditions such as access to information, locational sites, rules on hiring and firing labor, and access to potential customers in other firms. Entrepreneurship policies are designed to help potential entrepreneurs overcome these difficulties, although in practice the majority of them consist of loan programs for small firms.

Service centers

In the many successful Italian industrial districts, the practice of assisting existing firms in a series of concrete ways has emerged as a key method for public support of those communities of producers. Industry service centers are particularly devoted to spreading the costs for certain kinds of resources that single firms cannot afford for themselves alone, including systematic market research, foreign marketing, technology research and, in some cases, technology sharing, and on-line electronic networking facilities. In Italian regions, especially Modena, major industrial estates for small firms have been created, where state-of-the-art flexible configurations of space are made available to firms at below-market cost, not only permitting them to modernize their facilities, but also permitting them to remain together, thus enhancing communication and networking (Brusco, 1982). Service centers have also been involved in the promotion of regional brand names (something like *appellation contrôlée* for wine, but now applied to the market identities of other kinds of products), so as to enhance their non-substitutability on national and international markets.

The heterodox framework versus other policy approaches

There is hardly consensus about this sort of policy framework. Opposed to it are those whose point of departure is the rapid global transfer and diffusion of certain forms of technology and knowledge, and the increasing costs (hence entry barriers) of carrying out cutting-edge innovation projects. Their vision is of global technology-based oligopolies in competition where any national policy would have to reinforce the status of the nation's oligopolistic actors. For the USA, for example, this would mean weakening anti-trust laws (which are deemed to have outlived their purpose), either in a soft version to promote collaboration (la Sematech) or in a hard version, to promote concentration. Complementing this, some argue for neo-mercantilist trade policies. There may, in some cases, be a role for some such policies, a subject into which it is impossible to enter here. But there is little reason to believe that alone they would generate competitive technological learning and performance: the failures of concentration policy are well documented. Such failures often have to do with the absence of links between the resulting giant firms upstream to an effective national system of innovation and downstream to an effective production community. At the most, such strategies can play a limited role in the learning economy; and in some cases they may be harmful. The heterodox policy approach is quite the opposite in that it accepts as a given the openness of the trading system, the insufficiency of size alone, and in some cases, the disadvantages of concentration for competitive learning.

Another approach to policy is that of strengthening systems of innovation (SI) (Nelson, 1993). SI is also a heterodox neo-institutionalist approach to technological innovation. There are many different versions of SI extant at the present time. Almost all (except that of Edquist and Lundvall, 1993) share an emphasis on formal institutions, on scientific-engineering skills, and on the national level of formal institution-building. The major non-public institutions are firms and research laboratories; the major public ones are universities, government laboratories and procurement programs, and technical education. The heterodox approach differs in emphasis, although it is not in contradiction. The emphasis here is on: the plurality of worlds of production and innovation (science and engineering is only a part of the problem); 'small' processes of coordination via convention and relations; the circularity of conventions, relations and institutions; and hence the necessity for a significant meso-economic dimension to policy as well as a systematic national level.

THE DANGERS OF ORTHODOXY

The policy approach described above, like any set of measures that attempts to take a complex analysis of economic reality and create a policy formula based on it, runs the danger of missing its target. To avoid problems in the transformation of the current analysis into policy, both technical and substantive reductionism must be avoided. This analysis of learning is not inherently about small firms, networking, localism, or flexibility, per se; it is rather about adaptive technological learning in a territorial context. The proper goals of such policies are:

(a) for traditional or small-scale intermediate products, ongoing adaptation of products and processes, especially through product differentiation or moves up the price-quality curve, so as to respond to ongoing and inevitable entry by competitors, whether large firms or other regional systems; and

(b) for scale-intensive or new technology products, moves along the technological frontier, where that frontier is unknown or unknowable. The entire substantive thrust of any new-deal economic policy must be geared to these substantive goals, as specified in light of particular products and their worlds of production to be developed. New-deal economic institutions are only means to these ends.

The real danger exists, as theory now becomes packaged into policy, that such policies will become detached from this substantive content and necessary procedure of building convention, and instead devolve into mechanical formulas and self-referential content. Three particular tendencies are worrisome.

From framework to formula

Networking is now frequently discussed in policy literature as a sort of recipe for any form of communication between firms. This has no necessary relation to the precise conventional forms of interfirm relations which underlie successful worlds of production. Networking has to be a means to realizing a common developmental pathway characterized by learning. The content and shape of a network, as well as the degree of external network, will differ according to the products to be made and the specific way productive activity becomes a world of production.

The provision of *services to firms*, in substantive terms, represents a strong departure from traditional public goods provision. In the latter, public goods are provided where markets fail, due to the free rider problems that come when such goods are non-exclusive. As a result, public goods are provided which have non-specific assets: they are non-exclusive. But the provision of concrete, real services to real worlds of production involves public goods with asset specificities and, hence, a certain measure of exclusivity. It will not do to disguise service centers as mere providers of any old, generic public goods, and yet this is the tendency in the literature. Another danger is that service provision will be turned into a pretext for doing almost anything that supports local firms (especially the politically popular 'small' firms) with no substantive criteria for assessing the purpose of these services. Indeed, some services can have perverse effects. Modernization services, for example, can be used by some firms to distance themselves from local competitors and thereby to 'exit' from their local interdependencies. Many technological extension services are premised on the principle of survival for the fittest, not collective learning. Initially positive effects can then be followed by catastrophe (for example, the French *plan textile*). Services for learning in other words, only work when the goal is clear and when the services are consistent with the conventions of the world of production to be assisted, as understood by the participants themselves through talk.

Perhaps the most pernicious element of the current policy debate is the category of *small firms* as a goal. Small firms do play essential roles in many successful worlds of production. But smallness is not a goal, nor is there necessarily any commonality among firms merely because they are small. A small firm in a high-technology industry, whose products are evaluated according to their scientific-technological content, has virtually nothing to do with a small firm subcontractor to a major garment producer: their underlying conventions of work, product markets, interfirm relations, and so on, are totally different.

Finally, the category of *localism* has become important in the heterodox framework, because of its theoretical recognition of the agglomeration and territorial embeddedness or specificity of conventions in many learning-based production systems. The problem is that localism cannot be an end in itself: the territoriality of relations that go into learning is, in all cases, highly complex. If the strength of a particular local economy (one that corresponds to the jurisdictions of public institutions) is to be promoted, it is better to focus on learning and its conventional underpinnings than directly on localism. At its worst, localism could lead to an artificial closing off of the production system, reducing its flexibility and hindering the development of conventions that go beyond local borders but ultimately strengthen the local economy.

The dangers of cooperation

Nowhere is the danger greater than in the sudden stress on 'cooperation' as a key to world-class economic performance. Cooperation was, correctly, discovered as a dimension of certain kinds of highly successful industrial systems, principally in Italy and Germany, and its discovery has prompted a necessary corrective to the stress on competitive atomistic interaction of most economic thinking. But it is fully contradictory with the notions of sectoral diversity and the plurality of ways of successfully organizing modern production (the plurality of 'worlds' in other words), to hold up cooperation as a model for behavior in all cases. There are worlds of production where particular, conventionally rooted forms of cooperative coordination can be useful, but there is no general model of cooperation for all industries in all places.

Boilerplate approaches to the learning economy

The transformation of this new heterodox thinking about economic development into an all-purpose formula is dangerous as well. Porter's (1990) 'diamond' of development is perhaps the best known and certainly the most widely employed of such policy formulas. The framework has two main problems. The first is that it is superficial: for the most part, it restates the obvious *outcomes* of success as observed in many places (the four points of the diamond). It then 'reverse engineers' these outcomes, claiming that they were causes of success. But of course this does not follow. Attempting to create success by installing outcomes has always been the downfall of industrial policies; the fact that Porter has based his model on an admittedly more sophisticated analysis of real world experiences does not prevent the result from being equally prone to failure. Second, by abstracting across a wide variety of cases, that is, preferring an extensive form of reasoning to an intensive one, it turns a great diversity of experiences into a single formula, with potentially great errors (for example, all success is based on high levels of domestic intrasectoral competition, and so on). The record already shows that 'intangible factors play a central role in distinguishing cases of success in the new policy framework from dramatic failures' (Doeringer and Terkla, 1990).

Scientism and prescriptive rationality[13]

Many of the problems described above stem from the tendency of analysts to seek determinate causes of industrial performance and for policy-makers to extend that via prescriptive rationality. One of the greatest ironies observable at the present time is the transformation of an analysis explicitly inspired by 'non-Cartesian' and 'context and contingency sensitive' epistemologies into an all-purpose technocratic formula for development. The 'architecture' of a production system and of public, organized institutions is only interesting insofar as it helps understand the patterns of action which constitute production; the objects (technologies, tools, infrastructures) are themselves the outcomes of human practices and exist to facilitate such practices; rules, skills, and formal roles depend, for their efficacy on the identities of agents. The problem with much policy-oriented analysis is that it tends to reduce its vision to architecture, objects, rules, skills and roles, and to prescribe changes in them. Not only does this ignore the substantive object of analysis, but by attempting technocratically to prescribe behavior for the agents of the system, it has a high risk of failure.

The entrepreneurial state, 'Laboratories of Democracy'

The third great danger is that heterodoxy will be used as a pretext for a neo-conservative retreat of the national state from its appropriate duties, and the installation of a system of ferocious and destructive inter-regional competition. In recent years, the turn to the region in the United States was stimulated essentially by a retreat of the federal government from the economic development field. In a nation where industrial and regional policy have always been quite weak by comparison to Western Europe, this left a policy vacuum which many states and localities attempted to fill. In some cases, small tentative steps toward the support of regionally based clusters of firms have been taken, and certain elements of the policy framework described above have been set into place. But in many of the American cases, they resemble only superficially the framework discussed here; instead, what has been done is to set up public-sector centers for delivering services to individual firms on a local basis (often 'pay as you go'), where the collective and coordinative aspect of world-building has no place in the effort. These 'laboratories of democracy' (Osborne, 1992) are often nothing more than effective privatization and atomization of industrial policy (Sternberg, 1992). And recent federal programs, notably the Clinton Technology Policy, duplicate these problems by making federal resources available only via proposal-based inter-firm competition (Storper, 1995).

The attempted devolution and decentralization of industrial policy in certain areas of the European Union has a different starting point, of course. Many European nations have long had more activist policy frameworks and highly centralized states. It has become imperative to allow more initiative at regional level. France, for good reason, is now more than a decade into her experiment with administrative and policy decentralization. Still the results are mixed, in part because formal devolution of decision-making does not in and of itself lead to the creation of capacities for action at the regional or local level.[14]

It is essential that such European experiments not lead to the outcome which is already observable in the United States. There, a more pernicious form of localism in economic policy is known as the 'entrepreneurial' state (Maier, 1994). The locality and its governmental agencies are viewed as collective entrepreneurs in competition with each other. In practice, this often means simply attempting competitively to lower the price of labor, taxes, and so on, so as to attract inward investment. But even when it involves such politically correct measures as stimulating firm start-ups, the ideology of interplace competition serves to block out any fruitful discussion of the need for higher levels of government to set certain ground rules (such as on interplace price competition) and to provide certain kinds of services (for example, national education policies, infrastructure, and other generic public goods). The danger exists that the European Union's principle of subsidiarity will be reduced to savage interplace price-cost competition.

This points out that subsidiarity in economic policy needs to have certain kinds of boundaries, and that what is to be built at subnational levels is not entrepreneurial states, but what we might call – taking our cue from the East Asian development literature – 'developmental states'. These distinctly activist, strategically oriented, systematic state efforts differ entirely from the notion of state entrepreneurialism and are much more consistent with the analysis developed in this paper (Wade, 1990).

SUMMARY

At the end of this analysis, it will be helpful to draw the threads together. The institutions of the new economy consist of a complex circular relationship between specific, convention-bound, learning-oriented production systems which are themselves institutions, and various kinds of formal, organized institutions, notably firms, public governmental institutions, and other organizations such as universities, unions, and trade associations. Any policy framework which involves the creation of public institutions to build or sustain the institution of the learning economy has to be based on ways to cut into this circle, and must reject the traditional logic of 'public institution' versus 'private non-institution'.

We identified four major steps in the economic strategy in the new economy. The first is strategic assessment. The technical dimension is the determination of what kinds of products, where the product is the essential unit of analysis, and not the sector or the input–output system, are susceptible to being mastered in the economy at hand, where mastery is defined as ongoing competitive technological learning. There is a complex interaction between the product as a technology – a knowledge field – and its associated process technology. Just as products evolve through learning, so do processes, and both have dynamic parallels and complementarities which spill over their boundaries at a given moment.

However, strategic assessment is not only a technocratic task. Learning depends on the conventions which define collective identities of the actors in the production system by giving them access to a common context of coordination. Without this context, learning will fail, no matter how good the hardware is. The context cannot be produced by plans, nor bought by subsidies; in order to know whether the strategy is possible, it has to be known whether there is any reason to expect actors to go along. The circular relationship described here can only be broken into by talk. Talk is a necessary element in, and component of, strategic assessment.

The second step is the definition of the capacities for action and identities of actors which are associated with the world(s) of production to be assisted by policy. Each world – a specific, local or national concretization of Interpersonal, Market, Intellectual, or Industrial action and coordination – involves conventions, which coordinate interfirm relations, markets, labor markets, and so on. These are the substantive goals, the specific (and differentiated) end points of policy. They, too, can only be defined through the difficult and clumsy exercise of talk, in concert with analysis.

The third step is the implementation of specific versions of heterodox meso-economic policies, whose content is defined by combination of technical assessment and social process, especially talk. The substantive method of heterodox policies is not to attempt the construction of learning-based worlds of production from whole cloth, but rather to try to create precedents which build confidence and hence make possible the deepening and widening of conventions. Small experiments are one logical way to proceed.

Finally, and only at the end of this long and 'soft' process, can the need for further formal institution-building be realistically assessed and practically undertaken, the latter on the basis of confidence-precedent (and hopefully success in learning), and consequently emerging collective identities. There are other dimensions of formal institutions, that is, having to do with macro-competition rules, banking, education, and so on, which are not considered in this analysis. They, too, require links to the substantive concerns elaborated here. For example, education policies in different countries favor very different kinds of economic action, and push them down different routes of specialization. Some decisions about institutional structures at these levels can be taken with respect to strictly generic concerns (universal values of the society; inputs to any kind of modern economic activity); but a surprising number involve more concrete visions of the particular kind of productive economy and collective action which is desired. Here we have merely laid out the fragments of this way of thinking about the problem – the problem of constructing coherent conventions and frameworks of action in the learning economy.

NOTES

1. The author wishes to acknowledge the support of the Institute of Geography at the University of Copenhagen, and in particular John Jorgensen, during the time this paper was prepared. Thanks are also due to the Danish Fulbright Commission, directed by Mette Skakkebaek.
2. This is, of course, the position taken by contemporary institutional economics, where uncertainty is a result of universally opportunistic behavior, generating moral hazards, which are only overcome either by authority (internalization) or the law of large numbers (Williamson, 1985).
3. This is developed in detail in Storper and Salais (1997).
4. *See* the papers in Grabher (ed.) (1993).
5. Lundvall (1990) relies in part on Habermas (1976).
6. This is the basic assumption of modern transactions-cost economics: *see above*, note 2.
7. We have a detailed study of French successes and failures in Storper and Salais (1997), Ch. 6.
8. In general, the literature treats the function of reputation as a form of cross-check on behavior. It multiplies the probability of getting caught; and multiplies the consequences of getting caught. *See* the papers in Gambetta (ed.) (1988).
9. This is meant as a deliberate critique of the 'diamond' found in Porter (1990).
10. Even Porter (1990) admits this. *See also* Zysman (1994) and Wade (1990).
11. I argue this point in greater detail in Storper (1995); a similar argument may be found in Romer (1993).
12. What follows comes largely from: Storper and Scott (1995).
13. Thrift and Amin (1994).
14. We have a detailed analysis of decentralization in Storper and Salais (1997), Ch. 11.

REFERENCES

Amin, A. and N. Thrift (1993) 'Globalization, Institutional Thickness, and Local Prospects', *Revue d'Economie Régionale et Urbaine*, 3, pp. 405–30.

Arrow, KJ. (1951) *Social Choice and Individual Values,* Cambridge: Cambridge University Press.

Asanuma, B. (1989) 'Manufacturer-Supplier Relationships and the Concept of Relationship-Specific Skill', *Journal of the Japanese and International Economies*, 3, pp. 1–30.

Becattini, G. (1975) *Lo Sviluppo Economico della Toscana,* Florence: Guaraldi.

Brusco, S. (1982) 'The Emilian Model: Productive Decentralization and Social Integration', *Cambridge Journal of Economics*, 6, 167–84.

Buchanan, J. and G. Tullock (1965) *The Calculus of Consent,* Ann Arbor: University of Michigan Press.

Dei Ottati, G. (n.d.) 'Prato, 1944–1963: Reconstruction and Transformation of a Local System of Production', Florence, University of Florence, manuscript.

Doeringer, P. and D. Terkla (1990) 'How Intangible Factors Contribute to Economic Development: Lessons from a Mature Local Economy', *World Development*, 18, pp. 1295–1308.

Dosi, G., K. Pavitt and L. Soete (1990) *The Economics of Technical Change and International Trade,* New York: New York University Press.

Edquist, C. and B.-Å. Lundvall (1993) 'Comparing the Danish and Swedish Systems of Innovation', in R.R. Nelson (ed.) *National Innovation Systems,* New York: Oxford University Press, pp. 167–84.

Ergas, H. (1992) 'The Failures of Mission-Oriented Technology Policies'. Paper delivered to the international conference on 'Systems of Innovation', Bologna, October.

Ettlinger, N. (1994) 'The Localization of Development in Comparative Perspective', *Economic Geography*, vol. 70 (2), pp. 144–66.

Gambetta, D. (ed.) (1988) *Trust,* Oxford: Basil Blackwell.

Gereffi, G. (1995) 'State Politics and Industrial Upgrading in East Asia', *Revue d'Economie Industrielle*, 71, pp. 79–91.

Gereffi, G. and S. Fonda (1992) 'Regional Paths of Development', *Annual Review of Sociology*, 18, pp. 419–48.

Grabher, G. (ed.) (1993) *The Embedded Firm,* London: Routledge.

Haas-Lorenz, S. (1994) 'Apprentissage et proximité géographique dans une perspective volution-niste', doctoral thesis, University of Aix-Marseille, Faculty of Economics, Aix-en-Provence.

Habermas, J. (1976) Connaissance et Intérêt, Paris: Gallimard (orig. in German, 1968).

Hirschman, A.O. (1970) Exit, Voice and Loyalty: Responses to Decline in Firms, Organizations, and States, Cambridge, MA: Harvard University Press.

Keohane, R. (1993) 'International Institutions: Two Approaches', in J.G. Ruggie (ed.) Multilateralism Matters: the Theory and Praxis of Institutional Form, New York: Columbia University Press.

Krugman, P. (1990) Rethinking International Trade, Cambridge, MA: MIT Press.

Leamer, E.E. (1994) 'Third World Imports and the Unskilled in the West', UCLA Conference on the World Trading System after the Uruguay Round, December, UCLA Center for International Relations, Los Angeles.

Lorenz, N. (1992) 'Trust, Community, and Co-operation: towards a Theory of Industrial Districts', in M. Storper and A.J. Scott (eds) Pathways to Industrialisation and Regional Development, London: Routledge.

Lundvall, B-Å. (1990) 'From Technology as a Productive Factor to Innovation as an Active Process', Colloquium, Networks of Innovators, Montreal, 1–3 May.

Maier, M. (1994) 'Post Fordist City Politics', in A. Amin (ed.) Post-Fordism: a Reader, Oxford: Basil Blackwell.

Nelson, R. (ed.) (1993) National Systems of Innovation, New York: Oxford University Press.

North, D. (1981) Structure and Change in Economic History, New York: Norton.

Nuti, F. (1989) 'I Distretti dell'Industria Manifatturiera', Rome: report to the CNR, National Research Council of Italy.

Olson, M. (1971) The Logic of Collective Action: Public Goods and the Theory of Groups, Cambridge, MA: Harvard University Press.

Olson, M. (1990) 'Toward a Unified View of Economics and Other Social Sciences', in K. Alt and Shepsle (eds) Perspectives on Positive Political Economy, Cambridge: Cambridge University Press.

Osborne, D. (1992) Laboratories of Democracy, Cambridge, MA: Harvard Business School.

Patel, P. and K. Pavitt (1991) 'Large Firms in the Production of the World's Technology: an Important Case of Non-Globalization', Journal of International Business Studies, First Quarter, pp. 1–21.

Petit, P. (1993) 'Are Full Employment Policies Pass?', paper delivered to the Annual Meeting of the American Economics Association, Anaheim, CA.

Porter, M. (1990) The Competitive Advantage of Nations, London: Macmillan – now Palgrave Macmillan.

Putnam, R. (1992) Making Democracy Work, Princeton, NJ: Princeton University Press.

Rip, A. (1991) 'Meta-modeling and Technological Change', paper delivered to OECD TEP Conference, La Villette, Paris.

Romer, P. (1993) 'Implementing a National Technology Strategy with Self-Organizing Industry Investment Boards', paper prepared for the June 1993 Meeting of the Brookings Panel on Microeconomics, Washington DC.

Sabel, C. (1993) 'Constitutional Ordering in Historical Context', in F. Scharpf (ed.) Games in Hierarchies and Networks, Boulder: Westview Press.

Salomon, J.J. (1985) 'Le Gaulois, le Cowboy et le Samourai', report to the Ministry of Industry and Research, Paris.

Sayer, A. and R. Walker (1992) The New Social Economy, Oxford: Basil Blackwell.

Schmitz, H. and J. Cassiolato (eds) (1992) High Tech for Industrial Development: Lessons from the Brazilian Experience in Electronics and Automation, London: Routledge.

Sternberg, E. (1992) Photoelectronics and Industrial Policy, Albany: SUNY Press.

Storper, M. (1991) Industrialization, Economic Development and the Regional Question in the Third World: from Import Substitution to Flexible Production, London: Pion.

Storper, M. (1995) 'Regional Technology Coalitions: an Essential Dimension of National Technology Policy', Research Policy, vol. 24 (6), pp. 895–912.

Storper, M. and R. Salais (1997) Worlds of Production: the Action Frameworks of the Economy, Cambridge, MA: Harvard University Press.

Storper, M. and A.J. Scott (1995) 'The Wealth of Regions: Market Forces and Policy Imperatives in Local and Global Context', Futures (summer).

Thrift, N. and A. Amin. (1994) 'Socioeconomics, Democracy and Economic Policy', paper presented to the Innis Centennial Conference on 'Technology Regions and Policy', Toronto, September.

Tyson, L. (1987) *Creating Advantage: Strategic Policy for National Competitiveness*, Berkeley: BRIE.

Wade, R. (1990) *Governing the Market: Economic Theory and the Role of Government in East Asian Industrialization*, Princeton: Princeton University Press.

Williamson, O. (1985) *The Economic Institutions of Capitalism*, New York: The Free Press.

Wolfe, D. (1994) 'The Institutions of the New Economy', Ottawa: Carleton University, Dept. of Political Science, manuscript.

Zysman, J. (1994) *How Institutions Create Historically-Rooted Trajectories of Growth*, Oxford: Oxford University Press.

Chapter

2

WORK, EMPLOYABILITY, SUBJECTIVITY

This chapter explores a variety of literatures that deal with the question of the meaning of 'work', and I look at the ways that people are impacted by changes to how work is viewed, and how these views are processed by governments that influence particular political strategies intending to create employable, objectified subjects. I compare traditional views to more contemporary, modern, and even postmodern conceptualisations, to identify how common sense, discourses, and the hegemonies of ideas in a Gramscian understanding take shape in conjunction with social change and assumptions of human capabilities in the new and 'flexible' world of work.

The analysis and comparison of cross-national education and employment policy is particularly important in the context of a contemporary crisis of capital. Starting in 2008, the world was faced with an international economic crisis with unprecedented implications for the sustainability of capitalism as a global economic model. Although Europe had had an economic slump in the 1980s and East Asia experienced a regional crisis from 1997, a truly international crisis had not emerged with the same implications for the operation of the modern global financial architecture since its first incarnation at Bretton Woods in 1944. The November 2008 forecast set by the IMF indicated that global unemployment was going to rise to 6.1 per cent in 2009, as compared to 5.7 per cent in 2007 (ILO Jan 2009). In 2009 in the UK, unemployment rose to 6.3 per cent.[1] In South Korea, the rate of joblessness rose from 3.1 per cent to 3.3 per cent from November to December 2008, which was the only contraction within the previous three years for job growth. A sharp rise in applications for unemployment benefit was seen in January 2009 in South Korea. Also in January, 128,000 people went on the books for 'unemployment insurance', which was the biggest figure since 1996, just before the Asian economic crisis (AsiaPulse 2009). Singapore enjoyed five years of a consistent fall in unemployment from 2003 to 2008, during which time unemployment fell from 4.6 per cent to 2.1 per cent (Index Mundi 2009). However, Singapore was the first of the Asian economies to face a recession in the context of the global economic crisis, and in January 2009 the Finance Minister Tharman Shanmugaratnam announced that a stimulus package of USD13 billion would be applied to the Singaporean economy, since the recession had hit most of the sectors of Singaporean industry and manufacturing. Non-oil domestic exports fell by 7.9 per cent in 2008 particularly in the final months of that year, and the number of new jobs dropped by 26,900 net in the fourth quarter. Gross domestic product (GDP) growth dropped continuously over the year, and unemployment rose to 2.6 per cent (*International Herald Tribune* 2009). The rate of unemployment in Singapore was predicted to rise to 4 per cent and Singapore's National Wages Council announced that layoffs would be significantly higher in 2009, and advised firms to apply freezes or cuts on wages to save jobs (Lim 2009). International symptoms of the recession began to affect workers first, which is typical of economic contraction, but this recession was perhaps different from any previous downturn.

Neoliberalism is a peculiar offspring of liberalism, one that aims to stalk and control an increasing arena of social experience, and these intentions begin to invade policy that in turn affects day-to-day lives. This chapter sets up a theoretical framework to understand the use of a term which has become critical to discourse affecting work, employment and the workforce, or 'employability'. The terms 'employability', lifelong learning, and skills and competencies are increasingly seen in labour market policy reports and various binding statements across the three case studies identified in this book. These concepts are very much *subjectively* derived states of being and mind, and diverge dramatically from employ*ment*, and begin to affect people's experiences of the world and most importantly, subjectivities.

Both the notion of employability and, at its core, the idea of *work*, are negotiated, in the post-industrial era and in the context of our new 'knowledge based' global economy. Labour process theorists, sociologists, and psychologists have researched the evolution and significance of the concept of work as it has emerged in various epochs of specific production models and management strategies as well as production relations. The first section of this chapter looks at how *labour* has become *work*, and how this has impacted people's ability to have autonomy over their lives in a variety of guises. My argument is that work has taken a different significance for people with regard to identity formation in the climate of consumerism and rhetorical freedom of choice that has less to do with society and the family and more to do with individualism and accumulation. A seeming shift to new forms of work and creative 'play-bour' (in place of 'labour'),[2] usually discussed in the context of work in the entertainment industries, is heralded as emancipatory and generally liberating for workers. However, I argue that there is not yet an emancipatory angle to this new world of work stemming from the Quality of Working Life (QWL) model in the 1970s and emerging into the current KBE. Reasons for this lack of fulfilment of the 'promise' for workers have to do with what is done with the product of 'play-bour'. While workers cannot expect a guaranteed wage within this new world of work (Gorz 1999; Braverman 1974; Burawoy 1979; etc.), people are still expected to produce. Production or 'product', whether it is a form of commodified cognitive output or traditional physical items, is viewed and measured in light of others' production and presumably can be used to alter the employee relationship depending on its measure, but increasingly, at the macro-level people's productiveness with relation to people's employability and competency, is also viewed in light of company productivity and international competitiveness. So, simultaneous to the government-led skills revolution that places responsibility for workers' employability directly into the hands of those workers through personal self-management and lifelong learning abilities, workers are ironically being held accountable for nations' economies and economic health. Therefore the position of the worker is not only unstable according to supposedly immutable conditions of capital but, increasingly, is unstable unless personality and drive are freely available to all from some unknown resource found within subjective congruities.

The second section of this chapter then looks at the implications this has for the changing meaning of what it is now to be 'employable', in the context of the rapidly changing world of work and the new expectations of enterprise to become involved in increasing avenues of social life and society's institutions, such as education. To be generally 'employable', but not necessarily 'employed', means that people are required to take a new form of subjectivity and self-awareness as well as responsibility for learning and self-education in the form of lifelong learning. The study of employability as a newly relevant form of subjectivity is an under-researched area. The significance of its meaning is often used in such a way that it appears authors would like this idea to be taken for granted. However, as globalisation becomes an increasingly questioned idea in the context of the Asian economic crisis of 1997, and the global recession starting in 2008, and as people find themselves increasingly out of work for reasons that are attributed to a global problem, people's self awareness and identities are becoming increasingly removed from their physical workplaces. If people were identified previously by the work they did, now they are being forced to understand themselves as workless people, but still as labourers in the wider sense with a growing responsibility for their own identity creation as employable subjects.

So the chapter identifies 'employability' as a form of subjectivity that is intended to complement the contemporary, post-Fordist interpretations of work, work that is apparently more self-managed and creative and 'immaterial', but that has not yet eliminated the government and management structures that tend very successfully to undermine and control workers. In fact, the 'employability' revolution of subjectivities is one that governments have tried to incorporate and manipulate as part of a supposedly commonly accepted discourse, by way of the 'skills revolutions' they have initiated. So within this chapter I take an interdisciplinary approach to understand the ideas I have outlined, with the intention of looking at how skills revolutions are in fact passive revolutions in the Gramscian sense, in our current world of less-measurable labour time. In this sense, this seeming global 'skills revolution' is elite-led.

LABOUR AND WORK

'The notion of work [*travail*] is an invention of modernity or, more exactly, of industrial capitalism' (Gorz 1994: 53). Indeed, work only becomes work as we know it today in the context of commodity production. After people did not toil, drudge, construct, prepare (ibid.), or attend to subsistence production in villages there was no measure for production that could be used for all outputs and for all types of workers, in the same way that management had thought during the Fordist era. Hannah Arendt's distinction between labour and work is reflected in Gorz's insights. These authors are not ashamed to point out that Marx and Marxists paid/pay scant attention to the difference between manual and intellectual work, and focus on relations of production in a way that does not allow for historical updates. Rose points out that 'in nineteenth century capitalism – in mine, mill, and manufactory – work seems easy to picture in these terms. But over the course of the present century, types of work and conditions of working have radically changed' (Rose 1999: 56). This is particularly the case in the twenty-first century, during which time we are seeing the rise of post-industrial forms of labour and organisations of work, and increased flexibilisation and precarious forms of labour on the rise. In earlier times, that which was performed in the household was the basis for survival, and 'work' was considered a very negative, intrusive, and annoying matter to be avoided. Perhaps this view is romantic and gendered in a way that can no longer be accepted in the feminist line of reasoning. But, nonetheless, it allows insight into the transformation of how activities can be perceived in the different historical periods.

Arendt, and later Gorz, reasoned that work becomes a separate category of activity when production is no longer solely for the self, but fulfils a wider function for society, and is necessarily seen as having value outside the labour in and of itself. Work is done in the public eye, and is done for the greater good of society rather than private individuals. These two characteristics were apparently always the defining points of work, but one more has been added with the rise of industrial capitalism:

> Work must have a recognized social validity or value, and this will be attested by the possibility of exchanging it for a determinate quantity of any other kind of work whatever – or, in other words, by the possibility of selling it, of presenting it as a commodity. It is by its commodity form that it becomes social work 'in general', abstract work, participation in the overall social process of production. (Ibid., 54)

In the nineteenth century, a class of skilled industrial workers emerged, and 'work' took on a creative dimension, as the supposed road to prosperity and wealth, and the way to dominate nature. It is with this rise of a 'poietic' framework that work was considered to be a creative and productive act for the greater social good, an act that would ultimately provide mastery over nature. Work is supposedly now only to be carried out publicly, thus underplaying all traditional private sphere production, despite the fact that reproduction is clearly as relevant and necessary for the survival of social life.

As workers become increasingly skilled and management structures increasingly place emphasis on such activities as team working, mobile working, and flexibility (more often seen than flexisecurity, a set of policies applied for the Scandinavian workforces), the private sphere for some forms of work and production becomes public. The question becomes obvious: how does one separate *work* from free time, leisure time, and genuine creativity? Gorz talks about work as production in the contemporary workplace as a 'false work'. This new inheritance of the model of *work-as-poiesis* is being applied to new forms of work such as are seen within the service industry. Gorz points out that this work has very little to do with the types of work conducted by 'toolmakers, boilermakers, metal-turners, masons and rolling-mill workers' (1994: 56).

Rose (1999) is concerned with the changed face of work and the impact this has on workers' subjectivities. He outlines the way in which transformations to the 'conception, organisation, and regulation of work and the worker over this century involve relations between many aspects of thought and practice ... human technologies, and the techniques of the self have been brought into being by [these] new ways of thinking and acting on the economy, the workplace and the worker' (1999: 60). Particular networks of power were evident within Taylorist design and later post-Fordist management structures. Like Yahoda (1932/2002), Rose writes that, in times past, work gave people a sense of self-fulfilment, social identity, and personal satisfaction. However, a shift from the Protestant work ethic emerged particularly in the 1980s and we no longer see ourselves as merely producers, but we are now consumers with a choice of work and professions. We can choose how to live our lives, we can even choose our own 'selves' from a range of choices set out for us through various media.

Work is no longer something that allows social satisfaction and a type of inclusion with origins in the family/marriage or wider social structure. It is now seen as a tool for individual identity formation. Workers are not, in this subjective appearance, simply seeking financial gain through work, but are seeking to discover themselves. There is, Rose claims, no emancipation *from* work, but there should be emancipation *in* work in our new world of work. A new management style, or perhaps movement, emerged in the 1970s called QWL, probably originating from the US. This movement emphasised 'excellence' and 'humanising work' (Rose 1989: 102), and really took force in the

1980s. What we see now is an unprecedented psycho-technology of work, one that requires a specific psychology and subjectivity, as well as a management psychology. Peters and Waterman outline conservative management styles and associated required behaviours in their best-selling book, *In Search of Excellence: Lessons from America's Best-Run Companies* (1982). The authors suggest behaviours that seem almost like adages to the contemporary management guru, having to do with the fostering of innovation, teamwork, and so on. This influential text relies on a supposedly typical human psyche or human nature, and has a sub-text for how these behaviours would increase productivity of the humans it was intending to represent. This type of subjectivity must be held by the individual who craves security but is also in love with change, one who is competitive but also longs to work in groups, longs for success and achievement, and so on. This was to be a new kind of citizen who longs for self-fulfilment through work, but in a way that is not complementary to the society of the industrial age. What is now generally taken out of the equation is a guaranteed wage, and union involvement at the level of human resources, and the commitment from governments to provide anything but a resolve to inculcate higher education and training by way of a particular process that could produce such subjectivities.

Theorists of the emerging IPEW can learn much from a wide range of authors who are often overlooked in traditional IPE, such as seen in the work of Beynon et al. on the 'new realities of work' (2002); Rifkin on the 'end of work' (1992); Burawoy on work conditions and monopoly capitalism (1979; 1985); Spencer's *Political Economy of Work* (2009); Fine and Milonakis on 'the social' in economic theory (2008); and Fine (2001) on social capital versus social theory. Moreover, theorists who are interested in the world of work in the digital 'playground' are searching for new ways to measure work and labour in our new information economy, such as Cubitt (1998), and have begun to make investigations into how society is constructed objectively, subjectively, and the importance of inter-subjectivities (building on the work of Berger and Luckmann 1967). IPE has very few critical theorists to offer in the contemporary moment, although the work of Abbott and Worth (2002), Worth and Moore (2009), and others aims to rectify this. Montgomerie (2008) attempts to build bridges between competing 'critical' political economy perspectives by arguing for an end to the obsessive attacks on mainstream 'economic' approaches in favour of more collaborative efforts to offer an alternative theoretical and empirical method of evaluating the changing dynamics of present day capitalism. With reference to work and wages, Montgomerie demonstrates how individuals who rely on inflation-indexed wage increases have been drawn into global labour market dynamics as low-cost consumer goods produced in the Global South affect wage-growth of workers in the Global North through diffuse mechanisms of global trade relations and consumer-price index measures.

However, no IPE theorists are investigating the relevance of the contemporary 'necessary' subjectivities of the worker. Typically, sociologists or work psychologists have taken the lead in analyses of the subjective elements of work, such as Clark and Oswald (1996), and Clark (2005) (cited in Spencer 2009: xvii) who aim to find ways to identify life satisfaction as associated with subjective participation. The 'economics of happiness' (Layard 2005) thesis claims that happiness can be found through work, a philosophy that informs New Labour's unemployment and welfare-to-work policy in the UK, but Spencer (2009) is critical of this homogenising platform. A handful of mainstream work psychologists, including Holman et al. (2009, 2008), advocate well-being through specific work design models and goal-setting strategies. But these authors completely ignore the implications for why resistance is happening in the workplace and are interested only in reforming it according to pre-determined 'rules'. The emotional labour literature looks at emotion work and emotion labour as forms of alienation that occur particularly in the context of service labour, that is, hotel and shop work that forces people into 'suppression of the real self' (Brook 2009: 533). Hochschild distinguishes between emotional labour, which is the 'management of feeling to create a publicly observable facial and bodily display (1983: 7) and emotion work, which is the 'process of managing and presenting emotions in the private sphere of our lives such as among family and friends' (Brook 2009: 533).

The 'labour process' literature, on the other hand, is based around a category identified by Marx that referred to 'the simple elements of the labour process [which] are 1) purposeful activity, that is work itself, 2) the object on which that work is performed, and 3) the instruments of that work' (1976: 284). Littler states that the labour process is a category that lies in 'contradistinction to the valorisation process' (1990: 77). Valorisation (translated from the word *Kapitalverwertung*) is vital for the labour process, but this is often overlooked. While the translation of this term is not completely precise, valorisation is understood as the process of value creation and of the surplus value of work. So the labour process is not a theory in and of itself, but it is a process of production that Marx critiqued in his *Critique of Political Economy* (1976). The activity that makes this process affiliated with capitalism is the seemingly endless search for profitable accumulation, including profit for the capitalist, from workers' output. Paying a worker less for her work than the value that is added to the labour process as a result of that work, is at the heart of the capitalist employment relationship (Knights 1990: 4).

[handwritten marginal note: Valorisation]

The literature associated directly with the 'labour process' starts with Harry Braverman's *Labour and Monopoly Capital* published in 1974. Braverman's work was the first to analyse systematically the employee/employer relationship and the management structures of control to manage this relationship through deskilling workers; and, separating manual from mental labour, Braverman famously identified how scientific management separates conception from execution.

Several debates across academics were triggered by Braverman's groundbreaking book, to do with:

1 questions about deskilling and the attempt to construct a satisfactory model of skills changes;
2 questions about labour markets and the attempt to construct a satisfactory model of capitalist labour markets; and
3 questions about managerial strategy and control.

(Littler 1990: 46)

Littler notes these as the 'core' areas of the debates after *Labour and Monopoly Capital* was published. While Braverman's work caused significant discussion across the fields of industrial relations, sociology, and politics, it was not entirely above reproach, and perhaps the most important critique is that Braverman was too committed to structures, rather than with workers' subjectivities and their own experiences of the workplace. Several authors, most prominently Burawoy, voiced concern regarding the issues that were overlooked by Braverman. Braverman was concerned with '"objective" aspects of the labour process' (Burawoy 1985: 25) but did not consider the 'day-to-day impact of particular forms of "control", and specifically Taylorism, so the same one sided perspective leads him to compound Taylorism as ideology and as practice ... He makes all sorts of assumptions about the interests of capitalists and managers, about their consciousness, and about their capacity to impose their interests on subordinate classes' (ibid.). Burawoy aims to indemnify this lack of investigation and conducts extensive fieldwork in the factory to disclose how regimes of control operate. Where Burawoy builds on Braverman's influential analysis is his application to the workplace of Gramsci's thesis on hegemony and the absorption of workers' needs and interests through what he calls *concrete* coordination (ibid.: 10). Political and ideological research is crucial for the understanding of what actually occurs in the workplace, of how management structures of control are operationalised and how they are sustained, and why workers have not overthrown these structures of control. Braverman did not look at the 'subjective dimension' of class, and is restricted by an economistic view of externally defined class and one that predominantly looks at people's contribution to capital-accumulation processes despite his claims that classes are 'not fixed entities but rather *ongoing processes*' (1974: 409).

So, considering the absence of adequate analyses of subjectivity, how could this father of the labour process literature theorise resistance or dissent? While Braverman led the American Socialist Party, which had been a splinter group from the Socialist Workers' Party, he defended slaves' rights, and wrote in 1956 about American radicalism with the insight that, after the Second World War, there had been a crisis of the left (Braverman 1956). The following quotation indicates Braverman's earlier dedication to looking at resistance to the expansion of capitalism which he predicted:

> The Communist Party's number one dictum for years has been that 'socialism is not the issue,' but that confuses two things. If it is taken to mean that at present no direct struggle for socialism is possible in the form of mass activities or a broad national election campaign, that is quite true. But if it is taken to mean that on this account it ought to be discarded or shelved to a future millenium [*sic*], that is dead wrong. Exactly because now is not a time when the Left can move masses into struggle either for immediate demands or for socialism, its role as an educator, posing fundamentals and recruiting a serious following on a fundamental basis, comes to the fore. ... But organized labor in this country is a massive and slow-moving body where politics is concerned, and tends to move as a unit, out of timidity and conservatism, and fear on the part of each leader of getting out too far in front. This means that groups inside and outside the labor movement will tend to outrun it in pioneering attempts, as happened in Britain as a prelude to the organization of the Labor Party there. We will probably see many third-party attempts of various sorts before the twin-headed monopoly is finally broken. Radicals can and should take an active part in these advance-guard movements. (Ibid.)

With this in mind, Nikolas Rose explores the connections between material, social and economic changes, and workers' subjectivities:

> The changes in the conception, organisation, and regulation of work and the worker over this century involve relations between many aspects of thought and practice: the history of the large corporation, the changing relations of manufacturing and non-manufacturing industry; the elaboration of an expertise of management; innovations in the rationale and techniques of accounting to incorporate the human resources of the enterprise; transformations in macro-economic policy and much more ... the relations between governmental rationalities, social strategies, human technologies and techniques of self [that] have been brought into being by these new ways of thinking and acting on the economy, the workplace, and the worker ... new networks of power have been established, a web of calculations and technologies connecting macro-economic policy, the management of the enterprise, and the design of the labour process with human subjectivity itself. (1999: 60)

So what scholars have not yet done is to look specifically at how policy is affected by the policy and workplace changes that link with 'human subjectivity itself' (ibid.). Education has been targeted as a site for reskilling, and industry is repeatedly welcomed to take part in curricula development in an increased number of countries internationally.

In all of this, Michel Foucault cannot be overlooked. Foucault's groundbreaking work on power relations, governmentality, and subjectivation offers a great deal to the exploration of policy and its impact on people. Power is conducted through a multiplicity of forms, and Foucault identifies several ways this is applied, not least in the realm of the subject. The state is seen not simply as 'government', though government is often the form that we see at the helm of the objectification of the subject, in particular through the uprooting of the individual in a number of ways. The struggle against 'government of individualisation' is seen in a 'series of oppositions that have developed over the last few years: opposition to the power of men over women, of parents over children, of psychiatry over the mentally ill, of medicine over the population, of administration over the ways people live' (Foucault 2000: 329). The latter comment here is the area of interest for research into employability as a form of subjectivity and of subjectivation. Postmodern struggles are those that revolt against a 'technique, a form of power' (ibid.: 331) rather than perhaps a revolt against the elite, or against an institution as such. 'Where there is power, there is resistance, and yet, or rather consequently, this resistance is never in a position of exteriority in relation to power. Should it be said that one is always "inside" power, there is no "escaping" it, there is no absolute outside where it is concerned' (Foucault 1990: 94).

EMPLOYABILITY AS DISCOURSE AND AS SUBJECTIVITY

Employability within this supposedly 'excellent' world of work is a seductive term as it seems to provide a one-size-fits-all safety net for people's survival in an increasingly unstable labour market. But what does the rise in an 'employability' rhetoric seen across social policy and education programmes mean for workers, as well as jobseekers?

Starting in the 1960s and picking up considerable pace in the 1980s, leaders decided that change would be inevitable as a response to pressure to 'outsmart' rivals in the global political knowledge economy, and began to focus on ways to prepare labour markets and to promote workers' employability as a policy target for the sake of economic prosperity.[3] Despite the industry/education link has never been proven to be an effective or successful approach and a way to understand 'employability', governments have adopted it increasingly since the 1980s.

Garsten and Jacobsson (2004) offer several definitions for employability and note the transformations of the concept over time. In a series of 'waves' (2004: 7–9), the meaning of employability has responded to different forces. In the 1900s, someone was either available for employment and was thus employable or, alternatively, they were not. During the Great Depression, *dichotomic employability* was seen as a statistical measure to explain people's ability to work and get into employment. Modern versions emerged during a 'second wave' occurring in the 1950s and 1960s, and were more inclusive of ideas beyond the predominantly Anglo-Saxon model. Garsten and Jacobsson outline three different versions of employability developed and used by labour market policymakers and public sector professionals. The first wave genre is apparently 'socio-medical employability', which emphasises a range of qualities observed by potentially employable individuals with an emphasis on physical and mental health. The second version is more general in that it identifies social 'health', that is, whether someone has a criminal record or has a driving licence, and rehabilitation centres on these apparent detriments towards employability. This is called the 'manpower policy employability' because it by definition 'measures the distance between the individual's characteristics and the production and acceptability requirements on the labour market' (7). Both these versions assume authority of markets and do not question employer prejudice or forced social change. The third variation, developed in France in the 1960s, takes a more collective dimension but concentrates on *un*employability rather than employability through an observation of the amount of time it takes for unemployed groups to find work.

But over time, employability has become increasingly defined as the ability to *adapt* to flexible patterns of employment more than anything else, and has often been conflated with the idea of lifelong learning (Hillage and Pollard 1999; Tamkin and Hillage 1999; Worth 2003), rather than the ability to work in a socially sustainable and meaningful way. Companies were seen as unreliable for comprehensive training in economies that have begun to commodify knowledge, and government programmes appeared to focus on training people to achieve 'greater individual self-sufficiency over job stability and career advancement' (Worth 2003: 608; Walker and Kellard 2001). Experts have also measured employability as a unit of analysis and found that the general perception of employability tends to be higher during times of prosperity but that dual labour market and human capital factors also affect the level of perceived employability of workers regardless of structural factors (Berntson et al. 2006). What this means is that training is no longer associated specifically with job-related tasks, but consists of a more seemingly holistic preparation forum, with education/learning at the forefront and with individuals' self-improvement and a certain kind of self-management as a crucial value.

As a result, governments in each country reviewed in this volume have made explicit attempts towards building a high-skilled, value-added production capacity to accommodate technology-heavy industries through building links between education and industry. Policies in each case have demonstrated a people-centred or supply-side agenda and have made 'employability' a top priority rather than using the demand-led approach that uses a different set of criteria to interpret how industries are kept in 'business'. Contemporary skills revolutions, as this volume names them, have followed the human capital approach, which prioritises employability. The British government from 1997 to 2010, Labour, has also been claimed to increasingly follow the American model at many levels as well, or the welfare to work, 'workfare' model (Daguerre 2004: 20–4).

South Korea, the UK, and Singapore all made the effort to openly and publicly shift responsibility for decision making to external factors, from international organisations, to individuals, and to the not always tangible 'authority' of the market. International networks and regimes of responsibility include Korea's involvement with UNESCO Vocational Education and Training Council (UNEVOC), Singapore's ongoing relationship with foreign capital, both of these entities with the Association of Southeast Asian Nations (ASEAN), and the UK's ongoing membership of the International Network for Quality Assurance in Higher Education as well as the pressures of EU membership to adapt to the Lisbon Agenda. The nature of choices towards supranational governance involves frameworks of 'rules, institutions and practise at a level above the nation-state whose authority extends beyond just one state' (Kennett 2001: 31–3).

Marxist analyses have revealed inequalities and power relations as based on labour regulation within an industrial model, but new models of production and labour processes appear to differ from those of the industrial age. Labour process theory had been criticised for failing to address the importance of the subjectivity of the worker and the way in which exploitation of the surplus value of labour is not always explicit, but is a lived process that becomes internalised to the point that a version of 'consent' can replace the assumption of worker compliance (Burawoy 1979). Braverman had noted even earlier that 'as human labour becomes a social rather than an individual phenomenon, it is possible – unlike in the instance of animals where the motive force is inseparable from action – to divorce conception from execution' (Braverman 1974: 113). While 'conception' relied on management's exclusive power to define and manage work, responsibility was gradually transferred to workers themselves in unprecedented production environments, or what are now understood as work cultures. The cultural turn in this topical age throws a new light on the management of business and organisations (Lash and Urry 1994: 108), and has inspired a shift from bureaucratic, mechanistic, rationalist systems that constitute the firm of old. The term cultural economy is associated with the grand claims towards economies of signs, the network society, and the knowledge economy, highlighting a turn to culturalised organisational and economic life (Du Gay and Pryke 2002: 6).

Employability is increasingly described in the discourse as though it is a skill in its own right, which is a frightening development when this tenuous term is viewed as supposedly the most important/viable way to maintain employment. Historically, someone's employment, or waged relationship to his/her employer on its own, did not mean that the worker was employable strictly and exclusively according to market terms, in the way that the contemporary neoliberal market-place demands. People are subjected to labour processes in the same way as they were before Post-Fordism supposedly overturned this static waged relationship. Workers' labour becomes a commodity when sold to the capitalist, but in the case of the employability discourse, it is more than the work alone playing a role in this relationship. The worker who can demonstrate employability has begun a relation-ship of subordination to capital before even necessarily being employed, meaning that capitalism is successfully becoming integrated into increasing levels of people's everyday lives. But what is even more interesting is that this phenomenon looks increasingly similar in a widening territorial context, as capitalism continues its ascent to hegemonic status. 'Employability' is a highly subjective term, and requires the productive woman/man to become a citizen/worker, who is also labelled a learner worker (Williams 2005) and an 'incurable learner' (Harding 2000). Rather than specific skills and abilities alone, workers are expected to have particular 'labour attitudes' (Worth 2003: 608). The employable worker appears to demonstrate the following characteristics:

- Flexibile personality
- Incurable learner
- Learner worker
- Enriched communicator
- Entrepreneur
- Employable
- Self-managed/directed
- Innovator
- Independent thinker

- Individual
- Adaptable
- Job sharer

(Ibid.)

A perception of the 'employable' individual appears to be gradually replacing or at the very least, challenging, discussions for 'employment' or job creation. The ambiguity of the emerging debate seems to require a marriage of the productive individual (what Lefebvre calls 'productive man') with a contemporary form of idealised citizenship (or Lefebvre's 'political man') that in practice requires people to become entrepreneurs of their own fates in unprecedented campaigns, apparently triggered by unregimented globalisation.

Contu (Contu et al. 2003: 943) is very critical of the 'common *imaginaire*' that has emerged in the construction of a particular kind of learning discourse; one that aims to create an 'incurable learner' (Harding 2000) with campaigns that construct a certain set of standards for individuals' employability, and the campaign's crucial companion, lifelong learning. The campaign marginalises more than it includes, as it places a homogeneity of expectations on all people, demanding certain types of capabilities for learning, excluding for example autistics, manic-depressives, schizophrenic people, and perhaps 'eccentrics', just to name a few. Britain's, South Korea's, and Singapore's employability campaigns all demonstrate a significant shift in what is expected of citizens via the formulation of their subjectivities in a normalisation process that is consolidated by the private sector's renewed demands for skills.

Skills and subjectivity

The transformation of skills expectations is increasingly becoming internationalised, and is considered crucial for knowledge production and workers' employability, which includes methods of learning that require creativity, and andragogical learning capabilities that must become subjectively inculcated and personally developed for 'learner-worker's' (Williams 2005) ongoing employability. Sturdy et al. (1992) contrasts the concept of a manual worker who stops working when 'coercion is removed' (Mann 1973: 23 quoted in Sturdy et al. 1992: 116) and socialisation literature that discusses work ethics and other worker characteristics, which are somewhat indoctrinated via external training sources. Sturdy comments that the labour process literature has neglected discussions of 'subjective action' (1992: 117), as well as emerging cases of workers' resistance even in the forms seen in absenteeism, 'making out' (Burawoy 1979: 27), and day-to-day evidences of rebellion (de Certeau 1984).

As I describe, for example in the UK, the Learning and Skills Council (LSC) has begun to work towards a project that intends to

> transform the way people think, feel and act about learning and skills … we will achieve this ambition through a lasting, memorable and actively supported campaign which will be used and developed by everyone in Further Education. (LSC 2007)

The highly personal and invasive language used in the campaign begins to move stealthily into the territory of subjectivities and people's lives. 'Everyday life' has been ascribed by elite voices to working classes or to the supposed types of people/workers who are incapable of understanding or living in the enlightened and perhaps postmodern world, an assumption that has been heavily critiqued on the left. How does the employability campaign deal with 'everyday lives' but as a criticism of the way

Critical.

people may have traditionally chosen to live, that is, in a way that is not all-consumed with preparing oneself for the supposedly immutable instability of the labour market? Employability of the *self* is a concept that holds absolutely no meaning if it is not an experience lived and constructed by people whose relationship to their work is increasingly subordinated to global and local changes to labour markets.

Scientific analyses of creative processes stem from the 1960s, at which time psychologists even referenced late nineteenth century authors to explore the idea of creative thought in comparison to other knowledge processes. Campbell noted the conditions for general inductive gain, involving a process of the evolution of mechanisms for introducing variation, added to consistent selection processes, which finally was expected to reveal a mechanism for reproducing and preserving selected variants emerging from the former conditions. So knowledge production emerges from 'blind-variation-and-selective-retention'. Creative thought, on the other hand, requires 'substitute exploration of a substitute representation of the environment' (Campbell 1960: 384) by way of an exploratory thought process. This author cites Bain (1874) in this discussion of trials and errors for theorisation of the accurate and successful process termination, or the 'aha-erlebnis' of a final idea. Bain condones originality, emotion, adventurism, and energetic character traits for the success of creative thinking. More recently, sociologists and management specialists have begun to consider membership of the 'creative class' (Florida 2004) as important for workers' knowledge production capabilities and thus for employability, but still limit the final outcomes of creative thinking to assessment within an unwritten curricula. Furthermore, andragogy may be seen to have taken the place almost of pedagogy, which removes the metaphorical instructor from the workplace nearly completely. These shifts represent a transformation of hegemonies for knowledge production both within models for business interaction, and within the concept of workers' employability in the post-industrial KBE.

However, the 'skill' of creativity has now become a tool to divide classes. The Richard Florida Creativity Group has divided percentages of 'classes' of workers and wage shares. People with 'creativity' make the most money, according to the Creativity Group, a project founded by Richard Florida, a Carnegie Mellon economist. Creative capital is 'even more important to regional growth than human capital or high-tech industries', since the latter two items are 'shaped' by the former. Regions' economic gain can be specifically linked to the 3T's: Technology, Talent, and Tolerance; these items will attract creative talent in the emerging global competition for talent. The Creative Class demonstrates:

- Individuality: Members of the creative class exhibit a strong preference for individuality and self-statement. They do not want to conform to organisational or institutional directives and resist traditional group oriented norms.
- Meritocracy: The creative class favours hard work, challenge, and stimulation. Its members have a propensity for goal setting and achievement. They want to get ahead because they are good at what they do.
- Diversity and Openness: Members of this class strongly favour organisations and environments in which they feel anyone can fit in and get ahead.

(Florida 2002)

The action of creativity is understood generally as the creation of an idea, whereas innovation is a more complex concept. A group of researchers at the Institute of Work Psychology, University of Sheffield, critique their own discipline for advancing the generation of ideas without examining their implementation, which requires an extended range of skills and most importantly, innovation (Axtell et al. 2000).

Employee role orientation and self-efficacy are linked to innovation (Farr and Ford 1990; Bandura 1982; Anderson and West 1998) though innovation itself requires 'approval, support and resources of others' (Axtell et al. 2000: 269), and assumptions of individualism and rationality lie at the core of skills and production capacities.

But this line of reasoning still relies on unwritten curricula and on the epistemological 'truths' that determine and design measures for success. Workplace expectations for knowledge production are becoming normalised within the KBE and rely on employability of workers, revealing contradictions within this transformation. If employability is dependent on the 'accidental circumstances' (Mach 1896) that must be instigated by workers' energetic trial and error, how can potential employees possibly defend themselves and their abilities in a meaningful sense, or in a way that protects jobs and job security? Furthermore, experts rely on the assumption that the process as a whole externally provides foresight for overt behaviour; otherwise, the results could not be measured for success as the production of truly 'new' thought.

Resnick and Wolff (1987) claim that knowledge is a process and a conceptual response that 'continually extends, elaborates, and revises its conceptual apparatus according to the ever-changing determinations of its environment'. Responses demand creations of new concepts, rejections of other concepts, and a 'systematic ordering' of a growing body of accepted concepts. These authors credit Marx for this depiction of knowledge creation, citing *Critique of Political Economy*, in which Marx writes that 'it is not the consciousness of men that determines their existence, but on the contrary, their social existence determines their consciousness' (ibid.: 54). But these authors also rely on a line of reasoning that restricts the line of knowledge production as originating from the structure.

Jessop discusses critical semiotic analysis for a better understanding of knowledge production that critiques the variation, selection, and retention model understood within the aforementioned psychology circles. Jessop is interested in the way in which capitalism reproduces itself via social and, to a lesser extent, material constructions of historically specific networks of social relations and aggregations of institutions. He initiates a discussion of CPE that marries critical political economy with semiotics, which specifically looks at 'argumentation, narrativity, rhetoric, hermeneutics, identity, reflexivity, historicity and discourse', and Jessop looks at the 'intersubjective production of meaning [semiosis] to cover them all' (2004). It is thus appropriate to look at the production of knowledge regarding what makes employees employable and an investigation of the value ascribed to knowledge produced in the workplace from the CPE perspective, which allows for a critique rather than a reification of understandings. If OS is a site for the attainment of employability, then does it succeed in creating an alternative economic imaginary? Or is it reinvention, indeed redemption of the capitalist mode of production?

THEORISING 'EMPLOYABILITY'

The Bologna Declaration emphasises employability and encourages the 'adoption of a system of easily readable and comparable degrees, also through the implementation of the Diploma Supplement, in order to promote European citizens' employability and the international competitiveness of the European higher education system' (European Ministers of Education 1999). Employability is a term that is becoming accepted internationally and is thus part of an international discourse that encourages a particular form of power over subjectivities and bodies. It has, become almost a matter of common sense that informs policymaking. The difference in theorising discourse in the

Foucauldian framework and common sense from a Gramscian perspective is that Gramsci imagined a 'correct' way of thinking that is not evident in cases of common sense (in fact he designated the correct way of thinking as 'good sense'). The idea of discourse and power is that there are multiple ways of thinking that could become discourses, and Foucault was not committed to identifying the 'correct' way.

Often, confusion regarding definitions and interpretations of what employability represents is evident, and one study looks at the employability of geography graduates in Estonia, the US, Chile, Greece, the UK, Italy, and Spain. Employability is linked with education in these studies and countries' curricula are discussed to incorporate strategies to enhance graduates' employability (Rooney et al. 2006). The unemployable in the late nineteenth and early twentieth century were simply those who were unable to work (Welshman 2006) but the concept has altered dramatically to almost unrecognisable proportions as a result of globalisation and the changing relationship between industry and education.

Two threads run through the literature on employability: (1) a human capital approach and (2) an approach that stresses labour market attachment or work-first (Daguerre 2004). Overall, employability has shifted from the simple notion of those who are 'able' to work, to a reliance on workers' capabilities to adjust to changing labour markets, and how workers can be trained into this mentality is an issue discussed at increasing levels of government and governance alike. Employability is a concept that appears now to stretch beyond solely personal factors, but must include the awareness that individuals encounter a range of barriers to prevent access to the labour market due to 'globalisation'.

Braverman argued in his groundbreaking work (1974) that the deskilling of workers has always been a management imperative designed to maintain hierarchies and subordinate workers. Several authors with left political leanings aim to resurrect Braverman's ideas into present analyses, and look at the transposition of Taylorist employment relations into the present day. Clearly, dedicated orthodox management theorists see exploitation of labour as being simply that, that is, the extraction of value through workers' productive capability for the good of organisational aims, and absolutely see no need for normative explanations (Reilly 2001). Labour process literature has been critiqued for neglecting to fully engage with and explore the important subject of the subjectivity of workers (O'Doherty and Willmott 2001; Knights 1990; Willmott 1990; Sturdy 1992). Within Marxist literature, too much emphasis has been placed on the structure of management control and objective conditions that are viewed over and above 'workers' subjective feelings and identities' (Glenn and Feldberg 1979: 52). To restrict research to structural conditions is to offer an incomplete view of the labour process and of important relations of production, that is, employment relationships in the contemporary context wherein policy discourse relies on the gospel truths of what must be done in the neoliberal, globalised world. Lazzarato points out that in our new world of work, 'the worker's personality and subjectivity have to be made susceptible to organization and command' (1996: 133). Burawoy and several others began to attempt to put some meat on the bones of the corpus of ideas started by Braverman, with the understanding that what happens on the shop floor and production more widely are events that are formed around political and ideological factors (Smith 1990: 233).

But 'skill' has become more than specific knowledge about the execution of a job, but nonetheless it has become a competitive advantage within supposed knowledge economies, and contemporary governments have tended to forget their own rules for neoliberal laissez faire-ism and have begun to intervene through investment into education. A 'high skills approach' is thus taken in policymaking to remain competitive in the global knowledge economy. The concept of skill is increasingly concurrent with education, while industries have begun to operate a 'skills approach' (Pascail 2006). Pascail notes that higher education is no longer devoted to the transmission of knowledge alone, but has become a training ground to create a workforce that will directly become involved in the development of economies (ibid.).

The debate surrounding the extent to which higher education can or even should engage itself in this way seems to position itself on two sides. First, authors like Cranmer (2006) began to doubt that employable skills can be acquired in the classroom, and advocate a return to on the job training and learning by doing or, on the other hand, actual involvement of employers into curricula. One study by the Higher Education Funding Council for England (HEFCE) (Mason et al. 2006) throws doubt on the idea that educators in the classroom of higher education can actually have an impact or improve the chances for graduates' employability, but encourages increased direct involvement and investment of employers into education to aid in graduates' obtaining of employment.

This book thus highlights the urgency of discussions of work and production and looks at how in our supposed post-industrial world, in the context of global recession, subjectivity is less affiliated with people's work and employment and is more about a supposed core ability to posture oneself towards the market in a way that ultimately disallows creative self identification and self realised and managed subjectivity.

NOTES

1. The employment rate for people of working age [in the UK] was 74.1 per cent for the three months to December 2008, down 0.3 from the previous quarter and down 0.7 over the year. The number of people in employment for the three months to December 2008 was 29.36 million, down 45,000 over the quarter and down 37,000 over the year. While there has been a fall over the quarter of 78,000 people in full-time employment, the number of people in part-time employment has increased by 33,000' (UK National Statistics 2009).
2. Perhaps the idea of 'play-bour' originates in the gaming industry, wherein, for example, the modification of games, or 'modding' is seen as something IT developers do as a leisurely pastime. However, developers often are not able to translate their activity into something personally useful, and the output of modding is frequently used by the industry or by salaried developers to advance the quality of games, while modders remain in precarious forms of work. 'The relationship between work and play is changing, leading, as it were, to a hybrid form of "playbour"' (Kücklich 2005).
3. In Australia, a country that has recently had significant fallouts with its labour unions, the subjectivity of workers was explicitly avoided in any related policy until recently, when competent 'learner-workers' were expected to also acquire 'employability skills'. Williams (2005) warns that this kind of intervention will necessarily lead to ambiguities towards what is expected of workers, and contradicts previous commitments to keep personal attributes out of policy discussion. Events in Australasia reflect a similar redefinition of workers' relationship with employment in nations that reflect each of Coates' defined models of capitalism.

BIBLIOGRAPHY

Abbott, J. and O. Worth (eds), *Critical Perspectives on International Political Economy* (Palgrave Macmillan, 2002).
Anderson, N. R. and N. A. West, 'Measuring Climate for Work Group Innovation', *Journal of Organisational Behaviour* 19 (1998), 235–58.
AsiaPulse, 'South Korean Unemployment Benefit Filings Hit Record High in Jan', (Seoul, 09 Feb 2009). Online, Available (03/03/09) http://www.zibb.com/article/4851085.

Axtell, C. M., D. J. Holman, K. Unsworth, T. D. Wall, P. E. Waterson, and E. Harrington, 'Shopfloor Innovation: Facilitating the Suggestion and Implementation of Ideas', *Journal of Occupational and Organizational Psychology* 73: 3 (2000), 265–85.

Bain, A., *The Senses and the Intellect*, third edition (Appleton, 1874).

Bandura, A., 'Self-Efficacy Mechanism in Human Agency', *The American Psychologist* 37: 2 (1982), 122–47.

Berger, P. L. and T. Luckmann, *The Social Construction of Reality: A Treatise in the Sociology of Knowledge* (Anchor, 1967).

Berntson, E., M. Sverke, and S. Marklund, 'Predicting Perceived Employability: Human Capital or Labour Market Opportunities?', *Economic and Industrial Democracy* 27: 2 (2006), 223–44.

Beynon, H., D. Grimshaw, J. Rubery, and K. Ward, *Managing Employment Change: The New Realities of Work* (Oxford University Press, 2002).

Braverman, H., 'Which Way to a New American Radicalism?', *American Socialist* (1956). Online, Available (05/03/09) http://www.marxists.org/archive/ braverman/1956/04/radicalism.htm.

Braverman, H., *Labour and Monopoly Capital: The Degradation of Work in the Twentieth Century* (Monthly Review Press, 1974).

Brook, P., 'In Critical Defense of Emotional Labour, Refuting Bolton's Critique of Hoschild's Concept', *Work, Employment and Society* 23: 531 (2009), 531–48.

Burawoy, M., *Manufacturing Consent: Changes in the Labour Process under Monopoly Capitalism* (University of Chicago Press, 1979).

Burawoy, M., *The Politics of Production: Factory Regimes Under Capitalism and Socialism* (Verso, 1985).

Campbell, D. T., 'Blind Variation and Selective Retention in Creative Thought as in Other Knowledge Processes', *Psychological Review* 67 (1960), 380–400.

Contu, A., C. Grey, and A. Örtenblad, 'Against Learning', *Human Relations* 56: 8 (2003), 931–52.

Cranmer, S., 'Enhancing Graduate Employability: Best Intentions and Mixed Outcomes', *Studies in Higher Education* 31: 2 (2006), 169–84.

Cubitt, S., *Digital Aesthetics* (Sage, 1998).

Daguerre, A., 'Importing Workfare Policy Transfer of Social and Labour Market Policies from the USA to Britain under New Labour', *Social Policy and Administration* 38: 1 (2004), 41–56.

De Certeau, M., *The Practice of Everyday Life*, translated by S. Rendall (University of California Press, 1984).

du Gay, P. and M. Pryke, 'Cultural Economy: An Introduction', in *Cultural Economy: Cultural Analysis and Commercial Life* (Sage, 2002), 1–19.

European Ministers of Education (joint declaration), 'The European Higher Education Area', meeting convened in Bologna (19 June 1999). Online, Available (24/02/09) http://www.oest.oas. org/engineering/ingles/documentos/reference/Doc_03_Bologna%20Declaration.pdf.

Farr, J. L. and C. M. Ford, 'Individual Innovation', in M. A. West and L Farr (eds), *Innovation and Creativity at Work: Psychological and Organisational Strategies* (John Wiley and Sons, 1990), 63–80.

Fine, B., *Social Capital versus Social Theory: Political Economy and Social Science at the Turn of the Millennium* (Routledge, 2001).

Fine, B. and Milonakis, D., *From Political Economy to Economics: Method, the Social and the Historical in the Evolution of Economic Theory* (Routledge, 2008).

Florida, R., *The Rise of the Creative Class and How It's Transforming Work, Leisure, Community, and Everyday Life* (Basic Books, 2002).

Florida, R., 'Creative Class War: How the GOP's Anti-Elitism Could Ruin America's Economy', *Washington Monthly* (January/February 2004). Online, Available (05/09/09) http://www.washington monthly.com/features/2004/0401.florida.html.

Foucault, M., *The History of Sexuality. Volume I: An Introduction*, translated by Robert Hurley (Vintage Books, 1990).

Foucault, M., 'The Subject and Power', in James D. Faubion (ed.), *Michel Foucault: Essential Works of Foucault 1954–1984* (Penguin, 2000), 326–48.

Garsten, C. and K. Jacobsson, *Learning to be Employable: New Agendas on Work, Responsibility and Learning in a Globalising World* (Palgrave Macmillan, 2004).

Glenn, E. N. and R. L. Feldberg, 'Proletarianising Clerical Work: Technology and Organisation Control in the Office', in A. Zimbalist (ed.), *Case Studies in the Labour Process* (Monthly Review Press, 1979).

Gorz, A., *Capitalism, Socialism, Ecology* (Verso, 1994).

Gorz, A., *Reclaiming Work: Beyond the Wage-based Society* (Polity Press, 1999).

Harding, J., 'Creating Incurable Learners: Building Learner Autonomy through Key Skills', in S. Fallows and C. Steven (eds), *Integrating Key Skills into Higher Education: Employability, Transferable Skills and Learning for Life* (Kogan Page, 2000), 77–86.

Hillage, J. and E. Pollard, *Employability: Developing a Framework for Policy Analysis* (Department for Education and Employment 1999).

Holman D., S. Frenkel, O. Sørensen and S. Wood, 'Work Design Variation and Outcomes in Call Centers: Strategic Choice and Institutional Explanations', *Industrial Labour Relations Review* 62 (2009), 510–32.

Holman, D., D. Martinez-Iñigo, and P. Totterdell, 'Emotional Labour, Well-Being and Performance', in C. L. Cooper and S. Cartwright (eds), *The Oxford Handbook of Organizational Well-Being* (Oxford University Press, 2008), 331–55.

Hochschild, A. R., *The Managed Heart: Commercialisation of Human Feeling* (University of California, 1983).

ILO, 'ILO Global Employment Trends Report 2009 – Unemployment, Working Poor, Vulnerable Employment to Increase Dramatically due to Global Employment Crisis' (29 January 2009). Online, Available (03/03/09) http://www.ilo.org/asia/info/public/pr/lang—en/WCMS_101494/index.htm.

Index Mundi, 'Singapore Unemployment Rate' (2009). Online, Available (06/03/09) http://www.indexmundi.com/singapore/unemployment_rate.html.

International Herald Tribune, The Associated Press, 'Singapore Unemployment Jumps to 2.6 Percent' (30 January 2009). Online, Available (06/03/09) http://singaporenewsalternative.blogspot.com/2009/01/singapore-unemployment-jumps-to-26.html.

Jessop, B., 'Critical Semiotic Analysis and Cultural Political Economy', *Critical Discourse Studies* 1. 2 (2004), 159 74.

Kennett, P., *Comparative Social Policy* (Open University Press, 2001).

Knights, D., 'Subjectivity, Power and the Labour Process', in D. Knights and H. Wilmott (eds), *Labour Process Theory* (Macmillan, 1990).

Lash, S. and J. Urry, *Economies of Signs and Space* (Sage, 1994).

Layard, R., *Happiness: Lessons from a New Science* (Penguin, 2005).

Lazzarato, M., 'Immaterial Labour', in P. Virno and M. Hardt (eds), *Radical Thought in Italy: A Potential Politics* (University of Minnesota Press, 1996).

LSC (Learning and Skills Council), 'Entrepreneurial Spirit Sweeps the Nation', news release, publication number 446 (30 July 2007). Online, Available (27/02/09) http://readingroom.lsc.gov.uk/lsc/National/nat-entrepreneurial-nation.doc.

LSC (Learning and Skills Council), 'Our Future. It's in Our Hands', *What We Do* (July 2007). Online, Available (07/07/07) http://www.lsc.gov.uk/whatwedo/ourfuture.htm.

Littler, C., 'The Labour Process Debate: A Theoretical Review', in D. Knights and H. Willmott (eds), *Labor Process Theory* (Macmillan, 1990).

Mach, E., 'On the Part Played by Accident in Invention and Discovery', *Monist* 6 (1896), 161–75.

Marx, K., *Capital: A Critique of Political Economy*, Volume I (Penguin, 1976).

Mason, G, G. Williams, and S. Cranmer, 'Employability Skills Initiatives in Higher Education: What Effects Do They have on Graduate Labour Market Outcomes?', National Institute of Economic and Social Research, London (2006). Online, Available (24/02/09) http://www.niesr.ac.uk/pubs/DPS/dp280.pdf.

Montgomerie, J., 'Bridging the Critical Divide: Global Finance, Financialisation and Contemporary Capitalism', *Contemporary Politics* 14: 3 (2008), 233–52.

O'Doherty, D. and H. Willmott, 'Debating Labour Process Theory: The Issue of Subjectivity and the Relevance of Poststructuralism', *Sociology* 35: 2 (2001), 457–76.

Pascail, L. 'The Emergence of the Skills Approach in Industry and Its Consequences for the Training of Engineers', *European Journal of Engineering Education* 31: 1 (2006), 55–61.

Peters, T. and R. Waterman, *In Search of Excellence: Lessons from America's Best-Run Companies* (Harper and Row, 1982).

Reilly, P., *Flexibility at Work: Balancing the Interests of Employer and Employee* (Gower, 2001).

Resnick, S. and R. Wolff, *Knowledge and Class* (University of Chicago Press, 1987).

Rifkin, J., *The End of Work: The Decline of the Global Labour Force and the Dawn of the Post-Market Era* (Tarcher Putnam, 1992).

Rooney, P., P. Kneale, B. Gambini, A. Keiffer, B. Vandrasek, and S. Gedye, 'Variations in International Understandings of Employability for Geography', *Journal of Geography in Higher Education*, 30: 1 (2006), 133–45.

Rose, N., *Governing the Soul: The Shaping of the Private Self* (Free Association Books, 1999).

Smith, C., 'Technical Workers: A Class and Organisational Analysis', in S. Clegg (ed.), *Organization Theory and Class Analysis: New Approaches and New Issues* (Walter de Gruyter, 1990), 233–56.

Spencer, D., *The Political Economy of Work* (Routledge, 2009).

Sturdy, A., D. Knights, and H. Willmott (eds), *Skill and Consent: Contemporary Studies in the Labour Process* (Routledge, 1992).

Sturdy, A., 'Clerical Consent: "Shifting" Work in the Insurance Office', in A. Sturdy, D. Knights and H. Willmott (eds), *Skill and Consent: Contemporary Studies in the Labour Process* (Routledge, 1992), 115–48.

Tamkin, P. and J. Hillage, 'Employability and Employers: The Missing Piece of the Jigsaw', Report 361, Institute for Employment Studies (Brighton: Institute of Employment Studies, November 1999). Online, Available (15/06/10) http://www.employment-studies.co.uk/pubs/summary.php?id=361.

Walker, R. and K. Kellard, *Staying in Work: Policy Overview* (Department for Education and Employment London, 2001).

Welshman, J., 'The Concept of the Unemployable', *Economic History Review* 59: 3 (2006), 578–606.

Williams, C., 'The Discursive Construction of the Competent Learner-Worker, from Key Competencies to "Employability Skills"', *Studies in Continuing Education* 27: 1 (2005), 33–49.

Willmott, Hugh, 'Subjectivity and the Dialectics of Praxis: Opening up the Core of Labour Process Analysis', in D. Knights and H. Willmott (eds), *Labour Process Theory* (Macmillan, 1990).

Worth, O. and P. Moore (eds), *Globalisation and the New Semi-Peripheries in the 21st Century* (Palgrave Macmillan, 2009).

Worth, S., 'Adaptability and Self-Management: A New Ethic of Employability for the Young Unemployed?', *Journal of Social Policy* 32: 4 (2003), 607–21.

Yahoda, M., *Marienthal: The Sociography of an Unemployed Community* (Transaction Publishers, 1932/2002).

Chapter
3

KNOWLEDGE-INTENSIVE FIRMS

CHAPTER OUTLINE

- Learning Outcomes
- Introduction
- Types of Knowledge-Intensive Firm
- The Distinctive Characteristics of Knowledge Work and Knowledge Workers
- Facilitating Knowledge Work – Organizing as an Adhocracy
- Structural Constraints on Knowledge Work
- Cultural Conditions in Support of Knowledge Work
- Conclusions
- Case Study: Scienceco Managing an Expert Workforce
- Summary of Key Learning Points

LEARNING OUTCOMES

At the end of this chapter you should be able to:

- Understand the concept of knowledge-intensive firms and differentiate between different types of knowledge-intensive firm.
- Understand the structural and cultural conditions relevant to the management of knowledge-intensive firms.
- Understand the different ways in which these structural and cultural conditions interact to provide an enabling context for knowledge work in knowledge-intensive settings.
- Appreciate the importance of achieving a 'fit' between structure and cultural conditions for the successful management of knowledge workers.

INTRODUCTION

Here we focus our attention on firms where the majority or even the entire workforce consists of knowledge workers – hence the term 'knowledge-intensive firm' – and consider the distinctive management challenges posed by this particular type of 'expert' workforce. Even today in what many refer to as the 'knowledge based economies' of the developed world, knowledge workers are still a relatively scarce resource within the labour market as their particular knowledge, skills and expertise are not generally widely available (Horwitz et al., 2003). Knowledge workers therefore tend to have considerable choice and latitude regarding their place of work – particularly within knowledge-intensive firms – and management are required to find ways of attracting and perhaps more importantly, retaining an expert workforce as the costs of replacement in terms of time and money are significant.

Knowledge-intensive firms tend to be service-based organizations often competing in their respective sectors based on their ability to solve complex problems and provide solutions for clients. Law firms, accountancy practices, management consultancies, investment banks, architectural practices, advertising and public relations agencies are all good examples of knowledge-intensive firms. Many of these types of firms tend to organize in distinctive ways in order to (a) attract and retain knowledge workers and (b) promote innovation and in some instances creativity. Sustaining an expert workforce who are willing to create and share knowledge is crucial if knowledge-intensive firms are to achieve competitive advantage in the long term. Yet it is the workforce in these firms that to a large extent owns the means of production, not management. Developing and, more importantly, *sustaining* an expert workforce is therefore possibly the most important strategic issue that confronts management within these firms over time.

In this chapter we are going to consider the structural and cultural conditions which, in combination, support the management of knowledge work and promote the recruitment and retention of knowledge workers in knowledge-intensive settings. In so doing we focus on the *process* and *practice* of knowledge work. We illustrate the importance of the interaction and integration of these organizational elements through the case of ScienceCo. The distinctive organizational arrangements that developed in this firm, characterized by an atypical culture, serve as a useful example of the importance of creating an *enabling context* for the conduct of knowledge work – particularly the design of core work processes which involve creativity and innovation.

TYPES OF KNOWLEDGE-INTENSIVE FIRM

Alvesson defines knowledge workers as 'qualified labour' (Alvesson, 2004, p. 8). However, this is a somewhat broad definition. Here we use the term 'knowledge worker' to encompass both professionals and groups with other forms of disciplined-based knowledge or more esoteric expertise and skills, for example advertising, media, whose major work tasks involve the creation of new knowledge or the application of existing knowledge in new ways. It follows then that different types of firm employ different types of knowledge workers. Lowendahl (1997), for example, suggests that the crucial strategic difference between knowledge-intensive firms is the role of the professionals employed, that is, the characteristics of the resource base and the types of project targeted. She identifies three generic types of knowledge-intensive firm premised on the firm's strategic focus (see Table 3.1).

Alvesson (2004) distinguishes between two major types of knowledge-intensive firm; R&D companies and professional service firms. Professional service firms deal largely with intangibles and those employed often deal directly with clients while R&D companies typically produce tangible products and contact between employees and the customer are less direct. This largely concurs with Lowendahl's typology which only differentiates further on the basis of what is produced for the client in terms of either bespoke or readily adapted solutions/products (be they tangible or intangible). The term 'knowledge-intensive firm' is therefore used as a generic term to encompass many different types of firm operating across sectors. Traditional professional service

Table 3.1 – Types of knowledge-intensive firm

	Strategic focus	Resources	Examples
Client-based	Client relations	Individually controlled	Law and accountancy practices
Problem-solving	Creative problem-solving – innovation	Team-based	Advertising agencies, software development, web design firms
Output-based	Adaptation of ready solutions	Controlled by the organization	Some large management consultancy firms

Source: Adapted from Lowendahl (1997).

firms such as law and accountancy firms, for example, are seen as a subset of knowledge-intensive firms and have existed as long as the organized professions. These types of firm generally organize along partnership lines with recognized codes of practice and clearly defined 'up-or-out' career paths. Despite the changing nature of some of the established professions (Muzio and Ackroyd, 2005), the majority of professional service firms still tend to be structured and organized along similar lines – often referred to as the professional bureaucracy (Mintzberg, 1979). Professional bureaucracies are organized along traditional hierarchical lines. Legal professionals will occupy the senior positions within the firm and a range of non-legal professionals will manage discrete functions within the firm such as human resources, finance and so on. Small professional service firms tend to be organized along traditional partnership lines otherwise known as the P2 form whereby the senior partners of the firm also manage the firm (Greenwood, Hinings and Brown, 1990). Larger ones are often referred to as Managed Professional Bureaucracies (MPBs) (Cooper et al., 1996) and employ a variety of professionals as well as legal professionals and administrators to deal with the management and operation of the firm. Notably within the larger MPBs, professionals often work as part of large teams (i.e they do not necessarily individually control resources) addressing the needs of similar large, corporate clients. Professional service firms are characterized by a clear hierarchical, partnership structure and well-defined career paths, and the management of this type of firm is already well-documented in the management literature (Lowendahl, 2000).

Some knowledge-intensive firms, in particular large consultancy firms, are also often loosely referred to as professional service firms. The way in which the very large, global consultancies such as Accenture, McKinsey and Price Waterhouse Coopers organize does tend to resemble that of the traditional professional service firm (although they tend to be output-based rather than client-based). However, whilst these categories overlap, the features of knowledge-intensive firms are broader and, importantly, some of the features ascribed to the traditional professions are not necessarily apparent in all knowledge-intensive firms. For example, distinctive features of PSFs such as codes of ethics, strong professional affiliations and specific educational entry requirements leading to restricted access need not, and do not, exist in many knowledge-intensive firms.

More contemporary forms of knowledge-intensive firms emerged in the latter part of the twentieth century including media, advertising and public-relations agencies, software development companies, and many other high-tech and specialist consultancy firms. Around the start of the new millennium we also witnessed the emergence of virtual, Internet-based knowledge-intensive firms offering specialist services to both individual clients and the general public (e.g. Napster, Friends reunited). It is the issues around organizing and managing within these typically smaller, knowledge-intensive firms operating in knowledge-based sectors that are going to be specifically addressed here in this chapter.

Not surprisingly, a precise definition of a knowledge-intensive firm is elusive and it is clear from the term itself that it is a socially constructed, broad-ranging and yet quite ambiguous concept. Alvesson (2004, p. 17) loosely defines knowledge-intensive firms as 'organizations that offer to the market the use of knowledge or knowledge-based products . . . '. The core of activities in these companies is based on the intellectual skills of a very large proportion of the labour force deployed in development, and often also in the sale of products and in service work and he goes on to define a knowledge-intensive firm as 'an organization broadly recognized as creating value through the use of advanced knowledge' (p. 29). However, the term 'advanced knowledge' here is somewhat ambiguous. Unfortunately, because there is no precise definition there has been a proliferation of articles on the subject of knowledge workers and knowledge work in what might be considered fairly traditional work settings, which has led some commentators to suggest that all work is in fact knowledge work (Knights et al., 1993). However, in this chapter we are not using this broad definition but instead focus on those sectors in today's knowledge-based post-industrial economy which compete on the basis of their ability to create, apply and share professional and discipline-based knowledge. This includes sectors where the skills and expertise required are not necessarily acquired through formal education and qualifications but where knowledge is still the basis for competition. For example, many skills that are applied within the field of ICT, such as software development, web page design and so on, are skills that are often largely self-taught and almost develops intuitively by those individuals with a particular interest in IT. In many instances it is not necessary to have a degree in computer science in order to become a software expert or web developer. It is therefore quite difficult to give a precise definition of a knowledge-intensive firm in terms of the particular skills and expertise required.

From a critical perspective, Alvesson (1993, 2001) suggests that knowledge-intensive firms might be more usefully seen purely as 'systems of persuasion' – relying primarily on their persuasive strategies (esoteric skills) rather than expert knowledge or skills *per se* to convince clients of their superior ability and expertise to satisfy client expectations. This might be the case in some service-based knowledge-intensive firms, for example, some advertising agencies, but certainly not all knowledge-intensive firms. Whilst there is therefore a lack of clarity and a degree of ambiguity around the term 'knowledge-intensive firm', it is a useful one with which to encapsulate a broad range of firms operating across sectors in knowledge-based, post-industrial economies. What is indisputable is that many types of knowledge-intensive firm emerged in the late twentieth and early twenty-first centuries and now such firms constitute important industry sectors within a post-industrial economy. In this chapter we address the ways in which they organize and the drivers for particular modes of organizing. We next turn to describing the distinctive characteristics of knowledge work and knowledge workers.

THE DISTINCTIVE CHARACTERISTICS OF KNOWLEDGE WORK AND KNOWLEDGE WORKERS

Autonomy

Generally knowledge workers expect to have considerable autonomy in their work. The nature of the work, which is often characterized by creativity and problem-solving, demands autonomy. It is the knowledge workers themselves who tend to be the most appropriate people to decide how to initiate, plan, organize and coordinate their major work tasks. Unlike other kinds of workers, knowledge workers possess or 'own' the organization's primary means of production – that is, knowledge. They therefore expect and demand autonomy and management is not really in a position to deny them. This is not to say that knowledge workers work alone, typically they work in teams of varying sizes with varying degrees of inter-dependency. In addition, it is not always the case that management in knowledge-intensive firms shares the same levels of skills and expertise as the expert workforce they are trying to manage. Therefore, knowledge workers' demand for autonomy, in combination with an insufficient understanding of the work being conducted in some instances, means that management is typically not in a position to directly control or even manage knowledge work processes. Therefore, it is perhaps more appropriate within a knowledge-work setting to suggest that management's role is to provide the necessary *enabling context* that will *facilitate* knowledge work. Further evidence for this is provided in more recent research conducted by Amabile et al. (2004, 2005). Amabile and colleagues conducted research focused on the cognitive aspects of creativity and adopted a social psychology methodology. In total 222 knowledge workers, working in 26 teams across 7 companies and 3 industries completed a daily questionnaire which sought information to establish the relationship between positive affect (mood) and creativity. A positive mood was found to be positively associated with creativity and this lingered through to the following day (Amabile et al., 2005). Moreover leadership behaviour was found to have a significant influence on subordinates in that leader behaviours was found to precipitate subordinate perceptual and affective reactions, which in turn influenced subordinate creative performance (Amabile et al., 2004).

Knowledge base and working methods

Different types of knowledge worker rely, create, share and apply different types of knowledge in their work. Thus in different knowledge work settings distinctive 'epistemic cultures' can be found (Knorr-Cetina, 1999), epistemic cultures being 'those amalgams of arrangements and mechanisms. . . . – which, in a given field, *make up how we know what we know'* (Knorr-Cetina, 1999, p. 1; italics authors own). Such cultures are characterized by different social, discursive and material practices, including different levels of interaction with natural objects, sign systems and so on. When we consider the different epistemic cultures associated with different forms of knowledge work we start to appreciate the 'the complex texture of knowledge as practiced' (Knorr-Cetina, 1999, p. 2) and how this might differ across different knowledge work contexts. Robertson et al. (2003) found significant differences in knowledge creating practices across a scientific consultancy and a legal consultancy which was explained in terms of institutionally embedded means of legitimating knowledge across scientific and legal contexts. These included different emphases on experimentation versus interpretation, different forms of personal networking, and significant differences in the relative importance of codifying knowledge. In scientific professions for example, claims to knowledge are legitimized by the application of the scientific method (principally experimental) to natural and biological phenomena. Once established and replicated through the scientific method and validated by the scientific community, such knowledge claims transcend particular contexts (Collins, 1985). In contrast, 'lawyers point to the law finding of judges and the law making of legislatures' (Halliday, 1985, p. 426). Thus the knowledge claims of the legal profession extend only to particular jurisdictions and particular points in time. It is also important to recognize that, as well as the broad epistemological differences that exist between professions, such differences are also found amongst different specialisms within a broad professional grouping (Drazin, 1990). This has implications for management inasmuch as attempts to introduce standard work practices and procedures (e.g. Knowledge Management systems and tools), may be perceived as contrary to the ongoing epistemic practices and an unnecessary distraction from core work processes.

Co-location

Another distinguishing feature of the type of work conducted by knowledge workers in knowledge-intensive firms is that there is often the need to work remotely from the employing firm, typically physically located at the client firm. This physical co-location of knowledge workers can be an important management issue to be addressed. For example, client firms may well be inclined to offer permanent employment to knowledge workers who produce good results and who might prove to be a lot less expensive if employed directly by the client rather than on a consultancy basis. The client firm might therefore be in direct competition with the employing firm for the services of knowledge workers. Not only is management therefore required to focus on strategies to aid retention in relation to direct competitors to the firm, they must also consider the development of retention strategies in relation to their client firms.

In addition, knowledge workers are typically organized in teams with more or less interdependence depending on the nature of the task. Physical co-location can therefore also be problematic for team-working even when sophisticated ICT is made available. The complexity of knowledge working often makes face-to-face modes of interaction the only viable communication medium for sharing and creating knowledge at critical points in the process. Here then, management again is required to develop strategies and mechanisms that will enable the coordination and integration of knowledge work processes across the team without necessarily directly intervening in those processes.

'Gold collar' workers

The distinctive characteristics of knowledge workers and knowledge work processes led to the term 'gold collar' worker being applied to knowledge workers (Kelley, 1990). This term implies that these workers need to be managed skilfully, provided with excellent working conditions and generally afforded exceptional, or at least very good, terms and conditions of employment. There are exceptions to this naturally, particularly in large knowledge-intensive firms, such as large management consultancies (cf. Alvesson and Karreman, 2007). However, in small- and medium-sized knowledge-intensive firms, leaders and managers of the firm typically offer superior employment conditions which can be viewed as providing an enabling context for knowledge work (Baron et al., 2001).

In addition to terms and conditions of employment, modes of organizing need to be developed which will be conducive to knowledge work and viewed favourable by knowledge workers. Management must therefore pay careful attention to both the structural and the cultural conditions that exist within the firm. Knowledge-intensive firms thus typically need to organize differently compared to more traditional firms where workers are not necessarily the direct productive force of the organization and, in many respects, are easy to replace. There are still relatively few in-depth empirical studies of the management of knowledge-intensive firms (though see Alvesson,

1995, 2004). Articles on the topic however continue to proliferate and many focus on what is perceived to be the major problem of motivating knowledge workers (O'Neill and Adya, 2007; Thompson and Heron, 2006). These articles are somewhat limited in their focus and do not directly address aspects of the wider organizational context. Here however we are concerned primarily with developing a more holistic account and focus on what constitutes an enabling context for knowledge work within knowledge-intensive settings. The generic structural and cultural conditions which are considered to facilitate the management of knowledge-intensive firms are considered in conjunction with some of the structural or cultural barriers that might mitigate against successful outcomes from knowledge work processes.

FACILITATING KNOWLEDGE WORK – ORGANIZING AS AN ADHOCRACY

The way in which knowledge-intensive firms structure and organize internally will be crucial where innovation and creativity are the basis on which the firm competes. Whilst it will be particularly important for management to offer good terms and conditions of employment to knowledge workers, the way in which the major work processes are managed and coordinated will be equally significant. An approach to organizing needs to be developed that is synergistic with knowledge work and provides an enabling context for the practice of knowledge work.

The way in which many knowledge-intensive firms organize tends to reflect the more general trend towards flatter, less bureaucratized ways of organizing that are becoming more common across all sectors in the twenty-first century. In general terms, knowledge-intensive firms try to organize highly organically and flexibly, generally around teams. Henry Mintzberg (1979) identified five archetypal structural forms that characterize the way firms organize. He suggests that where creativity and innovation – typically in the form of developing novel solutions to client problems – are a conscious strategy, as often tends to be the case within knowledge-intensive firms, then an 'adhocracy' is the most appropriate organizational configuration. The adhocracy is almost the complete opposite of the traditional bureaucracy. An adhocracy genuinely de-emphasizes a hierarchical structure in preference to a dynamic organizational structure based on self-formed and self-managed project teams, decentralized decision-making and minimal formalization in terms of policies, rules and procedures. Within an adhocracy, Mintzberg suggests, control tends to be based on professionalism and shared, organizational values – referred to as cultural or normative control – rather than on more typical forms of direct control such as direct supervision and adherence to rules and procedures. To summarize this analysis, Table 3.2 highlights the distinctive characteristics of the adhocracy in comparison to the traditional bureaucracy.

The adhocracy can also be contrasted with traditional professional service firms where conflict can often arise between competing professional and organizational values (Raelin, 1991). For example, professionals will naturally want to complete client work to the best of their professional abilities, applying discipline-based knowledge (legal, financial, scientific) to client problems. However, time is always considered to be a precious resource in these firms and directly related to the fee structure. There can therefore, on occasion, be conflict between the professional values of the lawyer or accountant, for example, to do a 'good job' and the needs of the firm to manage the firm's resources across the client base as efficiently as possible. According to Raelin,

Table 3.2 – The bureaucracy and the adhocracy compared

Bureaucracy	Adhocracy
Multiple level hierarchy	Minimal hierarchy
Work processes organized around functional groups	Work processes self-organized around teams
Many formal rules, policies and procedures	Few or no formal rules, policies and procedures
Direct control characterized by supervision	Normative control characterized by self-management
Centralized decision-making	Decentralized decision-making
Coordination achieved through explicit rules and procedures	Coordination achieved though mutual adjustment
Highly mechanistic form	Highly organic form

managing partners within these types of professional service firm are required to find ways of mediating these conflicting tensions.

This conflict of values, however, is not necessarily so apparent in some more contemporary types of knowledge-intensive firm where the notion of 'professionalism' is broader and tends to refer to general beliefs and expectations around high standards of performance and a dominant work ethic. This is explored further later in this chapter. Thus, in general, the informal, loosely coupled organizational context of the adhocracy is considered to provide the necessary autonomous working conditions in which individuals can spend time experimenting with ideas and more generally engaging in creative and innovative work. Whilst it may seem somewhat atypical for management to choose to organize in this way, this approach tends to be adopted in many contemporary knowledge-intensive sectors such as software development, new media, specialist consultancies and so on. It has been shown that any significant shift from this mode of organizing can be highly detrimental to both organizational performance and employee turnover. Baron et al. (2001), for example, conducted a large-scale, longitudinal survey of software firms in Silicon Valley over a ten-year period which focused on modes of organizing, performance, CEO and employee turnover. Baron's team discovered that across a population of 173 software firms over time there were four dominant organizing templates. These templates were characterized by what was considered to be the primary motivation to work for the firm (attachment), the primary selection criteria and the primary means of co-ordination and control. Across the five templates the nature of the work conducted within the firm across the star, engineering and bureaucracy was considered to be the major means of attachment, attracting knowledge workers to these firms and promoting retention. The commitment template was characterized by knowledge workers' strong emotional attachment to the firm (love) and money was the major means of attachment in firms characterized as autocracies. Typically skills were the major selection criteria applied although firms adopting the star template selected on the basis of future potential. The star template firms also relied largely on self-control and professionalism as the basis for co-ordination and control, whilst the engineering and commitment templates relied on cultural control. These are summarized in Table 3.3.

The majority of firms in the sample were identified as either Engineering (34 per cent) or Commitment (13 per cent) types and 11 per cent of the sample were also identified as Star types. Only 6 per cent organized as bureaucracies and 7 per cent

Table 3.3 – Organizing templates that characterize high-tech knowledge-intensive firms

Type	Attachment	Selection	Co-ord/control
Star	Work	Potential	Professional
Engineering	Work	Skills	Cultural
Commitment	Love	Fit	Cultural
Bureaucracy	Work	Skills	Formal
Autocracy	Money	Skills	Direct

Source: Adapted from Baron et al., 2001, p. 968.

organized as autocracies where the CEO adopted a command and control mode of organizing. The remainder of the sample were classified as hybrids. The majority of firms therefore relied primarily on professional or cultural (normative) control (see below) rather than formal co-ordination and control mechanisms as a means to co-ordinate work. This supports the idea that an organic, informal and flexible mode of organizing is preferred in these types of knowledge-intensive firm (the notion of cultural or normative control is explored in depth later in the chapter). Notably, firms which adopted a bureaucratic or autocratic model had significantly higher employee turnover than those adopting a commitment or star model. Often over time, with a change in CEO came a change in organizing and the most de-stabilizing in terms of employee turnover, and firm performance was the shift from star or commitment types to the bureaucracy. This tended to occur when firms went public and shareholders demanded more traditional modes of management. The very few firms that shifted from a star model (arguably the template that most closely resembles the adhocracy) to bureaucracy experienced the highest employee turnover. Baron et al.'s research therefore clearly demonstrates that the majority of knowledge-intensive firms do tend to organize largely informally and traditional bureaucratic modes of organizing are not suitable if innovation is required.

More recent research by Robertson and Swan (2004) also highlighted that subtle shifts in organizing template from an adhocracy to a 'soft bureaucracy' (again largely legitimated by the public flotation of the firm onto the stock market) can also have a significant detrimental effect. Soft bureaucracy is considered to be a new, subtle form of bureaucratic control and domination characterized by 'ambivalent structures of governance, within which domination is not essentially exerted by means of, for example, violence, direct punishment or local hierarchical supervision, but through sophisticated managerial strategies' (Courpasson, 2000, p. 142). Control in 'soft bureaucracies' is thus characterized by four distinctive components: (1) a specific combination of impersonal and personal obedience; (2) centralization as a means of legitimating political decisions; (3) control based on soft coercion and protection; (4) control which fuses external and internal legitimacy. In short, the aim is to manage knowledge-intensive firms to be 'both simultaneously innovative (retaining the appearance of worker autonomy) and yet able to control innovation' (Robertson and Swan, 2004, p. 130). Ultimately however Robertson and Swan (2004) demonstrate that whilst soft bureaucracy may be one way of subtly controlling knowledge workers, the negative effect in terms of morale and subsequent performance may be significant. Their research also supports Baron et al.'s earlier research which highlighted that going public, and the demands of the market (shareholders) for greater formalization can start to erode the enabling context for knowledge work.

STRUCTURAL CONSTRAINTS ON KNOWLEDGE WORK

Development of organizational 'best practice'

Research has demonstrated that even when the structural conditions are generally supportive of knowledge work tasks, it is still very easy for creativity and innovation to be stifled (Starbuck, 1992). Firms are therefore cautioned to try and avoid the development of particular norms and practices that might constrain innovative behaviour. For example, informal routines that have developed over time can quickly start to become standardized ways of working embedded in physical capital, routines and even organizational culture. These informal routines can develop into knowledge that becomes codified into firm-specific 'best practice' templates, such as systematic auditing procedures and tools for project planning and development. As the usage of these tools spreads and comes to be seen as almost mandatory within the firm, then innovation can be constrained as consideration of new tools, concepts and ways of working tends to be precluded. This, however, is perhaps less likely to happen in scientific contexts where experimentation is a dominant epistemic practice and notions of 'best practice' are somewhat redundant.

Monitoring of time

Starbuck also highlights that in many knowledge-intensive firms, such as consultancies and advertising agencies, time spent working on client projects is often monitored and rigorously accounted for, as it is billable time and needs to be carefully documented to the satisfaction of management and the client. This monitoring, however, can often inhibit innovative behaviour even when timescales have been mutually agreed between the project team and the client – as should be the case in a genuine operating adhocracy. Where this is common practice knowledge workers often reduce or ultimately fail to spend time searching for, creating or acquiring new knowledge and actively learning. This 'redundant' time (Nonaka, 1994) is considered to be particularly crucial for innovation and yet is simply not available within those knowledge-intensive firms that are intent upon monitoring and controlling billable time.

Growth

Starbuck also emphasizes that, over time, knowledge-intensive firms often have a tendency to attempt to diversify and grow and this is not always a sensible strategic decision. Increasing growth and diversification often lead to increasing formalization, layers of hierarchy and increasing numbers of support staff which can all ultimately lead to the firm experiencing problems. As Starbuck states, 'when support staff come to outnumber experts greatly, or when knowledge-intensive firms (KIFs) claim expertise in too many domains, KIFs lose their halos of expertise and their credibility' (1992, p. 737). Mintzberg in fact suggests that the adhocracy is a typical organizational form only in young, start-up, entrepreneurial firms. He argues that over time adhocracies evolve into other archetypes – in the case of knowledge-intensive firms they often evolve into professional bureaucracies. The firm necessarily becomes more formalized, introducing, for example, levels of professional management in an attempt to manage basic requirements such as efficiency improvements.

As discussed earlier in the chapter, this shift in structure and organizing may however be counterproductive where innovation is the basis on which the firm competes. Research conducted by Lowendahl (1997) demonstrated that a strategy of growth can be counterproductive, particularly for those firms that compete on the basis of their ability to solve complex problems for clients. A compromise, however, might be achieved by creating new, autonomous business units as soon as the firm reaches a particular size or introducing internal markets around a project based form of organizing. These new business units should ideally be led by those who recognize the need for an enabling context and the importance and significance of low levels of formalization and decentralized decision-making for knowledge work processes. A number of high-tech firms operating in Cambridgeshire in the United Kingdom (often referred to as 'Silicon Fen') have adopted this strategy. 'Spinning out' new firms as opposed to organizational growth is the approach these firms have adopted in order to manage the exploitation of new innovations developed in-house. These firms are therefore consciously attempting to continue to operate as adhocracies-stimulating innovation but avoiding organizational growth.

CULTURAL CONDITIONS IN SUPPORT OF KNOWLEDGE WORK

Many knowledge-intensive firms do attempt to structure and organize along the lines of an adhocracy, recognizing that this approach provides an enabling context for knowledge work. However, as discussed in the previous section, this highly informal approach to organizing can often be problematic to sustain in the long run. In order for an organization to survive in the long term, it must be able to achieve and sustain a competitive level of profitability. When firms organize predominantly around self-formed and self-managed knowledge-based teams, it can be very difficult for the leaders of such firms to both develop and manage efficiency criteria even when the firm remains small.

The nature of much of the work that is carried out can be both ambiguous and intangible and is therefore difficult to measure, control or even quantify. For example, advertising agencies develop 'ideas' for clients and specialist consultancy firms develop bespoke solutions to client problems. In these cases, it is extremely difficult for managers or even knowledge workers themselves to estimate the resources required in terms of time, expertise and skills to successfully complete client projects. In addition successful outcomes cannot always be guaranteed as innovation is an inherently uncertain process. In many instances successful outcomes can only be measured by the degree to which the client is satisfied with the outcome. Rational, qualified judgements that highlight means–ends relationships are difficult or impossible to make.

Furthermore, it has already been emphasized that knowledge workers will, to a greater or lesser extent, resent any attempt to directly monitor and control their work, demanding and requiring as they do high levels of autonomy in order to carry out their major work tasks. The leaders of knowledge-intensive firms are therefore always seeking ways to manage the fundamental underlying tension that exists between efficiency and autonomy. Whilst structural conditions which emphasize flexibility and self-managed team-working are important preconditions facilitating knowledge work tasks, the cultural conditions within the firm will be at least as important in ultimately creating an enabling context for knowledge work processes that are largely conducted autonomously. It is the cultural conditions within a knowledge-intensive firm that primarily promote 'responsible autonomy' (Friedman, 1977), where employees use their work autonomy to advance the interests of the organization and not just their own personal interests.

Cultural (normative) control

Whilst leaders of knowledge-intensive firms will be keen to employ individuals with particular skills and expertise, their general requirements will be rather broad, recognizing that diversity across the workforce is considered to be a significant factor promoting innovation (see, e.g. Grant, 1996; Lowendahl, 1997; Nonaka, 1994). It was highlighted that the nature of knowledge production is changing and increasingly knowledge production relies on the combination of knowledge from a variety of fields and disciplines. Not only does this create a challenging environment in which to work from the perspective of the individual knowledge worker, diversity also generates significant management challenges in a very loosely organized environment. A form of management grounded in cultural or normative control has been suggested to be an appropriate approach to adopt within these organizational environments. The suggestion is that leaders of these types of firm are in a position to create and develop a corporate culture which workers will want and choose to identify with. By identifying with the organization it is assumed that workers internalize the dominant organizational ideology – values, beliefs and norms – and consequently behave in the interests of the firm.

The arguments around the role of corporate culture have been developing at least since the 1980s and the 'business excellence' ideas of that period (Peters and Waterman, 1982). Deal and Kennedy (1982), Kanter (1984), Schein (1983, 1992), also promoted the idea that it is the primary task of leaders of organizations to develop and actively reinforce *strong* organizational cultures. 'Improvements in productivity and quality, it is argued, flow from corporate cultures that *systematically* recognize and reward individuals, symbolically and materially, for identifying their sense of purpose with the values that are designed into the organization' (Willmott, 1993, pp. 515–516; italics author's own). Naturally this 'leader-led' organizational culture will be characterized by an organizational (core) value system that represents the long-term interests of the firm. This represents the basis of cultural (normative) control in organizations.

Importantly, in this literature strong organizational cultures are those that are shared across the firm, strengthening the firm through integration and enhanced productivity. This integration perspective on organizational culture (Martin, 1992) and much of the literature that advocates the promotion of a strong organizational culture posit culture as an organizational variable that can be directly shaped by the behaviour and core values of the leaders and management of the firm. These core beliefs permeate the whole organization over time and serve to influence the values and norms of behaviour of the rest of the workforce. There is an emphasis on homogeneity, consensus and, importantly, within the context of a knowledge-intensive firm, predictable behaviour which, in this context, is characterized by an impressive work ethic and communitarian loyalty (Alvesson, 2004). This view has persisted over time and more recent literature in this area reinforces the idea that normative control is an important aspect of the enabling context for knowledge work (Pyoria, 2007). What tends to be overlooked here, however, is that whilst predictable behaviour is sought with regard to knowledge workers displaying responsible autonomy, in other respects predictable behaviour is not advocated as this may not necessarily lead to innovation and creativity.

The way in which leaders of firms can actively create and shape organizational culture is explained in detail in Schein's work (1982, 1993). He suggests that leaders are in a position to implement primary embedding mechanisms and secondary reinforcement or articulation mechanisms, which will symbolically reflect and are consistent with the dominant, core values held by the leaders. Specific employment policies and practices such as the criteria used for recruitment and selection, performance management and reward are examples of what Schein refers to as primary embedding mechanisms. Organizational design and structure together with formal statements of organizational philosophy typically found in firms' mission statements are examples of secondary reinforcement mechanisms. Schein suggests that if leaders of firms implement all 12 mechanisms in a consistent and coherent manner then, over time, core organizational values will become shared values across the workforce leading to performance and productivity improvements. Alvesson (2004) also emphasizes the importance of symbolism and symbolic leadership, as an important aspect of creating and sustaining a strong organizational culture within knowledge-intensive settings.

From this perspective, if the leader of a knowledge-intensive firm wished to emphasize the importance of knowledge sharing – as might be expected in knowledge intensive firms – then mechanisms that directly or indirectly rewarded knowledge sharing would need to be introduced. For example, knowledge workers might be financially or symbolically rewarded for contributing to projects they were not directly employed to work on. In this way, by implementing this embedding mechanism in conjunction with other mutually reinforcing mechanisms, Schein suggests that knowledge sharing behaviour in the firm can be encouraged and promoted as knowledge workers begin to recognize that knowledge sharing is a core value within the firm.

Multiple perspectives on organizational culture

There is an overriding assumption in Schein's work and all of the business excellence literature that it is feasible and practicable for leaders of firms to actively create and shape an organizational culture which promotes integration and consensus around dominant organizational values. An expert, highly skilled and often highly educated and diverse workforce might, however, quite naturally hold a wide range of beliefs and values, particularly when diversity extends to national culture. Therefore it cannot simply be assumed or taken for granted that knowledge workers in knowledge-intensive firms will necessarily be willing to subsume their identity and personal value systems to those of the firm. The integration perspective on culture (Martin, 1992), which this literature reflects, assumes certain structural preconditions such as a well-defined hierarchy and highly centralized decision-making. These, as we have seen, are often not in place within knowledge-intensive firms – particularly those that organize as adhocracies. It may therefore be highly problematic to operationalize this approach to 'culture management' in a knowledge-intensive setting. The extent to which the leaders of such firms are in a position to shape beliefs, particularly in such an informal organizational context, is in fact highly questionable.

Leaders of knowledge-intensive firms may therefore have to acknowledge that knowledge workers will naturally hold a variety of beliefs, which cannot necessarily be altered or subsumed within a single organizational value system. This is referred to in Martin's (1992) work as the fragmentation perspective on culture. The fragmentation perspective suggests that culture is better viewed as a metaphor rather than a variable – something an organization *is* rather than something an organization *has*. From this perspective culture is only loosely structured and partially shared, emerging dynamically as organizational members experience each other, events and the organizational context over time.

The fragmentation perspective provides support competing and contradictory value systems held by individuals across the firm, which is often the case in knowledge-intensive firms populated by a highly skilled, diverse workforce. This perspective acknowledges ambiguity, recognizing that within organizations individuals might experience a lack of clarity or simultaneously hold multiple meanings and beliefs. Lack of clarity can result from unclear structures, fuzzy boundaries or imprecise goals. These are likely to be apparent within a knowledge-intensive firm organized broadly as an adhocracy. It may well be the case, then, that knowledge-intensive firms display cultural characteristics more reminiscent of the fragmentation perspective rather than the integration perspective.

Leaders of such firms therefore need to acknowledge and accept that differentiation and fragmentation rather than integration might predominate, and recognize that they are only in a position to loosely manage organizational culture, for example, by promoting perhaps just one specific value or belief that knowledge workers will naturally wish to identify with. Research by Alvesson and Robertson (2006) demonstrated that in several different types of consultancy settings, leaders and management employed a variety of strategic and symbolic mechanisms to construct an elite organizational identity with which consultants readily identified; this served as an overarching way of integrating knowledge workers within these firms. Consultancy firms appear to be particularly appropriate settings for the construction of elite social identities because of the type of people employed (often of high academic ability) and the nature of much of the work that is conducted (ambiguous and intellectually demanding). Consultants in these firms provide their expertise to other professionals – the majority of their clients are highly skilled themselves – therefore a high level of self-confidence is required. A construction of self and the organization as elite and therefore clearly superior in vital respects can be important resources on which to draw to promote and reinforce the required self-confidence. Moreover an elite identity was found to be a significant mediator of consultancy work for a variety of reasons. First, an elite identity was found to promote self-discipline which sustained a desire to accomplish high standards of performance. Secondly, perceiving these firms to only recruit 'the very best' served to attract applicants and generate high retention rates. Finally, a shared belief that consultants themselves and the firm as a whole were 'elite' generated a strong image that generated high calibre clients.

Typically, organizational elites have been considered the privileged few who control organizational resources and have considerable power and influence both organizationally and to some extent at a societal level (Hill, 1995; Kabanoff and Holt, 1996). Thus in much of the extant literature the elite is located at the apex of an organization. Alvesson and Robertson, however, demonstrated that the notion of belonging to the elite can exist across whole firms. By promoting an organizational ethos that is more or less generally accepted and shared, rather than attempting to instil and reinforce a dominant core value system, there is a greater likelihood that knowledge workers will start to see the firm as a 'good' place to work. As far as is possible in such a diverse, loosely structured environment, this approach is more likely to aid retention and promote responsible autonomy within the firm. One example of this is provided by Timothy Koogle, the founder of Yahoo!, a leading web portal, who argues that his organization became successful largely because he promoted the idea that employees should communicate freely with one another and as far as possible engage in genuine consensual decisions making (Greenberg and Baron, 2000). This ethos was considered to be essential in the fast-paced world of the Internet and at the same time intuitively appealing to the knowledge workers employed.

CONCLUSIONS

This chapter has highlighted the structural and cultural conditions that provide an enabling context for knowledge work processes characterized by creativity and innovation in knowledge-intensive settings. Some of the conditions that can act as barriers to knowledge work were also discussed. It needs to be emphasized, however, that the limited research that has been conducted in such firms highlights that there is no single 'best management practice' here. Many knowledge-intensive firms operate in niche markets – offering very specialized services – and the way in which many of these firms choose to organize is often quite unique and highly context-sensitive. Generally, the structuring and organizing of these firms will be loose, informal and flexible characteristic features of the adhocracy. Whilst the adhocracy might appear to be a somewhat chaotic, relatively unmanaged context, it is perhaps useful to consider the way in which this configuration has been operationalized in a scientific consultancy firm based in the United Kingdom. The way in which structural and cultural conditions interact to promote knowledge work processes is explained in the following case study and illustrates the complex conditions actively promoted over time which have ultimately mediated the tensions around efficiency and autonomy within a knowledge-intensive setting. First the case is described and then two questions are posed.

We focus on the actual process of knowledge creation or knowledge generation and adopt a micro-level of analysis. We move from a firm-level analysis of the way in which modes of organizing and organizational conditions can develop in support of knowledge work processes to an analysis of the dynamics of knowledge creation processes within a project team setting.

CASE STUDY

SCIENCECO MANAGING AN EXPERT WORKFORCE

ScienceCo was founded in 1980. It is a medium-sized, technology-based consultancy company, located on the outskirts of London. It operates today on a global basis. At the time of its inception, the founder wished to create a consultancy environment that would not only develop solutions in response to client problems, but also stimulate invention and innovation more generally. Eighty-five per cent of the workforce are highly educated scientists and technologists, who rely primarily on their expertise and knowledge rather than equipment or systems to provide inventions and innovative solutions for manufacturing, engineering and pharmaceutical companies around the world.

Since 1980, the firm has grown from a small entrepreneurial business employing a handful of scientific consultants specializing in engineering and communications to a medium-sized company employing about 200 people and incorporating other scientific disciplines such as biotechnology, applied sciences and information systems. The workforce is truly international, incorporating 19 different nationalities. In defining the type of projects that ScienceCo conducted for their clients, it is important to understand the difference between invention and innovation. Consultants working in interdisciplinary project teams develop completely new concepts and products that are marketed as intellectual property rights (IPR) to clients and project teams. They also develop innovative solutions to client problems using existing concepts, ideas and technologies in new ways. The firm has been responsible for the invention of major scientific and technological developments that are recognized and used throughout the world. One such item is the electronic security tag, which since its invention has been manufactured and marketed by the Swedish firm Esselte. ScienceCo is primarily in the business of creating new knowledge and applying existing knowledge in new ways.

A crucial issue for management at ScienceCo has always been attracting and retaining a highly skilled, expert workforce of international standing in order for the firm to grow and successfully compete on a global basis. Thus developing an appropriate organizational environment in which expert consultants are keen to work has been of paramount importance. The following sections outline the organizational structure, human resource practices, patterns of IT usage and organizational culture that have developed within the firm over time.

ORGANIZATIONAL STRUCTURE

Attempts have been made to maintain a fairly flat organizational structure throughout the firm's development. Even today, there is fundamentally only one level of management, consisting of the founder (now Executive Chairman), Chairman and Managing Director. Decision-making within the firm has typically involved significant numbers of consultants as well as management. A worker committee, the Board of Management, which consists primarily of consultants and one or two support staff, make recommendations to management regarding day-to-day operations and organization. Management communicates constantly with the whole of the firm (generally using e-mail) regarding new projects and potential future projects. Turnover and profitability are also communicated to everyone on a monthly basis. Consultants are encouraged to innovate outside of client project work, and they can request financial resources for this through the Innovation Exploitation Board. This forum includes consultants from across the firm, as well as the management team, who meet regularly to discuss the feasibility of new ideas proposed by consultants. All members of the management team are also active consultants, contributing to project team-working within the firm.

Consultants are organized across three divisions within the firm according to their particular scientific expertise. These are Business Innovation (BI), Technology, Internet, Media and Entertainment (TIME), and Engineering (ENG). While divisional managers head up divisions, there are actually no hierarchical levels either within or across divisions. Divisional managers tend to be those individuals who are prepared to take on some minimal adminis-trative responsibilities such as recording revenue generation and monitoring the projects that are being managed by consultants within their own division. In many cases, divisional managers are actually remunerated less than other consultants within their division (see section on 'Performance management') and they also actively contribute to project working across the firm.

Divisions have emerged, merged and disbanded in a reactive manner over time, based on the client project work in hand. In 1980, there were only two skill groups, Engineering and Communications. However, in 1990, a divisional structure was introduced in order to provide improved financial accountability. By 1996, seven divisions existed including two business consulting divisions, Information Systems and Applied Sciences. The Life Sciences division emerged at this time from the Applied Sciences division when enough biotechnology projects had been secured to ensure the divi-sions' sustainability in the medium term. By 2000, however, Life Sciences had again merged with the Engineering division together with Applied Sciences. Business Innovation by this time incorporated both business divisions and the Information Systems division. Despite the existence of divisions, consultants tend to work in an interdisciplinary manner across divisions within small project teams. This occurs because the nature of client requirements generally requires cross-disciplinary skills and expertise. These project teams are self-forming and self-managed. Project team-working is discussed in more detail within the section on 'Perform-ance management'.

RECRUITMENT AND SELECTION

For many years, the firm did not employ a Human Resources (HR) manager. However, in 1995, based on predicted and expected project work, the firm was faced with a requirement to increase the expert workforce by 15 per cent (and this was projected to continue annually, compounded). The firm recruited a Human Resources manager to develop a more formal recruitment and selection process, and to develop ways of maintaining high retention rates across the firm.

In the past, consultants had typically been recruited informally by word of mouth, drawing upon consultants' global personal networks of colleagues and contacts. In order to make the recruitment process more effective, the HR manager developed good relationships with two international recruitment agencies that had offices throughout the world. Once provided with a person specification and a brief that described very broadly the type of work carried out by the firm, they provided shortlists of candidates on an ongoing basis. In terms of the selection process, the founder had always insisted that candidates take an AH6 intelligence test and Cattell's 16PF personality test. Given that the majority of candidates shortlisted by the agencies generally had a PhD in a scientific discipline, it was virtually impossible for any candidate to fail the AH6 test. It was also difficult to 'fail' the 16PF because the firm did not look for an 'ideal' profile other than 'openness' and a 'willingness to experiment'. Consultants were simply keen to see what sort of personality profile candidates had. Thus, almost all candidates who had been shortlisted proceeded to an initial short interview with the HR manager and the relevant divisional manager.

During this preliminary interview, the HR manager stated that candidates were expected to demonstrate a strong understanding of their own and, more importantly, other disciplines, because of the need to work in interdisciplinary teams sharing knowledge. They were also expected to be 'almost naturally innovative' and have a strong commercial awareness. The HR manager stated,

> It's quite a unique mix we are looking for. All the way through the selection process, we give out big indicators to say the sort of organization we are. It's quite aggressive maybe, and I'm sure interviewees will pick up quite a lot of arrogance on the part of the company. But the messages we are giving out are more about confidence in what we do and how we do it rather than us thinking we are better than anyone else.

And approximately 25 per cent, which typically equates to four candidates, progress to a second interview. The firm was not overly concerned about the high numbers of candidates rejected. Management is only interested in individuals with either a PhD or particular expertise within a scientific discipline, who are fluent in English, have some commercial/industrial experience, and who are prepared to adopt the role of a consultant. This role involves marketing their own and, more generally, the firm's abilities and expertise. It is therefore a relatively unique set of characteristics which is sought in candidates.

The second interview focuses on assessing the candidate's ability to market to clients, their overall level of expertise, and their ability to work within interdisciplinary project teams. This second interview is a panel interview involving a number of consultants from several divisions, who 'quiz' the applicant in some depth on their knowledge of their own and other science- or technology-based fields. Panel members are randomly drawn from across the firm, based on availability at the time of the interview. If the panel agrees on a candidate, then the candidate will be recommended for appointment to the MD.

In 1996, typically, 16 candidates were interviewed for each post, and for each of those interviewed, approximately ten CVs would have been received from the recruitment agencies. The selection process is described as 'rigorous' by the HR manager. He emphasized that the interviews focus primarily on the candidates' ability to 'fit in' to the ScienceCo way of working. This involves willingness and ability to collaboratively share knowledge across different science- and technology-based fields, both within project teams and more generally. The HR manager commented,

> You get a CV, and the person has a PhD, and they've worked for a pretty high-powered research agency, and that's brilliant. You've got to see them, but you know that there is a pretty strong chance that the moment you meet them you're going to know what they're not – they're not one of us.

PERFORMANCE MANAGEMENT

Only one formal system exists at ScienceCo, and this is the performance management system that was introduced in 1990. This system was introduced at the same time as consultants were allocated to divisions. Before this, individual consultants' performance had not been managed. The system focuses on divisional revenue targets (DRTs) and personal revenue targets (PRTs). Management establishes these targets at the beginning of each financial year, and they are monitored monthly. The same monthly PRT applies to all consultants, regardless of age, experience and so on. Hence, DRTs are the accumulation of PRTs, premised on the number of consultants within the divisions. By default, then, the larger divisions had to generate more revenue.

Revenue is generated through project work that is generally priced at a flat rate rather than a fee rate. A lead consultant emerges on client projects. Typically, this is the consultant who has the most contact with a particular client. The 'lead' consultant is responsible for negotiating the value of the project with the client, after careful consideration of the resources that will be required in terms of breadth of expertise and time. Lead consultants will use e-mail to inform consultants throughout the firm about potential new projects and the skills and expertise that will be required. Once the value of a project has been determined with the client, it is the responsibility of individual consultants who want to work on the project to negotiate with the lead consultant regarding the amount of project revenue they will be allocated. As there are no formal systems to record these negotiations, e-mail messages serve as a record of any negotiations that take place. The allocation of project revenue contributes to the individual consultants' PRT and the DRT to which they are assigned.

Management described PRTs as a scheme for making people sell their skills to other people in an effective manner:

> It is a micro economy. It is a free market for expertise. Over the years it has been the subject of much controversy as it puts a lot of pressure on people, and it is in this way that we try to maintain a competitive (some would say combative) environment. It does create tension, but at the same time, it enhances innovation given by the rate at which new ideas come out of the organization.

In order to achieve PRTs, consultants generally work on a small number of projects at any one time, commanding a percentage of the overall revenue from each one. Achievement of PRTs consistently over time is expected of everyone, other than the most inexperienced consultants and recent recruits. The majority of consultants usually achieve their PRT. However, consistency across whole divisions is problematic and occasionally divisional managers find it difficult to achieve their DRT. At the end of each financial year, divisional managers performance-rank those within their division, based on achievement of PRTs and contribution to overall sales. This is a transparent process and individual consultants are free to discuss, and in some instances dispute, their overall ranking position. When divisional managers have agreed on their rankings within their division, they meet with the management team to agree on overall ranking across the firm. Individual consultants are then awarded percentage increments according to their ranking. Underperformers are tolerated in the medium term. Consultants who do not achieve PRTs over time will not receive a salary increment, but they are actively encouraged and helped by management to improve performance the following year. Management has never introduced salary scales within the firm, and no formal career structure exists because there is a no formal hierarchy. Individual consultants are therefore awarded a percentage increase based on the salary they have personally negotiated with the MD on their appointment to the firm.

It is also important to recognize that consultants manage their own time both within and outside of project working. Consultants are free to choose their hours of work and length of vacations. This means that some consultants work continuously, occasionally for months at a time and then take extended vacations, up to 2–3 months at any one time. Other consultants choose to work regular hours and take shorter breaks. Divisional managers only expect to be made aware of vacations (time and length) and consultants are trusted to manage their time effectively.

TRAINING AND DEVELOPMENT

Professional development is particularly important to all consultants at ScienceCo. In order to stay at the top of their professional fields, consultants must be aware of any developments in their field, and they need to participate in activities that offer the opportunity for further professional development. Again, consultants are responsible for identifying their own requirements in terms of courses, conferences and workshops. Management simply provides the necessary financial resources, which in some cases are considerable. It is assumed that consultants will organize their workloads accordingly, in order to participate in professional development without any significant disruption of project work occurring.

Training for consultants has never been considered an issue within the firm. Management has always believed that the quality of the people employed negates any need for systematic training. It is assumed that if dedicated training is required, for example, in the use of particular software application for project work, then consultants are sufficiently skilled to train themselves at times that suit them.

IT USAGE

Significant resources have always been made available for investment in any technology that might facilitate project working. An e-mail system was introduced in 1990 to facilitate communication between consultants. By this time, the firm had grown to around 100 consultants, and the opportunities for regular face-to-face contact with everyone were rapidly diminishing. The e-mail system began to be used extensively almost immediately, as there were very few formal systems or procedures in use for communication, and on any 1 day, significant numbers of consultants would be working remotely at client firms. By 1996, consultants were receiving between 100 and 150 e-mails each day, and despite attempts to curtail the use of e-mail for trivial matters, consultants today still receive about this number. This is because no protocols are used to classify mail sent, other than to attach a prefix of SOC for 'social' communication and INNOV for an e-mail where the sender is searching for information.

It is the e-mail system that is generally used to broadcast requests for information when putting together proposals for clients. Anyone who wants to be involved in a potential project initially communicates in outline their potential contribution, in terms of skills and expertise, via e-mail. The system works well in this respect as the medium is good for communicating low-level information, quickly and across the whole firm. However, the level of e-mail communication consultants are exposed to on a daily basis is recognized generally as a significant burden. Norms have developed, such as sending replies to everyone in the firm and failing to edit the title of e-mails to ensure that it relates to the content of the e-mail. These norms, while making the use of e-mail relatively thoughtless, informal and simple, have generated a somewhat chaotic and haphazard system of communication. For example, some consultants, when faced with ever-increasing numbers of e-mail, choose not to bother reading the majority, and only use the system when absolutely necessary.

Other technologies such as groupware technologies are occasionally used and intranets have been set up in and across divisions. Consultants are aware that packages such as Lotus Notes can provide useful project documentation. However, the majority of projects continue to be documented in a highly idiosyncratic manner because project leaders are free to provide documentation in whatever way they deem appropriate. Client requirements need to be fulfilled in this respect. However, if the client is satisfied with the documentation produced, no further effort is directed at producing, recording and classifying project documentation in a consistent manner across the firm. Again, consultants are trusted to produce high-quality project documentation, without recourse to formal standards, systems or procedures.

The use of both groupware and intranets tends therefore to be spasmodic and piecemeal. For example, groupware, such as Lotus Notes, only tends to be used when geographical constraints impose a need to work in this fashion. Consultants prefer project team-working to be face to face, rather than via Lotus Notes discussion threads. Groupware technology is not generally considered rich enough to adequately convey some types of information and knowledge required during project work. In many instances, when significant decisions or results need to be shared across a project team, the technology is simply used to schedule a telephone conference call.

CULTURE

As stated in the introduction, from the outset the founder wanted to promote an innovative environment and one that would stimulate creativity. With this in mind, he attempted to develop and perpetuate an environment characterized by an absence of hierarchy, rules and formal procedures. An emphasis was placed on maintaining an egalitarian environment, one in which everyone was in principle free to contribute to decision-making, and one that allowed individuals' relative freedom to be creative. While the founder was keen to promote a corporate culture around a small set of core values specifically regarding the importance and value of creativity and innovation, to both the firm and society more generally, he respected individuals as individuals. He did not, therefore, attempt to develop a strong culture that encompassed particular norms of behaviour. The ScienceCo way of working is therefore characterized by a lack of prescription, informality and idiosyncrasy.

The heterogeneity and diversity of the workforce exemplify the importance placed on individuality within the firm. Not only are 19 different nationalities represented, there are also significant differences across the firm with regard to age, experience and general attitudes and behaviour. Individuality often tends to be manifest symbolically in dress, ranging from the bizarre (e.g. running shorts and vest in the depths of winter!) to the more traditional conformist dark suit and tie. During project working, however, diverse groups of individuals with differing expertise are expected to work together jointly, developing solutions to client requirements or problems. While conflict inevitably arises across such a range of diverse individuals, the environment is one in which individuals feel free to speak out without recrimination. Consultants are trusted to resolve any differences that might arise without recourse to the management team, so that ultimately client requirements are satisfied.

While everyone agrees that the environment is highly informal and this is considered to be one of the major attractions of working in the firm, consultants do have different perceptions of what constitutes organizational reality. For example, while everyone agrees that the organization is almost flat, it is widely recognized and acknowledged that a dynamic, informal hierarchy exists based on expertise. However, consultants do differ (in some cases quite considerably) in their opinions as to the hierarchical ordering based on their own personal experience of working with others in the firm. As one consultant stated,

> Nobody in theory has a job title. Single status applies but obviously some people are seen as more powerful, more influential, higher status than others – based purely on what they are seen to contribute to the organization in terms of big projects or particularly innovative ideas.

Individuals across the firm can therefore command powerful positions within the informal hierarchy. Their position will be based on their ability to both acquire new business and command large proportions of project revenue that contribute to their PRT. Positions within this informal hierarchy, however, are transient and relatively ephemeral, as new clients and new projects requiring different skills and expertise are acquired over time.

Questions

- Define and explain six critical organizational factors that have contributed to ScienceCo's growth and ability to retain an expert workforce.
- What are the potential problems that might arise over time in this organizational context?

Summary of Key Learning Points

- Knowledge-intensive firms rely on their workforce for their competitive advantage. Therefore employee retention is a crucial strategic issue within these types of firm.
- 'Knowledge-intensive firm' is a generic term that encapsulates a broad range of firms operating across sectors in a post-industrial economy.
- Knowledge-intensive firms can be classified as client-based, problem-solving or output-based.
- Knowledge workers are often referred to as 'gold collar' workers, acknowledging the autonomy and exceptional working conditions they are generally afforded.
- The adhocracy, characterized by a dynamic organizational structure based on self-formed and self-managed teams, is considered to be an appropriate configuration where innovation is the basis on which a firm competes.
- Structural constraints on knowledge work include the development of organizational 'best practice' templates, monitoring of knowledge workers' time and organizational growth.
- Responsible autonomy is more likely to be achieved if management acknowledges that organizational culture is likely to be characterized by differentiation and fragmentation rather than consensus and integration. Hence management should only attempt to loosely manage culture, aiming to promote an organizational ethos that knowledge workers find accessible and can readily identify with, rather than a dominant core value system.

REFERENCES

Alvesson, M. (1993). Organizations as rhetoric: Knowledge-intensive firms and the struggle with ambiguity. *Journal of Management Studies*, 30(6), 997–1015.

Alvesson, M. (1995). *Management of Knowledge-Intensive Companies*. Berlin/New York: De Gruyter.

Alvesson, M. (2001). Knowledge work: Ambiguity, image and identity. *Human Relations*, 54(7), 863–886.

Alvesson, M. (2004). *Knowledge Work and Knowledge-Intensive Firms.* Oxford: Oxford University Press.

Alvesson, M. and Karreman, D. (2007). Unravelling HRM: Identity, ceremony and control in a management consulting firm. *Organization Science*, 18(4), 711–723.

Alvesson, M. and Robertson, M. (2006). Going public: The emergence and effects of soft bureaucracy within a knowledge-intensive firm. *Organization*, 11(1), 123–148.

Amabile, T. M., Elizabeth, A. S., Giovanni, B. M. and Steven J. K. (2004). Leader behaviors and the work environment for creativity: Perceived leader support. *Leadership Quarterly*, 15(1), 5–32.

Amabile, T. M., Sigal, G. B., Jennifer, S. M. and Barry, M. S. (2005). Affect and creativity at work. *Administrative Science Quarterly*, 50(3), 367–403.

Baron, J., Hannan, M. and Burton, D. (2001). Labor pains: Change in organizational models and employee turnover in young, high-tech firms. *American Journal of Sociology*, 106(4), 960–1012.

Collins, H. (1985). *Changing Order; Replication and Induction in Scientific Practice*. London: Sage.

Cooper, D., Hinings, R. and Greenwood, R. (1996). Sedimentation and transformation in organizational change: The case of Canadian law firms. *Organization Studies*, 17(4), 623–647.

Courpasson, D. (2000). Managerial strategies of domination: Power in soft bureaucracies. *Organization Studies*, 21(1), 141–162.

Deal, T. and Kennedy, A. (1982). *Corporate Cultures: The Rites and Rituals of Corporate Life*. Reading, Mass.: Addison-Wesley.

Friedman, A. (1977). *Industry and Labour*. London: Macmillan – now Palgrave.

Grant, R. (1996). Prospering in dynamically competitive environments: Organizational capability as knowledge integration. *Organization Science*, 7(4), 375–387.

Greenberg, J. and Baron, R. (2000). *Behavior in Organizations*, 7th edn. Englewood Cliffs, NJ: Prentice-Hall.

Greenwood, R., Hinings, C. R. and Brown, J. (1990). 'P2-Form' strategic management: Corporate practices in professional partnerships. *Academy of Management Journal*, 33(4), 725–755.

Halliday, T. (1985). Knowledge mandates: Collective influence by scientific, normative and syncretic professions. *The British Journal of Sociology*, 36(3), 421–439.

Hill, S. (1995). The social organization of boards of directors. *The British Journal of Sociology*, 46(2), 245–279.

Horwitz, F., Heng, C. T. and Quazi, A. (2003). Finders keepers? Attracting, motivating and retaining knowledge workers. *Human Resource Management Journal*, 13(4), 23–44.

Kabanoff, B. and Holt, J. (1996). Changes in the espoused values of Australian organizations 1986–1990. *Journal of Organizational Behavior*, 17(3), 201–220.

Kanter, R. (1984). *The Change Masters*. London: Allen & Unwin.

Kelley, R. (1990). *The Gold Collar Worker – Harnessing the Brainpower of the New Workforce*. Reading, Mass.: Addison-Wesley.

Knorr-Cetina, K. (1999). *Epistemic Cultures: How the Sciences Make Knowledge*. Cambridge, MA: Harvard University Press.

Lowendahl, B. (1997). *Strategic Management of Professional Service Firms*. Copenhagen: Copenhagen Business School Press.

Lowendahl, B. (2000). *Strategic Management of Professional Service Firms*, 2nd edn. Copenhagen: Copenhagen Business School Press.

Martin, J. (1992). *Cultures in Organizations*. New York: Oxford University Press.

Mintzberg, H. (1979). *Structures in Fives, Designing Effective Organizations*. Englewood Cliffs, NJ: Prentice-Hall.

Muzio, D. and Ackroyd, S. (2005). On the consequences of defensive professionalism: Recent changes in the legal labour process. *Journal of Law and Society*, 32(4), 615–642.

Nonaka, I. (1994). A dynamic theory of organizational knowledge creation. *Organization Science*, 5(1), 14–37.

O'Neill, B. and Adya, M. (2007). Knowledge sharing and the psychological contract. *Journal of Managerial Psychology*, 22(4), 411–436.

Peters, T. and Waterman, R. (1982). *In Search of Excellence: Lessons from America's Best-Run Companies*. New York: Harper & Row.

Pyoria, P. (2007). Informal organizational culture: The foundation of knowledge workers' performance. *Journal of Knowledge Management*, 11(3), 16–27.

Raelin, J. A. (1991). *The Clash of Cultures: Managers Managing Professionals*. Boston, Mass.: Harvard Business School Press.

Robertson, M. and Swan, J. (2004). Going public: The emergence and effects of soft bureaucracy in a knowledge intensive firm. *Organization*, 11(1), 123–148.

Robertson, M., Scarbrough, H. and Swan, J. (2003). Knowledge creation in professional firms: Institutional effects. *Organization Studies*, 24(6), 831–857.

Schein, E. (1983). The role of the founder in creating organizational culture. *Organizational Dynamics*, Summer; 12, 13–28.

Schein, E. (1992). *Organizational Culture and Leadership*, 2nd edn. San Francisco: Jossey-Bass.

Starbuck, W. (1992). Learning by knowledge-intensive firms. *Journal of Management Studies*, 29(6), 713–740.

Thompson, M. and Heron, P. (2006). Relational quality and innovative performance in R&D based science and technology firms. *Human Resource Management Journal*, 16, 28.

Willmott, H. (1993). Strength is ignorance; slavery is freedom: Managing culture in modern organisations. *Journal of Management Studies*, 30, 515–552.

KNOWLEDGE MANAGEMENT SYSTEMS

CHAPTER OUTLINE

- Learning Outcomes
- Introduction
- The Historical Roots of Current Enterprise Systems
- Enterprise Systems and the Spread of 'Best Practice' Knowledge
- The Fallacy of 'Best Practice' Knowledge
- The Possession View and Knowledge Management Systems as Repository
- The Practice View and Knowledge Management Systems as Networking
- Conclusions
- Case Study: International Consultancy Company (ICC)
- Summary of Key Learning Points

LEARNING OUTCOMES

At the end of this chapter you should be able to:

- Understand two types of ICT that influence knowledge work and knowledge workers – Knowledge Management Systems (KMS) and Enterprise Systems.
- Understand how Enterprise Systems have evolved from earlier approaches that attempted to capture and standardize 'best practices'.
- Recognize the constraining and facilitating influences of Enterprise Systems on knowledge work and knowledge workers.
- Differentiate between channel/network and platform/repository KMS.
- Develop a critical appreciation of the role of ICTs as 'Knowledge Management Systems'.
- Recognize the difference between structural/possession manifestations of ICTs to support knowledge work and processual/practice approaches.
- Appreciate the potential of new forms of ICT that can expose knowledge processes as well as knowledge content.

INTRODUCTION

We considered how ICTs do not, in and of themselves, change the way work is done on a daily basis, nor the knowledge that is processed across an organization. Unfortunately, as we will see in this chapter, many organizations assume that ICT *does* drive organizational change and assume that introducing some type of ICT will more or less automatically improve Knowledge Management processes. Thus, organizations interested in improving the management and flow of knowledge focus typically on two types of ICT: Knowledge Management Systems (KMS) and Enterprise Systems. KMS are the dominant type of 'KM' initiative and are used to capture, store, search, connect, transfer and, so, reuse information and knowledge across individuals, for example using intranets or e-mail (Alavi and Tiwana, 2003). Enterprise Systems are a different type of ICT but are still important in relation to understanding the role of ICT in knowledge work. Thus, Enterprise Systems are used to support (and control) all types of work, being designed to ensure that standardized and integrated work processes are used across a distributed organization. The idea is that Enterprise Systems embed knowledge about 'best practice' in a software package, so that when an organization adopts an Enterprise System they are also adopting the industry 'best practices' in relation to how best to organize work (Wagner et al., 2006). Below we will explore these technologies, and their historical roots, and also identify their constraining and facilitating impact on knowledge work and knowledge workers and more generally, their effectiveness in supporting Knowledge Management processes.

The deployment of both types of technology is usually based very much on an 'epistemology of possession' approach and are structural in nature – knowledge is viewed as a cognitive resource, a possession, that can be captured and transferred across people using ICT (Schultze and Leidner, 2002). KMS/Enterprise Systems try, then, to transfer knowledge, assuming that it is an entity that can be captured and moved fairly easily across people, places and time. Thus, organizations rely on codifying knowledge that can either be transferred to the particular individual(s) who needs it – typically using e-mail – or put into a repository of some kind – an intranet, for example – where it can be stored and searched, and hopefully found, by those who will find it useful. Or they may rely on embedding knowledge in an Enterprise Systems package that then dictates how work shall be completed to ensure maximum efficiency. Much effort, therefore, goes into codifying knowledge (converting tacit to explicit knowledge, for example) that can be used in distributed locations (transferring it from the individual to the collective), rather than relying on personal networks and collaborative practices.

The dominance of these structural KMS/Enterprise Systems approaches is perhaps not surprising, given that many organizations today are very large and/or geographically distributed. New organizational forms often make it challenging or impossible for organizations to rely on face-to-face communication and personal networks for the sharing of information and knowledge. This is the case whether this be:

1 General communications for the whole organization (e.g. the organizational vision, goals or values) that are communicated through platform technologies, or,
2 Communications for a sub-group of employees (e.g. the budget statement for all VPs, or information about progress for all those involved in a large software project) that are communicated through channel technologies.

While KM initiatives are often structural in nature, there are also new forms of ICT that can potentially accommodate a more processual/practice orientation. These allow observation of the processes and practices through which knowledge is created, and

accept that the same content can be interpreted differently across communities. With the advent of what is sometimes called Web 2.0 or Enterprise 2.0, for example, it is now possible for documents to be created collectively using technologies like google. doc, sharepoint and wikis of all kinds. These technologies crucially allow people to engage in a process of joint knowledge creation and as well as to observe the product of that effort (McAfee, 2006). Moreover, with social networking software applications (including Facebook, Myspace LinkedIn, various kinds of blogs and YouTube), it is now possible for people to conduct online discussions and share a variety of multimedia content. These technologies, in other words, can facilitate interaction and expose practices of knowing as individuals create and recreate content in cyberspace. We will explore these practice-based KMS at the end of this chapter once we have discussed the dominant structural approaches of KMS and Enterprise Systems.

We illustrate in this chapter the problems of an exclusively structural KMS-approach to managing knowledge through exploring the ICC case at the end of the chapter. This consulting company had introduced a KMS in order to facilitate knowledge sharing between people geographically distributed across its global network. However, it did not produce the results that were anticipated.

THE HISTORICAL ROOTS OF CURRENT ENTERPRISE SYSTEMS

Enterprise Systems (a more generic term for the kind of Enterprise Resource Planning or ERP systems) are currently very popular in organizations because of their potential ability to streamline business processes across the value chain (Davenport, 2000; Kumar and Hillegersberg, 2000). Enterprise Systems (also based very much on an epistemology of possession) assume that knowledge about successful organizational practices within a particular industry can be identified, captured and embedded in software and so transferred across organizations. From this perspective, current Enterprise Systems initiatives can be seen as a direct descendant of the much earlier Scientific Management tradition developed by F. W. Taylor. Thus, while Taylor sought to transfer the knowledge that existed in worker's heads to their managers, and the Ford production system sought to transfer workers' and to an extent managers' knowledge to the assembly-line technology, Enterprise Systems seek to transfer knowledge of presumed 'best practices' across an industry sector by embedding the knowledge in a software package (Gratton and Ghoshal, 2005). Moreover, like Scientific Management and Fordist production, an Enterprise Systems seeks to impose the same kind of standardizing control on the ways work gets done, even in the context of knowledge work.

Taylor's so-called Scientific Management philosophy can be understood as an early attempt at Knowledge Management. Taylor believed that it was necessary to extract the knowledge from the workers and give it to managers who would then devise standardized work processes that each worker would be forced to follow. In this sense, Taylor supposed that there was 'one best way' to accomplish tasks – very like the current philosophy behind Enterprise Systems packages. How Scientific Management and the related Fordist production system had negative effects on the workers. More importantly, perhaps, such approaches also restrict flexibility since it is much more difficult to change workflows when control is embedded in complex production technologies that cost a lot, in terms of time and money, to change. This is demonstrated today very clearly with many very large car companies, especially in the United States, being very slow to respond to what has been a fairly dramatic change in customer preferences for cars – changing production lines from producing gas-guzzling SUVs, which customers no longer want because of high fuel costs, to small cars, which are more attractive because they are energy efficient, takes several years to accomplish, for example. Dramatic losses in market share are occurring in those companies that did not foresee this change and that, therefore, are not able to make adjustments quickly enough. These limitations on work and workers can be similarly recognized in today's very popular Enterprise Systems, discussed next.

ENTERPRISE SYSTEMS AND THE SPREAD OF 'BEST PRACTICE' KNOWLEDGE

While some of the underlying assumptions about human nature were clearly naïve in these early Scientific Management/Fordist approaches to managing work, the general idea of standardizing work practices through the use of technology remains dominant, only today standardization covers not just manual work but also a lot of non-manual work, including what might be considered knowledge work, and occurs through the use of ICT rather than through designing specific work tools, like spades, or machines, like assembly lines. Enterprise Systems exemplify this trend.

Enterprise Systems have their roots in earlier technologies for managing production processes – Manufacturing Requirements Planning (MRP), Manufacturing Resource Planning (MRP2) and Enterprise Resource Planning (ERP) (Wallace and Kremzar, 2001). The generic term 'Enterprise Systems' is used to describe, then, a range of ICTs that are designed to support workflows across an enterprise. All are based on the same assumption about the importance and efficacy of integrating and standardizing work practices for all types of workers.

The standardization of practices within an Enterprise System begins, so the rhetoric goes, with the capture of knowledge of 'best practices'. This is typically done by consultants working for software companies, and is based on their interpretation and benchmarking of how particular types of work are performed (e.g. the process of accounts payable or goods received) in what they define to be leading firms. This knowledge of 'best practices' is then embedded in the software packages that, when implemented in a given organization, will theoretically mean that the adopting organization acquires this 'best practice' knowledge (Gratton and Ghoshal, 2005). This is because the Enterprise System controls workflows by requiring data is input in a particular way and also requiring that data move in a certain way across a work process. Such Enterprise Systems packages are thus marketed as knowledge processing systems – a way for any given company to learn (i.e. acquire knowledge) to operate in the same way as the very successful companies in their industry, since by adopting the package the organization will be forced to reorganize its workflows to fit the work process models in the Enterprise System.

This is why there is so much emphasis from Enterprise Systems software companies, and the consultants involved in supporting implementations, on sticking to a 'vanilla implementation'. A 'vanilla implementation', means that the adopting organization should not customize the software to support different work processes to those embedded in the software because, if they do this, then they are losing the advantage of using the Enterprise System to support their adoption of the 'best practice' knowledge. Typically, however, there are configuration options which can supposedly accommodate important differences between firms, for example, in terms of their structure or geographical and so language and legal environments. However, such options are to be kept to a minimum so, in principle, when an organization adopts the Enterprise System, they will supposedly be adopting 'best practices' as defined for their particular industry. In this sense, context is not seen to matter that much, since it is assumed that there are 'best practices' that are broadly applicable across a wide range of situations.

The central idea behind an Enterprise System is that there should be a single database that stores data from across functions of a business (Gattiker and Goodhue, 2005). For example, all sales data will be stored in the single repository in the same format so that it is possible to integrate data from distributed sites as well as compare data across sites. This, it is claimed, provides a powerful system infrastructure for a business based on codifying 'best practice'. For example, in a consultancy organization a Customer Relationship Management (CRM) system might be used to standardize customer data used across departments; in a healthcare setting, an Electronic Health Record (EHR) system might be used to standardize patient data to be shared across different doctors; while in a university, an e-learning system might be used to create a standard learning environment for sharing information with students. Achieving this integrated system infrastructure depends on instituting standardized business/organizational practices so that the same processes are followed, meaning the data is consistent and standard across the organization.

Knowledge workers are certainly not immune from the influences of such standardizing processes. For example, university teachers are often required to use an e-learning course management system or some other kind of educational repository to communicate with their classes. 'Blackboard', for example, is designed around a particular 'best practice' vision of what a 'class' consists of and what type of information needs to be communicated between a teacher and their students. So, there is a button for announcements, syllabus, course documents, assignments, communication and so on that presumes a particular type of lecturing practice. Of course, individual professors will use this functionality somewhat differently, but nevertheless, the material design of the ICT constrains what they can do. Moreover, the system may well be a mechanism used by administrators to control the behaviour of knowledge workers – the Blackboard website can be looked at, for example, by a chair of department to ensure that an individual faculty member is conforming to expectations around norms of 'good teaching practice'.

THE FALLACY OF 'BEST PRACTICE' KNOWLEDGE

In the section above we considered the rhetoric of Enterprise Systems as carriers of 'best practice' knowledge. In this section we look at the limitations of this view. These limitations relate to:

1 the ways users enact (rather than simply adopt) technologies;
2 the myth that 'best practice' can be defined independently of the specific context;
3 the restrictions on flexibility and;
4 the creation of competitive value.

Taking each in turn, first, research has shown that individuals often find ways to work around the restrictions imposed by Enterprise Systems (or indeed other types of standardizing KMS). Users enact a technology, they do not simply adopt it. For example, sales people often maintain their legacy Excel spreadsheets to organize their customer leads and only input into the Enterprise System information that they want their boss or their colleagues to know about. For example, they may not record every sales contact (as the system says they should) because they do not want to share potential sales opportunities with colleagues. Similarly medical doctors maintain paper records on their patients but may only record partial information on the EHR system – the equivalent of an Enterprise Systems in a healthcare setting – either because they find this easier or because they do not want to record all of the information for wider consumption (Orlikowski, 2002). This demonstrates one of the limitations of assuming that the adoption of an Enterprise Systems will automatically embed 'best practice' knowledge in an organization.

Second, there is considerable debate and criticism of the very notion of 'best practice' given the very different history and culture of each organization. Crucially, you should be thinking about how the process and practice approaches to knowledge work, would suggest that the very idea that an Enterprise System embeds knowledge of 'best practice' ignores the importance of context and disregards the processes through which knowledge is negotiated. Thus, Wagner et al. (2006) illustrate that the definition of a 'best practice' is a socio-political process of negotiation, rather than an objective reality. In this sense, implementing an Enterprise System is an organizational change project. Organizational change, however, is never straightforward. Thus, research has shown that during an Enterprise System implementation there is often conflict with some end-users resisting the technology as they fight over what is 'best practice'. This is because individuals in different locations will carry out ostensibly the same practice (e.g. medical doctors making a diagnosis) somewhat differently. The introduction of an Enterprise System poses constraints on these localized work practices, with the software's integrated design encouraging the institutionalization of one approach to practice while silencing other ways of working. This is why the introduction of an Enterprise System to manage knowledge work (and knowledge workers) is often fraught with difficulties, as individuals and groups (perhaps in different locations or different departments) fight to get their existing practices imposed as 'best' and fight against the standard 'vanilla' processes (Wagner and Newell, 2004).

Third, questions have been raised about how, in attempting to manage knowledge work, Enterprise Systems may restrict the very organizational flexibility that such work requires, so becoming the 'legacy' systems of the future (Galliers, 2006). Thus, it now seems clear that organizations need to be able to differentiate between what is standard and what is their unique 'value added'. One estimation is that around 75 per cent of work processes can be considered standard so that following 'best practice' workflows by instituting the 'vanilla' Enterprise Systems may be most efficient (Davenport, 2000). Nevertheless, even in these 'standard' cases (referred to as commodity processes) it may be possible to use knowledge of what will create added value for a customer to differentiate the process and provide some competitive edge to knowledge work (Huang et al., 2007). For example, wake-up calls in hotels today rely on a fairly standard technology – everything is automated and hotel staff do not usually make the wake-up calls in person. However, some hotels have slightly modified this technology to influence greater customer satisfaction. Thus, some hotels in Disneyland now allow guests to select which Disney character will wake them up in the morning! Customizing some commodity processes may, therefore, be useful.

However, and fourth, deciding the 25 per cent of processes that can differentiate an organization is extremely problematic, especially because the software companies and consultants who sell Enterprise System technologies have a vested interest in trying to ignore this aspect of an Enterprise System adoption because their main selling point is that *all* 'best practice' knowledge is embedded in the software.

All of this suggests that the notion of 'best practice' knowledge that underpins Enterprise, and other Knowledge Management, Systems is more about convenient rhetoric than about actual practice. Despite this, it is important that we recognize both the constraining and facilitating influences of Enterprise System on knowledge work and workers. Enterprise System do constrict the way knowledge workers carry out their daily work tasks (as with the example of Blackboard given above) but they also potentially assist such workers by providing them with information on what is happening across an organization that feeds into their decision-making processes. For example, before the advent of Enterprise System it was very difficult for a senior manager of a large company to be able to compare business units because each business unit collected data in a different format. Today, with the integrated database, it is easier for managers to compare business units and to draw distinctions about which is doing relatively better or worse. This ability to draw distinctions is a core feature of what it means to have knowledge. However, we also need to recognize that the system in itself does not automatically draw these distinctions – these rely on the managers' prior experience and interpretation of the context. In this sense, Enterprise System do not, in effect, constitute KM systems, despite claims to the contrary. They are actually information systems (Galliers and Newell, 2003) – the individual uses knowledge of the context and processes to make sense of the information that is provided by the Enterprise System.

Nevertheless, Enterprise Systems are often marketed as systems that can support Knowledge Management – they are sold as systems which embed knowledge of 'best practice' and as systems which facilitate the production of knowledge. We have discussed the fallacy of such an idea. These limitations are also relevant to the second group of technologies that we will look at in this chapter which are actually often described as 'Knowledge Management Systems' – that is they are systems that are specifically designed to transfer information and knowledge across an organization. We turn to look at these KMS next.

THE POSSESSION VIEW AND KNOWLEDGE MANAGEMENT SYSTEMS AS REPOSITORY

Like Enterprise Systems, KMS also assume a possession/structural view – valuable knowledge, located inside people's heads (i.e. the input) can be identified, captured and processed via the use of ICT tools so that it can be applied in new contexts (i.e. the output) (Tseng, 2007). The aim is thus to make the knowledge inside people's heads or knowledge embedded in successful routines widely available. Indeed, 'Knowledge Management' is frequently reduced to the implementation of ICTs for knowledge transfer (Jennex and Olfman, 2003; Scarbrough and Swan, 2001). Thus, surveys of firms introducing what they describe as 'Knowledge Management initiatives' show that these are dominated by ICT implementations. For example, Ruggles (1998) reports on a survey of 431 organizations and describes what firms are actually doing to 'manage knowledge'. The four initiatives that were the most popular were all related to ICT developments – creating an intranet, data warehousing, decision-support tools and groupware. Similar findings were reported by Alavi and Leidner (1999). A more recent survey in Australia (Xu and Quaddus, 2005) found that nearly 70 per cent of the 1500 participants indicated that they had some type of KMS. The range of what is defined as KMS has been expanded over time, but the same technologies still dominate. Thus, Xu and Quaddus identified the following as examples of KMS (with the % in brackets indicating their popularity):

E-mail (92%)	Video conferencing (43%)	Electronic bulletin boards (29%)	Best practice database (22%)	Extranet (17%)
Internet (90%)	Online discussion systems (40%)	Electronic meeting systems (26%)	Corporate yellow pages (22%)	Issue management systems (16%)
Databases (86%)	Workflow systems (39%)	Learning tools (25%)	Online analytical processing systems (21%)	Knowledge directories (15%)
Intranet (80%)	Data warehousing/ mining (37%)	People information archive (23%)	Knowledge repositories (21%)	Expert systems (8%)
Document management systems (60%)	Search and retrieval tools (36%)	Decision support systems (23%)	Knowledge portals (19%)	Artificial intelligence (5%)
Customer management systems (48%)	Executive information systems (34%)	Groupware (22%)	Lessons-learnt databases (18%)	

Alavi and Tiwana (2003) categorize these different KMS in terms of the knowledge processes that they aim to enhance (knowledge creation, storage, transfer and application), as depicted below:

Knowledge process	Knowledge creation	Knowledge storage	Knowledge transfer	Knowledge application
KMS	– E-learning systems – Collaboration support systems	– Knowledge repositories (data-warehousing and data-mining)	– Communication support systems (e-mail) – Enterprise information portals (intranets/internets)	– Expert systems – Decision support systems

This is helpful in the sense that it recognizes that different types of ICT will be more or less useful for different knowledge processes. At the same time, the Xu and Quaddus (2005) study demonstrates that it is the storage and transfer technologies which are most popular in terms of the types of KMS that are used in practice.

In relation to the storage and transfer processes, we can contrast two different types of KMS: McAfee (2006) describes these as 'platform' and 'channel' technologies; while Alavi (2000) distinguishes between 'network' and 'repository' technologies. Channel or network technologies (e.g. e-mail) can be used where it is clear that a particular individual or group needs specific information and knowledge from another individual – for example, a software project manager needing information from sales about the client requirements for a new system. Channel technologies are thus used to pass information and knowledge from a source to one or more recipients. In other cases, however, it is not known in advance who will need, or find useful, particular information and knowledge, either right now or in the future. In this situation some kind of platform or repository technology (e.g. an organizational intranet) is used so that people can store and search/retrieve information and knowledge as they need it. The fact that so many organizations have adopted these two types of KMS implies that decision-makers believe that sophisticated ICT tools can help in the capture, storage and transfer of knowledge.

Many commentators, however, are more sceptical about the utility of new ICTs for delivering organizational performance improvements (Blair, 2002). Thus, many organizations have put a lot of effort into putting content on to their intranets – a type of platform technology (McAfee, 2006), where documents can be stored and searched – but research has found that users do not always find these platform technologies useful. Davenport (2005), for example, found that only 44 per cent of survey respondents felt that it was easy to find information they needed by looking on the company intranet. The other very popular type of KMS involves channel technologies, such as e-mail (McAfee, 2006), which allow the sharing of documents between particular individuals, either one-to-one or one-to-many. This research finds that those involved in knowledge work rely more heavily on the channel (e.g. e-mail) than the platform (e.g. intranets) technologies, reflecting the extent to which knowledge work is a social activity dependent on joint production of knowledge. However, even the channel tools have problems with regards their ability to enhance knowledge processes. For example, Davenport (2005) found that 26 per cent of people in a survey felt that e-mail was over-used in their organization; 15 per cent felt that it reduced their productivity; and 21 per cent actually felt overwhelmed by the amount of e-mail that they received.

One reason for the limitations of these KMS, the mutual relationship between technology and organization. A KMS *per se,* will not in itself, improve the capture, storage and sharing of knowledge. It depends on how the KMS is perceived and used as part of people's everyday work practices. From all the many studies that have been done on the implementation of all kinds of ICT in an organization, we know that adoption of technology and its subsequent use are not straight-forwardly linked.

Another issue in understanding the problems with this kind of KMS is to reflect on why some knowledge may not readily lend itself to capture and codification. There are a number of reasons for this, including:

1 *Difficulty*: Some knowledge may just be too difficult to express in written form and so may be more effectively communicated through face-to-face interaction or learning by doing. For example, it may be far easier to simply show a person how to set up, log on and use a computer than to ask them to follow a set of detailed written instructions on how to do this. The complexity of computer manuals and the continued attempts by designers to create 'user-friendly' help services attests to this. The telephone helpline where knowledge can be communicated through two-way interaction is often preferred to the text-form help databases available on the computer itself.

2 *Uncertainty*: Some knowledge may be too uncertain. For example, I may feel that I 'know' that the best way to design a training course is to include humour and anecdotes. However, this is based on personal experience and intuition, and so I am uncertain of its accuracy. I am therefore not likely to write it down (in case it is wrong), although I may well share this 'knowledge' informally.

3 *Dynamism*: Some knowledge may be subject to continuous change. For example, 'process mapping' attempts to articulate and represent in written form the underlying processes involved in work tasks. However, organizational routines are subject to almost continuous change such that by the time the processes are mapped they are almost immediately out of date or wrong in some detail.

4 *Context-dependency*: Some knowledge may be highly context-dependent. For example, knowledge about how customers react to a particular new humorous marketing campaign is likely to be unique to a particular country, given what we know about national predispositions in humour. Reusing the same campaign in a

different country, ignoring the importance of context, is likely to prove ineffective and may even produce the opposite effects to those expected.

5   *Cost*: Some knowledge may cost more to codify than to learn by trial and error. For example, writing down in detail instructions about how to use a simple mechanical device, like a stapler in an office environment, is not likely to prove very useful. This may sound like a trivial example, but it does not take much imagination to realize that there is an awful lot of material 'written down' in an organization, which is rarely if ever referred to.

6   *Politics*: Some knowledge may be politically too sensitive to codify. For example, very important knowledge when managing a project relates to who is a good team player and who is likely to be obstructive and difficult. It is very unlikely that someone will formally share this knowledge with others, stating on a database that 'Sue is a pain to work with!' (and in any case it might well be considered libelous if it were formally codified).

All these issues mean that what is actually available on the organizational KMS may be trivial and unhelpful while the really important knowledge continues to reside in everyday practices. Moreover, not only are there problems in actually codifying some knowledge, but also it must be recognized that people may be reluctant to even attempt to 'brain dump' what they 'know' onto a database because knowledge, or knowing, is also a key source of personal power within organizations. Ironically, in cases where knowledge really needs to be shared – that is, where it is both in short supply and central to the organization – there may be a particular reluctance amongst people to share it with others. This is because knowledge, or knowing, confers personal advantages – it means that some people can do things that others are not able to – and so is kept secret by the 'knower'.

More fundamentally, the practice view of knowledge suggests that KMS are limited by the very possession view of knowledge that they assume. Thus, the practice approach views knowledge (unlike data) as something that cannot simply be possessed and transferred; rather it is continuously recreated and reconstituted through dynamic, interactive, and social, action and interaction.

THE PRACTICE VIEW AND KNOWLEDGE MANAGEMENT SYSTEMS AS NETWORKING

The epistemology of practice – that underpins both process and practice-sensitive accounts of knowledge work – starts from the premise that, truth, and so knowledge, is contestable, which means that knowledge cannot be transferred between people through ICTs in any straightforward way. A particular version of 'truth' can be transferred but, were this to be understood by the intended recipients (and this in itself is problematic), it may not be accepted given alternative 'justified true beliefs'. Knowledge, or rather knowing, cannot, therefore, be disassociated from the beliefs and experiences of those people that use it. ICTs marketed as 'Knowledge Management Systems' obscure and/or deny this socially constructed nature of knowledge. Instead, those promoting such systems imply that, by introducing standard processes and ICT-supported communication channels which link people and groups, 'best practice' knowledge can be shared throughout a global organization. However, unlike data, knowledge cannot be simply transferred from a sender to a receiver. Data can be directly transferred but their interpretation, which involves the process of 'knowing', may be highly variable (Galliers and Newell, 2003).

The knowledge-as-practice view highlights the importance of relationships, and shared understandings and attitudes to knowledge formation and knowledge sharing (Kofman and Senge, 1993). It is important to acknowledge these issues since they help to define the likely success or failure of attempts to implement KMS. The knowledge-as-practice view suggests that it is likely to be fairly easy to share knowledge between individuals who are relatively homogeneous in terms of their practice, because they share a common understanding and meaning/belief system. For example, globally distributed software engineers, with a similar training and understanding, may be able to work collaboratively without much difficulty and to share information via a KMS. However, it is extremely difficult for such globally distributed collaboration to occur where the individuals have heterogeneous beliefs and understandings. Yet, the sharing of knowledge across functional, organizational and/or national boundaries is precisely the goal of most KMS initiatives. Paradoxically, then, this means that attempts to manage knowledge using KMS may actually be most problematic in the very conditions where the need is greatest – that is, where there are significant divisions of practice.

Developments in ICT do, however, open up opportunities for knowledge work and knowledge workers from a practice perspective. In particular, new material properties of ICT, in particular the development of the so-called Web 2.0 and Enterprise 2.0, can facilitate the types of interaction that support knowing in practice. These developments led *Time* Magazine in 2006 to nominate the person of the year as 'You'. This was to celebrate how all kinds of content – news, entertainment, information of all kinds, reviews and so on – was being created, not by dedicated corporations who would then transmit this content to passive recipients, but by everyone using Web 2.0 technologies. Web 2.0 is a term used to describe the new type of software that allows users themselves to create content and share directly with each other, whether through social networking sites like Facebook, MySpace, YouTube and LinkedIn, or through wikis and blogs. The Internet has thus become a tool for collaboration and networking rather than a repository.

In the context of an organization, McAfee (2006) uses the term 'Enterprise 2.0' to define these same kinds of technologies, but used within the firewall of an organization. The key characteristic of these 2.0 technologies, according to McAfee, is that they not only allow the sharing of documents (i.e. outputs of knowledge work) but also make visible the *practices* of knowledge workers and interdependencies between practices (i.e. valuable process knowledge not just content or product knowledge). Thus, Web 2.0 technologies allow users to observe the processes of knowledge production, as well as the output – who adds/deletes/amends something over time and what they have added/deleted/amended. McAfee suggests that there are six key features of 2.0 technologies that differentiate them from traditional ICT:

1 Search – new tools that make it possible to search for information rather than having to rely on navigation options.
2 Links – dynamic links between content, reflecting how people have actually moved across pages and sites, make it possible to identify related content, thus facilitating users in finding useful content.
3 Authoring – blogs (enabling individuals to author content that others can add to), wikis (enabling groups to author content in an iterative fashion) and YouTube (enabling individuals or groups to produce multi-media content for others to view) provide everyone the opportunity to author content that others can read or view – many people are now actively engaged in either producing or consuming this user-generated content.

4 Tags – allow individuals to have control of categorizing the content of their digital material (e.g. del-icio.us allows users to tag websites with bookmarks). These user-generated categorization systems are called folksonomies – a folksonomy emerges over time depending on what users find useful to group together based on the information structures and relationships that are actually used in practice.

5 Extensions – systems can also go beyond this tagging process to develop algorithms based on the pattern of use of different information which then allows for automatic referrals to individuals who have shown interest in a certain type of content. This is done by Amazon very effectively to make recommendations to their customers of other books they might enjoy reading, based on their pattern of consumption to-date as compared to the millions of other customers.

6 Signals – given the sheer amount of information that is digitally available, it can also be helpful to have certain information automatically pushed to users based on their interests. Signals are the means of doing this, alerting users to the fact that new information is available that they may be interested in. RSS (really simple syndication) is now a popular technology that provides this kind of signal.

All of these features of 2.0 technologies suggest a very different environment as compared to a repository environment. McAfee (2006), thus, argues, that

> Enterprise 2.0 technologies have the potential to let an intranet become what the Internet already is – an online platform with a constantly changing structure built by distributed autonomous and largely self-interested peers. On this platform, authoring creates content; links and tags knit it together; and search, extensions, tags and signals make emergent structures and patterns in the content visible and help people stay on top of it all. (p. 26)

In reality, however, many organizations have yet to take advantage of 2.0 technologies. A major reason is that they can reduce managerial control and may be used by some to express negativity, which many senior managers want to avoid. For example, individuals can use blogs to broadcast weaknesses in a company's strategy or to deride organizational decision-makers. Some may fear that chaos may rein if knowledge workers are allowed to add or change content on their departmental website without this being vetted by a central authority. Nevertheless, we can expect that KMS will change over time in organizations as the potential of these new 2.0 technologies become more fully understood, especially in support of knowledge work, and more accepted in practice. For now, repository systems remain dominant.

CONCLUSIONS

In this chapter we have considered the fallacy of assuming that the adoption of Enterprise Systems or KMS such as company intranets will allow an organization to painlessly improve the management of knowledge processes within an organization. We have recognized the importance of engagement in practice as an essential vehicle for developing, what Orlikowski (2002) refers to as 'knowledgeability'. Taking the position that knowledge is an outcome of participation in practice, and not just something possessed by individuals, we have indicated how traditional KMS systems do have a role but that their limitations must be acknowledged. In fact, we would suggest that it is a misnomer to call many of these systems KM systems – reverting to the, albeit less sexy, label of 'information systems' may in fact provide a more fruitful way forward in terms of thinking about how such systems can enable (or disable) knowledge work. Newer Web 2.0 and Enterprise 2.0 technologies provide promise for the future as tools that play a role in the generation of knowledge as well as supporting traditional sharing of documents. In particular, these newer tools are important because they can help to make visible ongoing practices of knowledge workers. The case of ICC, presented next, illustrates the major challenges of KMS outlined in this chapter.

CASE STUDY

INTERNATIONAL CONSULTANCY COMPANY (ICC)*

ICC is a medium-sized, private, US-based management consulting company, which operates out of 16 offices located worldwide in the American, European, Japanese, Chinese and Indian markets. It turns over approximately $250 million per year, employing around 800 employees, of which approximately 600 are consultants. Its core business lies in counselling established firms across different industry sectors on how to improve their operational strategy, and how to achieve product, supply chain, customer experience and business technology innovations. It claims to differentiate itself from competitors through its focus on implementation, driven by a highly engineering-oriented workforce and culture. Its client base includes many market-leading companies across a large variety of industry sectors, including healthcare, government, and electronics and computing. The company structure is organized geographically with one global managing director and three regional managing directors, who are respectively in charge of the Americas, Europe and Asia regions. The rest of the consultants can be classified into the roles of directors, principals, managers, associates and consultants, sorted in a hierarchically descending order. Directors are the owners and shareholders of the company.

   The management consultancy grew steadily and reached a size and global span, which made it difficult to harness the knowledge that was being developed throughout the organization. Directors recognized that this situation would only worsen over the years, as plans to expand in new, emerging markets were already under way. In addition, other management consultancies had already implemented KMS and it was thought that such technology would be instrumental to stay abreast of the competition by providing clients with a better service in less time. Hence, in 2003, the company implemented the SharePoint KMS developed by Microsoft and built a team of two knowledge managers to handle it.

THE KMS AT ICC

The KMS at ICC functions as a repository of documents. In terms of the supply side, at the end of every project, consultants are encouraged, although never coerced, to upload what is termed a knowledge closeout. A knowledge closeout is a standard template document, which consultants fill in with information of the project they are currently staffed on. The form requires them to input information about the type of project, the steps undertaken, the lessons learned and so on. Once this is done, consultants should go to a specific web-page on the KMS and upload the document onto the system. Before this, however, they are required to supply the metadata that will allow for the document to be searchable once it is on the system. The metadata to be input consists of

---

* This case was authored by Michael Vellat.

name, date, type of practice, type of service delivered, document importance and so on. Document importance refers to the value of the document: consultants can decide to tag a particular document as 'premium content'. Knowledge closeouts are not the sole documents that are uploaded. PowerPoint presentations detailing common frameworks and processes applied throughout projects can be frequently found. Yet, the vast majority of documents are stored and presented from a project-perspective, as opposed to a topic- or time-perspective. What this means is that although you can search documents from different angles, when they are retrieved and downloaded, they always present knowledge in terms of the different steps and processes undertaken in a project, as dictated by the knowledge closeout template.

In terms of the demand side, consultants can go on the home page of the KMS and use the search facility to search for relevant articles. The site is tailored to the specific characteristics of the organization and allows consultants to perform searches according to authors (i.e. director who led the project), client type, practice areas, service areas and industry type. For instance, if you go into the industry areas and click on electronics and computing, then the KMS will display the titles of all the documents that pertain to that industry sector in order of importance (i.e. premium content is displayed first). Alternatively, if the consultant searches for a particular keyword, such as 'product development', the KMS will retrieve all the documents that have metadata matching that keyword.

There is also a special section termed the 'People Section' on the KMS, which does not possess content related to projects. Instead, it allows searching for the profiles of other consultants. Such profiles usually contain information on the education of the consultant, her/his work undertaken prior to joining the company, and the types of projects she/he has been involved in with the management consultancy so far.

The KM team is responsible for monitoring and fostering the use of the KMS. They publish a monthly KM report, which gives an overview of metrics aimed at assessing the performance of the KMS and the use made of it by consultants. Metrics most commonly used include number of monthly searches undertaken, number of monthly searchers and so on. These reports show that of the 600 consultants, about two-thirds use the KMS and most of the searches are directed to the 'People Section'.

Factors affecting the KMS use

Access: Most of the time, consultants are either on the road or on a client site. Only rarely do they come to the office. This forces them to access the KMS from the client location or over a wireless connection. The problems with this are threefold: first, the procedure is highly cumbersome; secondly, the connection is much slower; thirdly, the client may not always grant the consultants access to their network:

> So, the big challenge we have is that as we try to keep the system secure we have to have some safeguards as to accessibility. On the flipside our ability to access the system is not always seamless based on where we are. For example, one of my main clients I have worked with almost continuously over the last 5 years and with whom the management consultancy has worked for over 12 years blocks our VPN from usage. So, we have alternative connectivity technologies

around our portal software that do allow us to access the KM system, but quite frankly they are less convenient to use and they do somewhat inhibit the use of the KM system. So, for example if somebody sent me a link to a particular document in the KM system I cannot directly access that link going through our portal.

Uploading: Consultants find the process of uploading documents on the KMS highly cumbersome and complex. The reason behind this was the large amount of metadata that the system requires to be submitted along with the document. Consultants work in a highly pressurized environment where they have very little spare time. Coercing them to fill in lengthy metadata forms for the submission of every single document saps their incentive to contribute to the system:

> So, every time you want to upload anything, you got to put in your name, the day it was created, the category, and I understand why that information is important, but it takes a lot of time to upload a document. And people that are in this industry and people that work for the management consulting company are extremely busy and overloaded that no one is willing to take the time that requires to fill in all the additional information.

Layout: The problems do not merely plague the access to the system or the uploading process, but also the surfing of the KMS. The layout of the website is perceived by some as user-unfriendly:

> I also find it that sometimes it is not clear how I get back from where I came from. Sure, hit the back button, but from a structural perspective I wasn't clear how I could get back to a similar area to where I was before [. . .] . I wanted to go back and I wanted to find a logical way to go back, but for most areas the layout changes quite completely.

Search: Lastly, the searching facility provided by the KMS was perceived to do a bad job at ranking content:

> But one thing we found out is that when we put keywords into the searching system, usually the best results do not appear at the top, which means that we have to flip over different pages and then maybe you find something you want. Sometimes the result is not accurate in reflecting the information you wanted to search for. I think that is an area that can be improved.

KMS USE AND CONSULTANT EXPERIENCE

The KMS is used differently by consultants with under two years of experience – referred to as less experienced consultants or LECs – and those with more experience (MECs). LECs tend to undertake what we can term a gap/synthesis analysis – they sift through the documents to learn how past projects have been undertaken and understand what common practice is. They seek to make up for their relative inexperience by acquiring knowledge about those activities that have been performed for years within the management consultancy and which are widely documented and similar throughout projects. The KMS is not necessarily used to solve a particular problem, but simply to familiarize and understand what will be required of them and what they are expected to do:

> I download typically more than 20 or 30 files, which are related to the topic or the kind of project we are working on [. . .]. We are addressing similar issues as the ones addressed in the documents even though they are not exactly the same. So, we use some of the approaches in the documents to help us. So, we use the documents to figure out which way is the best to deal with the particular client. [. . .] That helps us generate some ideas and understand what the traditional way is to approach a client.

MECs, on the other hand, use the KMS much less frequently, mostly because when they need knowledge it is new knowledge:

> If we've never done it, it would be really hard to find it, even if we have done something similar to it, because it would never be tagged appropriately, or no one would have ever thought about it. So, it is only the second or third time you are looking for something that you could rely on a system. And I find that most of the requests you get from people are new things, which we haven't done yet. You know, these are things that are on the edge of something I ike you have painted your room blue before and now you are painting it blue with stripes, but we've never done stripes. I can find something about painting blue, but I have no idea what to do about the stripes [. . .].

MECs make much more use of the 'People Section' on the KMS and sift through the backgrounds of other consultants in terms of the projects they have undertaken and what practice they belong to in order to select people who may help them with the new knowledge they are looking for:

> [. . .] The number 1 reason I go onto KM now is actually to go find people's profiles and look at the resumes of consulting staff, for instance for staffing a new project or get in contact with someone who knows about something I need. And that is a reason for me to log into the system, access the system, and get familiar with the system.

However, despite its existence, the 'people section' was never developed to fulfil this purpose and does not provide contact details, such as e-mail or phone number.

THE KMS AND COLLABORATION

All consultants expressed a strong need for direct collaboration, shedding light upon the limits of the collaboration capabilities of the current KMS. Even in this instance, however, consultants diverged in their opinions of what would provide an appropriate direct collaborative technology. In fact, MECs called for highly interactive and on-demand collaboration that would address their specific knowledge needs as they surfaced. LECs, on the other hand, requested more content-based and incremental collaboration through time, which relied less on human interaction. In fact, LECs seemed to be very enthusiastic about the possibilities from a wiki as a collaborative tool:

> I think that a wiki could help us share ideas about a particular topic. For example, you might want to look at the issues surrounding product development or sourcing and supply chain issues and whilst you have

> some ideas, you don't know exactly how to solve the client's problems. So, if people all go to the same place and share some ideas with you, even if they are not on the same project that could be very useful. Yes, I think that if such a technology could be used that would be very useful.

MECs, on the other hand, thought wikis would be less of a panacea:

> I don't see that playing a major role to be honest with you. [. . .] I don't want something else that I have to check every day. I read emails every day, I get a million phone calls every day, I don't need a new thing such as a wiki [. . .]. Maybe for some people that would be great, but for me that would not be helpful. It's not like working at an office [. . .].

Questions

- What do you see as the main strengths and limitations of the KMS at ICC?
- How would you describe the problems of the KMS at ICC – technical, organizational or a combination of both?
- Why do you think there are differences between the MECs and LECs in terms of their use of the KMS at ICC?
- What recommendations would you make to ICC to improve their KMS?

Summary of Key Learning Points

- Two types of ICT are often defined as supporting 'Knowledge Management' – Enterprise Systems, which supposedly embed 'best practice' knowledge, and Knowledge Management Systems, which supposedly facilitate the transfer of knowledge across individuals and groups.
- Enterprise Systems follow the historical trajectory of attempting to standardize work and embed knowledge in systems (rather than in workers). However, the idea that they can embed 'best practice' knowledge is inherently problematic.
- The most prevalent KMS initiatives involve the introduction of ICTs, for example, e-mail, intranets, databases, groupware.
- The majority of current KMS can be described as either platform or channel technologies.
- Both platform and channel KMS have limitations because they are based on a structural 'epistemology of possession' view and so neglect process and practice and the socially constructed, context-dependent nature of knowledge.
- Newer forms of ICT – Web 2.0 and Enterprise 2.0 – have the potential to expose knowledge practices and so, potentially, can play an important role in the future in encouraging knowledge sharing and knowledge creation.

REFERENCES

Alavi, M. (2000). Managing knowledge. In R. Zmud (Ed.) *Framing the Domain of IT Management*. Cincinnati, Ohio: Pinnoflex Educational Resources Ltd. Chapter 2, pp. 15–28.

Alavi, M. and Leidner, D. (1999). Knowledge management systems: Issues, challenges and benefits. *Communications of the AIS*, 1(5), 1–35.

Alavi, M. and Tiwana, A. (2003). Knowledge management: The information technology dimension. In M. Easterby-Smith and M. Lyles (Eds) *Handbook of Organizational Learning and Knowledge Management*. Oxford: Blackwell. Chapter 6, pp. 104–121.

Blair, D. (2002). Knowledge management: Hype, hope or help. *Journal of the American Society for Information Science and Technology*, 53(12), 1019–1028.

Davenport, T. (2000). *Mission Critical: Realizing the Promise of Enterprise Systems*. Cambridge, MA: Harvard Business Press.

Davenport, T. (2005). *Thinking for a Living*. Boston: Harvard Business School press.

Galliers, R. (2006). In Agile information systems, K. DeSouza (editor) pp. 163–177.

Galliers, R. and Newell, S. (2003). Back to the future: From knowledge to data management. *Information Systems and E-Business Management*, 1(1), 5–14.

Gattiker, T. F. and Goodhue, D. L. (2005). What happens after ERP implementation: Understanding the impact of inter-dependence and differentiation on plant-level outcomes. *MIS Quarterly*, 29(3), 559–585.

Gratton, L. and Ghoshal, S. (2005). Beyond best practices. *MIT Sloan Management Review*, 46(3), 49–57.

Huang, J., Newell, S., Poulson, B. and Galliers, R. (2007). Creating value from a commodity process: A case study of a call center. *Journal of Enterprise Information Management*, 20(4), 396–413.

Jennex, M. and Olfman, L. (2003). Organizational memory. In C. Holsapple (Ed.) *Handbook of Knowledge Management*, 2nd edn. New York: Springer, pp. 207–234.

Kofman, F. and Senge, P. (1993). Communities and commitment: The heart of learning organizations. *Organizational Dynamics*, 22(2), 5–22.

Kumar, K. and Hillegersberg, J. V. (2000). ERP experiences and evaluation. *Communications of the ACM*, 43(4), 23–26.

McAfee, A. (2006). Enterprise 2.0: The dawn of emergent collaboration. *MIT Sloan Management Review*, 47(3), 21–28.

Orlikowski, W. J. (2002). Knowing in practice: Enacting a collective capability in distributed organizing. *Organization Science*, 13(3), 249–273.

Ruggles, R. (1998). The state of the notion: Knowledge management in practice. *California Management Review*, 40(3), 80–89.

Scarbrough, H. and Swan, J. (2001). Explaining the diffusion of knowledge management: The role of fashion. *British Journal of Management*, 12(1), 3–12.

Schultze, U. and Leidner, D. (2002). Studying knowledge management in information systems research: Discourses and theoretical assumptions. *MIS Quarterly*, 26(3), 213–242.

Tseng, S. (2007). The effects of information technology on knowledge management systems. *Expert Systems with Applications*, 35(1–2), 1–11.

Wagner, E., Scott, S. and Galliers, R. (2006). The creation of 'best practice' software: Myth, reality and ethics. *Information and Organization*, 16, 251–275.

Wagner, E. and Newell, S. (2004). Best for whom: The tension between 'Best Practice' ERP packages and diverse epistemic cultures in a university context. *Journal of Strategic Information Systems*, 14(4), 305–328.

Wallace, T. and Kremzar, M. (2001). *Making It Happen: The Implementers' Guide to Success with ERP*. New York: John Wiley.

Xu, J. and Quaddus, M. (2005). Adoption and diffusion of knowledge management systems: An Australian survey. *Journal of Management Development*, 24(4), 335–361.

Chapter

CHALLENGES VS. OPPORTUNITIES: COMPETITIVE INTELLIGENCE AND GLOBAL STRATEGIES

ABSTRACT

In today's highly competitive global marketplace, a company that owns knowledge and information is no longer enough to compete adequately. It is imperative firms implement competitive intelligence (CI) programmes to meet present and future challenges. This needs to occur or firms run the risk of losing their share of the market. Global CI is instrumental in enabling firms to successfully launch products, compete effectively or enter a new market in a timely and specific manner, it assists in facilitating effective decisions. This paper highlights the challenges and opportunities of global competitive intelligence.

INTRODUCTION

Economic globalisation and the development of the Internet have created great opportunities for competitive intelligence (CI) professionals, how to grasp the opportunity is totally up to individual firms and their CI professionals. A good sense of history, politics and cultural and business knowledge is a prime requirement in building a global CI programme. These are the tools a CI analyst must possess to understand cultural realities and trends. By doing so the CI practitioner can fully understand the effect religion, ethnic backgrounds and histories bring to a culture. With this knowledge, the analyst is then able to piece together the puzzle of global competitive intelligence. In today's highly competitive global village, knowledge and information has to be analysed and converted to intelligence to be effective and worthwhile. Only in this way can the firm be assured of success in the global market.

The term competitive intelligence was originally used by the military in terms of obtaining the secrets and information of opposing forces for strategic planning. In the business world competitive intelligence is used to identify realistic threats and opportunities, to avoid surprises and to improve a firm's competitive position within a particular market. More specifically, it is defined as any information obtained from sources external to the firm, which can help improve the firm's performance. It is a special strategy that helps a firm anticipate and ultimately survive the rigours of increasingly competitive markets, it is the process of converting raw information by analysis into intelligence.

It is expected that international labour distribution and various international marketplaces make it possible for firms to seek profitable opportunities internationally. There is a pervasive belief that having a presence, or an infrastructure, around the world will assure business competitiveness and, therefore, success.[1] How to assess foreign industry, international competitors, suppliers, foreign marketplaces and the intricacies of doing business abroad are sometimes overlooked, however. This is the role global CI satisfies.

In spite of the growing number of international businesses, there is little knowledge of how firms gather information in the global arena. This lack of information not only affects firms in terms of international competitiveness, but also has a negative impact on the efficient use of global resources. It is necessary, therefore, for the business world to study international competitive intelligence and to find a solution for the effective conduct and implementation of global competitive intelligence. This paper highlights the challenges and opportunities of global competitive intelligence. The first section details the challenges; the second indicates current organisational practices; and the third presents opportunities and the way challenges are overcome. The report concludes with a description of how an international CI programme can be developed. It is very important for the business world to realise that conducting an international competitive intelligence programme is very different to a domestic one.

CHALLENGES: CROSS-CULTURAL FACTORS IN INTERNATIONAL COMPETITIVE INTELLIGENCE

Before discussing the challenges it is useful to begin with several basic issues concerning CI at a strategic level. Competitive intelligence as a business strategy for any firm should start, according to CI scholars,[2,3] by the CI professional answering the following questions:

- what are the characteristics of my industry
- who are the players
- what are the current positions of my competitors
- what moves are my competitors likely to make
- what are the probabilities attached to each strategic alternative
- what companies might have the potential to enter the market
- what moves can I make to achieve a competitive advantage?

These questions cover most of the fundamental issues in the CI field.

Competitive intelligence professionals usually rely on publicly accessible, open-source information. These sources include academic publications, trade shows, magazines, news reports, trade journals, speeches, websites and the Internet. Governmental reviews, benchmarking reports, the Securities Exchange Commission, career advertisements, lawsuits and bankruptcy filings, and patent registrations also provide vital information. Competitive intelligence professionals use all their resources to collect information. They then analyse the information collected in order to provide recommendations and solutions to decision-makers.

The core factor in the CI process is the information flow: how to get the information, process it and how to make use of it. In international CI, obtaining information from foreign markets is essential for developing successful market entry or defensive strategies. The process is the same as that in the home market but the analysis has to consider the characteristics and nuances of the foreign environments, such as cultural issues.[4] Normally, companies fail in their entry into foreign markets because of serious errors and misjudgments concerning the social, cultural and political environment. Obviously, conducting CI on a global basis is much more complicated than on a domestic one.[5] Prescott and Gibbons identified five reasons for this:

- countries vary in the types, timeliness, accuracy and motives for data collection
- the attitudes concerning individuals attempting to collect data and the ethical standards for acquiring information vary from country to country
- the technologies for the production, storage, movement, analysis and timing of information vary dramatically across countries
- language barriers are important for both the collection and analysis of information
- country-specific idiosyncrasies need to be addressed.[6]

In an attempt to address country-specific qualities the CI analyst needs to consider culture. Cultural factors have a major influence on the result of the analysis. Simpkins has identified eight cultural variables to be considered:

- action: is the culture relationship-centred where stress is placed on working for the experience rather than the accomplishment? Or is it more task-oriented where stress is placed on actions that achieve the goal? This would be the societal view of achievement and work as goals
- competitiveness: is more emphasis placed on competition for rewards, or cooperation for the benefit of life and relationships
- communications: are communications high context, meaning that shared experiences make certain things understood without the need to express them verbally, or low context, where explicit knowledge and facts must be expressed. Are communications direct or indirect? Is the preference for explicit one-to-one communications, or more of an implicit dialogue and avoidance of conflict? Are communications formal, where emphasis is placed on protocol and social customs, or informal, where restrictions are dispensed with
- environment: do people feel they can dominate the environment to fit their needs, should they live in harmony with it, or do they feel that their world is controlled by fate and chance
- individualism: is the individual more important than the group, or are the needs of the individual subordinated to the group interests? Is loyalty to self or society
- structure: a society may either lean towards order, with its predictability and rules, or flexibility, where tolerance of unpredictable situations and ambiguity are acceptable
- thinking: does the culture favour inductive reasoning based on experience and experimentation, or deductive reasoning based on theory and logic
- time: is there a concentration on one task at a time, with a commitment to schedules, or an emphasis on multiple tasks, with relationships being the most important? Is punctuality precise and fixed, or is it fluid and loose?[7]

In addition to the above, Sheinin provides the following variables:

- power and authority: the dominant views of authority versus subordinates. The power distance between individuals
- union and management: the extent of union–management cooperation to achieve a successful company

- social values: the dominant view of wealth and material gain — attitudes towards and the desire for material wealth versus religious satisfaction, the good life or other non-material stimuli found more in traditional societies
- risk view: the view of risk taking as a measured calculation of anticipated success
- change and innovation: the view of change or innovation — do people in a society embrace and adapt to change which promises to improve productivity or do they maintain their basic faith in traditions or old ways of doing things
- ethical values: the view of ethical standards and moralities
- gender: the degree of masculinity *vs.* femininity.[8]

The objective of the CI practitioner in a global setting is to research and gather high quality, accurate and relevant information to complete an analysis. If the analyst does not consider the above variables, serious errors of judgment can be made. The CI investigator may inadvertently impose their cultural bias or make culturally-based assumptions, or be oblivious to the perceptions of the host nationals to the individual CI professional cultural conditioning. After all, analyses flawed by a lack of cultural awareness will affect strategic entry decisions.

LESSONS AND EXPERIENCE: A CRITICAL REVIEW OF CURRENT PRACTICES

Competitive intelligence as one of a dynamic business's functions is relatively new to managers, let alone the international CI programme. Calof reports that many managers are careless in their international collection efforts; not enough emphasis is given to global CI even when firms are entering a new foreign market. He further maintains that there is an abundance of studies on how to gather information in the home country but it is not known whether these findings apply in an international context. Calof found that even when it was something as important as the decision to open up a foreign branch, few executives did anything more than discuss it with a few friends. Only 35 per cent of companies conducted a formal study, 18 per cent considered alternatives for international entries.[9] The reasons could be many, but the crucial point is that the executives are not well exposed to the international environment.

Business competition in the end is the competition in the marketplace. The traditional international or multinational approach to business concentrates largely on geographic markets, developing a distinct marketing mix for each market. Traditional approaches negate experience curve effects that can be gained by using the same marketing mix in more than one market. Global business, in contrast, concentrates on product, emphasising their similarities regardless of the geographic areas in which they are located. It does not, however, ignore differences; these differences are taken into account when implementing the marketing programme. For instance, advertising is translated into different languages for different national markets. And different distribution strategies are developed for areas with different distribution structures.[10]

All these business decisions should be based on a good understanding of differences across national boundaries as well as cross-culturally. By the same token all these differences need to be seriously considered before conducting international CI programmes. Many current international CI practitioners neglect this crucial point. For instance, Griffith notes that many US marketers are hard pressed to understand the French government's actions in restricting retail store size, especially given the success of efficient supermarkets.[11] It is certain, however, that if US marketers want to penetrate the French market they need to know this information to avoid business loss.

The above does not mean that all current international CI practices are not on the right track. In fact, many intensive exporters, as Calof[12] and other scholars found, have been proficient in obtaining information from abroad. These exporters are more likely to utilise any source of information than less intensive exporters; they try to understand the host country more in depth and successfully implement international marketing strategies. For instance, to be successful in the Persian Gulf most American franchisers have to have some adaptability and flexibility in their operations and policy because of cultural sensitivity.[13]

In international IC practice, the more intensive exporters can also use personal contacts abroad for the most important sources of information. For example, one of the authors once worked as an international business consultant for a Canadian firm. He used his personal connections/relations to research useful information to help the Canadian firm successfully develop a China project. This type of information resource was named the social capital pool and its values are flexible depending on how individual organisations wish to implement it in its business practice.

ON-LINE INFORMATION: OPPORTUNITIES AND CONSTRAINTS

The advancement of technology has had some very positive effects on this industry. The communication superhighway or the Internet, apart from reshaping the business environment, is providing benefits to CI practitioners. The Internet not only makes it easier to obtain good quality secondary and primary information as well as providing value to existing products or services; it also helps develop competitive or business intelligence.[14] Another use of the Internet is what is termed 'collaborative intelligence'. This refers to the process whereby CI professionals team up with colleagues in other divisions to leverage the firm's intellectual capital — helping design and publish 'knowledge bases'. At the same time, it is a way of identifying and developing ways to overcome hurdles to information sharing and collaboration. Educating senior executives about the Internet, and authoring 'learning modules' to help other employees learn information-seeking skills is another function of a collaborative intelligence programme.[15]

The Internet allows analysts to monitor competitors' activities by using on-line newsgroup postings or on-line discussion groups. Government agencies such as embassies also provide free on-line information. Obviously, the international CI practitioner should begin by obtaining free resources; this can be achieved by visiting competitors' websites, their suppliers and the specific industry in the new country. If time or the likelihood of obtaining the data is limited, there are now on-line business directories where this information can be purchased.

The problem with the Internet is the difficulty of determining the quality of the source. A criticism of the Internet is that standards for citing and classifying publications by subject, date, and origin are neither well established nor enforced. Another problem the authors are concerned with in their practice is that although over 90 per cent of the information on the Internet is in English, other languages are becoming more and more widely used. In practice, it is unlikely that CI professionals alone could locate useful information for CI purposes, collaboration between CI professionals and translators is necessary. This raises the costs of conducting CI through the Internet. On the other hand, due to technological problems, many languages are not yet supported on the Internet; this limitation makes it difficult to dig out more specific information pertaining to foreign competitors.

Accordingly, we also need to conduct international CI through other information channels. In fact, our experiences indicate that public and/or university libraries contain extensive amounts of information. Books provide insights into the psyche of corporations as well as the thought processes of key decision-makers. In addition, magazines and periodicals can provide details on competitors' actions. Trade journals and local and international newspapers also provide relevant and detailed information. Nor should personal contacts as sources of international information be forgotten. Relevant facts can also be gathered from the organisation's own sales force, customers, trade shows and distributors.

Once the CI unit has collected, evaluated and analysed the raw data it needs to disseminate the information to the decision-maker. In most cases, however, a comprehensive study also requires primary information, which may include surveys, interviews, observations and word of mouth. In practice, after obtaining data from inexpensive secondary sources, the firm is in a better position to conduct field studies in order to acquire true details. After obtaining secondary information and detailed primary data, a firm has a holistic perspective, which can provide an advantageous lead. We suggest that CI practitioners establish strategic alliances across national and cultural boundaries, so that the necessary back up information and in-depth analyses can be obtained when needed.

THE PROCESSES OF DEVELOPING A GLOBAL CI PROGRAMME

To win the competition in today's globalised economies it is necessary for firms involved in international business to design and develop a global CI programme. Such a programme should reflect the needs of the firms, facilitate information processes and assist strategic decision making by management. The structure and the scope of global CI programmes are various and totally depend on the individual firms. Based on previous research[16] and our own experiences we suggest that in establishing a formal international CI programme, a firm needs to follow an eight-step process. These eight steps are:

- define needs
- appoint a dedicated project leader
- identify the main international competitors
- assess available resources
- set CI programme objectives and budget
- design the programme structure
- data processing
- presentation.

Step one: Defining requirements

The CI practitioner must perform a needs assessment to determine what type of information the company requires. Knowing what information is required is key, it can make the research flow faster and more easily. A clear definition of the project needs to be made in writing with input from all function areas or departments as an effective CI programme potentially requires all staff to gather information. Asking the right questions and examining the business strategy may lead to areas that need to be addressed. At this stage, the coordinator has to be aware of cultural, social and economic differences between the home country and the potential host country.

The seven basic questions posed earlier provide a good guideline for the issues that need to be addressed, and thus suggest research/analysis areas. It is suggested that regulatory and legislative differences between the target country and the home culture, as well as all related changes that affect the competitive market are critical components for inclusion while assessing new markets and competitors' strengths and weaknesses. Contextual content, time prioritisation and sensitivity, as well as multitasking skills will deepen the analytical content and the effectiveness of the intelligence delivered.[17]

Step two: Assign a leader

Although most staff should be encouraged to acquire competitive information, the programme should be coordinated by one individual; this person should be open to cultural differences and be able to develop an action-oriented programme. It is suggested that this leader should have solid knowledge and be aware of global issues and diversity, active reading and listening skills, flexibility in scheduling time, and a patient, open and curious disposition towards people and cultures.[18] A person familiar with different cultures, fluent in more than one language and able to listen for content without being strictly bound by context should be the right candidate.

The person heading the programme should also be able to convert mountains of information into actionable intelligence. In addition, the CI analyst needs to build an international network of professionals. In this way primary information can be readily obtained. Having analysed the information, the CI practitioner must then keep the organisation informed about the general state of their industry and competitors. Prescott and Gibbons suggest building a project-oriented approach.[19] This means emphasising temporary involvement by different individuals 'funded' by different interested managers. The benefit of this type of participation is the exposure the programme has and the common perspective gained by a majority of staff. The end result is having employees acquainted with the programme and capable of being rapidly deployed to address critical business issues if required.

Step three: Identify the main competitors

It is important for firms that are involved in international businesses to conduct a competitive analysis as part of the CI programme. The purpose of competitive analysis is to better understand one's own industry and main competitors in order to develop a strategy that will enable the firm to gain a sustainable competitive advantage. This competitive advantage will in turn achieve continuing performance results that are superior to one's industry and competitors. For instance, a Canadian firm once hired one of the authors to conduct an international competitive intelligence. According to the client's needs, he first analysed the characteristics of that company's industry in the world, then he identified five major competitors to the company and located the positions of those five competitors in the industry worldwide. Based on the best information resources and his propounded analysis, he predicated what those five competitors were likely to do in the marketplace individually; and made some suggestions to the company as to the actions that should be taken to achieve a competitive advantage. The result turned out to be excellent.

This case, although a single one, not only demonstrates the importance of identifying one's competitors in conducting CI, it also illustrates that it is much more difficult to get information about one's international competitors. This is particularly true in industries where the market is not concentrated and competitors are widely distributed. In such a situation it is important for the CI professionals to focus on the major competitors.

Step four: Assess resources

The company needs to determine what information there is within the organisation. An assessment of knowledge, expertise, foreign national employees, and on-site materials can prove beneficial in a gap analysis. Furthermore, expatriates who have returned can provide valuable sources of competitive intelligence. At this stage it is suggested that the strategies include interviewing experts who are familiar with the subject concerned and who have lived, worked or studied in the country in question. Evaluating internal resources should be completed prior to the collection and analysis of external resources.[20]

Step five: Setting CI programme objectives and budget

The objectives of a CI programme should be seriously considered and decided, the earlier the better. The objectives, based on our own experiences, are influenced by various factors, such as the company's marketing strategy and available resources. At the same time, the objectives of a CI programme can influence every other step of the CI process. We suggest that two dimensions need to be addressed when defining the objectives, one dimension is to separate direct objectives from indirect objectives; another is to distinguish the comprehensiveness of the assignments and the type of assignments for the CI programme.

Once the objectives are defined the project coordinator has to consider the budget his/her group will need. Decisions pertaining to country visits need to made early due to scheduling, visas and inoculations that may be required. According to Robertson, the budget can sometimes dictate the number of trips that need to be made abroad.[21]

In addition to general administration expenses, the following need to be considered:

- the acquisition of new physical sources (books, maps, periodicals)
- additional part-time or full-time staff for collection and analysis of information translation and other aspects of the collection process
- training on cultural, trade or international business issues
- specialised conferences and/or association memberships
- on-site visits for collection of information.

Step six: International CI structures

At this stage, there needs to be an analysis of staff requirements for projects. If there are limited human resources then the CI analyst may need to cover the entire world. Robertson suggests that if the CI team is able to hire staff specifically for an internationally focused intelligence assignment, background and living experience in that culture may be preferable, but education and international orientation are the primary objectives.[22]

Relying on individuals who have first-hand knowledge of the country will prove to be most beneficial. According to Werther these individuals will be able to understand and deal with issues of comparative politics and development.[23] They need to under-stand and deal with:

- processes of rapid societal change
- clashing cultural norms
- historical animosities and friendships among groups and nations, and their various impacts on regional market performance

- economic trends
- national stability
- and, ultimately, questions of corporate strategy.

At the same time it is important to develop a common language for CI, an ethical framework for the collection of information including a code of conduct, skill-building workshops related to CI topics, and a vision of how CI fits with the mission of the firm.[24] The code of ethics and conduct must be flexible and suitable for use in different cultures and countries or it will be irrelevant. Moreover, the CI programme needs to be able to counteract current threats and facilitate or establish a learning organisation. By so doing it will enable the firm to continue surviving even if competitive conditions change.

Step seven: Data gathering and processing

Prior to leaving for the international site a few things need to be arranged. Interviews with a variety of sources need to be set up to learn as many details of the industry in the foreign country. Also, information that can be exchanged when interviewing should be prepared, since leaders recognise the value of trading facts. The CI analyst also needs to define the specific requirements and goals the visit should fulfil. For example, visiting proposed plant locations may be expected, but examining the distribution channels would also be an important part of the visit.[25]

Everything should be recorded with the intention of using it to complete the competitor intelligence puzzle. While at the site the CI practitioner needs to keep in mind the cultural challenges. The person should have an intimate knowledge of the effects of social, cultural and political factors on market performance along with more traditional reliance on financial, business and economic factors to gather relevant and worthy material. Failure to understand the social and political dynamics can lead to a waste of time, resources and money.[26]

Step eight: Presentations

Having acquired, interpreted, analysed and transformed the information, the last remaining step is to distribute or disseminate the intelligence. The CI programme needs to be designed to deliver proficient and complete solid analysis to people who can act on it. It has to assist in making timely, effective and competitive decisions. There might be different formats in terms of presentations but the fundamental content should be basically the same. It is up to individual CI professionals according to the management preferences to decide what types of format are the best to present the findings and recommendations. One important point for all CI professionals to keep in mind is that the final presentations should be available and accessible only to those who need the information, failure to do this may lead to great loss in terms of intellectual property.

CONCLUSION

The highly competitive global village demands that firms implement global competitive intelligence programmes to meet present and future challenges. It is undeniable that global CI is instrumental in enabling firms to successfully launch products, compete effectively or enter a new market in a timely and specific manner; it assists in facilitating effective decisions. For the CI professional, a good sense of history, politics, cultural and business knowledge is a primary requirement in building a global CI programme. These are the tools a CI analyst must possess in order to understand cultural realities and trends. Although, it is impossible to be able to understand every culture there can be an evolution towards a *global mind*.

It is very important for CI practitioners to know that conducting a global CI programme differs from that of a domestic one. This is where intellectually and socially curious people can acclimatise to the orientations of those worlds in which they are functioning without trying to assimilate the culture of their hosts. By doing so the CI practitioner can fully understand the effect that religion, ethnic backgrounds, and histories bring to a particular culture. With this knowledge, the analyst is then able to piece together the puzzle of global CI.

In today's highly competitive global village, knowledge and information has to be analysed and converted to intelligence to be effective and worthwhile. It is important for any company to know its competitors in terms of their products, their distribution channels and their marketing strategies. It is crucial in those cases where two companies produce similar goods and compete directly for the same market. Only in this way can the firm be assured of success in the global market.

If competitive intelligence as a dynamic business function has only recently been established, then the global CI programme is just in its introduction stage. At this time both academic scholars and business practitioners are short of theories and practices to research, much more work needs to be done for the practice of global competitive intelligence to mature. The authors' experiences and practice demonstrate that CI alone will not guarantee success in today's environment but, if CI, in some form, is not a part of the decision-making process, sooner or later a company will lose a crucial marketplace battle to a competitor. We hope our research will be useful to all those who are interested in either research about or practice in the fields of global competitive intelligence.

REFERENCES

1. Simpkins, R. (1998) 'The global mind', *Competitive Intelligence Magazine,* Vol. 1, No. 2, July–September.
2. Terpstra, V. and Sarathy R. (1997) 'International marketing', (Seventh edition), The Dryden Press, Forth Worth, TX.
3. Vedder, R. and Vanecek, M. (1998) 'Competitive intelligence for IT resource planning', *Information Strategy,* Vol. 15, No. 1, Fall.
4. Tian, R. G. (2000) 'The implications of rights to culture in trans-national marketing: An anthropological perspective', paper presented to the Society for Applied Anthropology 2000 Annual Meeting, San Francisco, 21st–26th March, 2000.
5. Feiler, G. (1999) 'Middle East CI sources: Problems and Solutions', *Competitive Intelligence Review,* Vol. 10, No. 2.
6. Prescott, J. and Gibbons, P. T (1993) 'Global competitive intelligence: An overview', Society of Competitive Intelligence Professionals, Alexandria, VA.
7. Simpkins (1988) *op. cit.*
8. Sheinin, C. (1996) 'Assessing global competition', *Competitive Intelligence Review,* Vol. 7, No. 3.
9. Calof, J. (1997) 'So you want to go international? What information do you need and where will you get it?', *Competitive Intelligence Review,* Vol. 8, No. 4.
10. Tian (2000) *op. cit.*
11. Griffith, D. (1998) 'Cultural meaning of retail institutions: A tradition-based culture examination', *Journal of Global Marketing,* Vol. 12, No. 1, pp. 47–59.
12. Calof (1997) *op. cit.*
13. Martin, J. (1999) 'Franchising in the Middle East', *Management Review,* June, pp. 38–42.

14. Graef, J. (1997) 'Using the Internet for competitive intelligence: A survey report', *Competitive Intelligence Review*, Vol. 8, No. 4.

15. Calof (1997) *op. cit.*

16. Robertson, M. (1998) 'Seven steps to global CI', *Competitive Intelligence Review*, Vol. 1, No. 2.

17. *ibid.*

18. *ibid.*

19. Prescott and Gibbons (1993) *op. cit.*

20. Robertson (1998) *op. cit.*

21. *ibid.*

22. *ibid.*

23. Werther, G. (1998) 'Doing business in the new world disorder: The problem with "Precision" ', *Competitive Intelligence Magazine,* Vol. 1, No. 2, July–September.

24. Prescott and Gibbons (1993) *op. cit.*

25. Robertson (1998) *op. cit.*

26. Werther (1997) *op. cit.*

INTELLIGENCE SYSTEMS METHODOLOGY: A SYSTEMIC APPROACH TO THE ORGANIZATIONAL INTELLIGENCE FUNCTION

ABSTRACT

Organizational intelligence can be seen as a function of the viable structure of an organization. With the integration of the Viable System Model and Soft Systems Methodology (systemic approaches of organizational management) focused on the role of the intelligence function, it is possible to elaborate a model of action with a structured methodology to prospect, select, treat and distribute information to the entire organization that improves the efficacy and efficiency of all processes. This combination of methodologies is called Intelligence Systems Methodology (ISM) whose assumptions and dynamics are delimited in this paper. The ISM is composed of two simultaneous activities: the Active Environmental Mapping and the Stimulated Action Cycle. The elaboration of the formal ISM description opens opportunities for applications of the methodology on real situations, offering a new path for this specific issue of systems thinking: the intelligence systems.

INTRODUCTION

Intelligence is a recurrent term in organizational studies, having acquired several different meanings. In this paper, focused on organizational behaviour, intelligence is understood as the search for information in the environment and its treatment in order to find out relevant elements to support organizations' decision-making processes.

The understanding of the intelligence role in organizations requires the comprehension of their structure characteristics, which depends on the approach applied to build up the structure relation model. One well-known example of such approaches is Stafford Beer's Viable System Model (VSM) that is a systemic methodology for internal organization arrangement that establishes a visual concept about the dynamic relations among organizational process actors and their roles. The use of VSM to create a full concept of the intelligence role in the organizational interactions is justified by the need for a consistent systemic model to determine the operation's relations between the organization's internal components and the environment. As pointed out by Beer (1981), Espejo *et al* (1996) and Jackson (2000), the VSM is based on recursive internal references of systemic functions and actors, a model of organizational features arrangement that could be applied for any kind of viable system. The idea of recursion refers to the replication of the whole model's structure in each of its parts. The intelligence function of VSM is not the only source of information in the system, but the core level of the processing information obtained by the other functions.

The VSM is based on a five-level hierarchical systemic arrangement, embedded in neurocybernetics, qualified by Jackson (2000) as the richest and most flexible system. The viability of a system is determined by its capacity to respond to unpredictable environmental changes, based on the interaction of its components with the external actors. In order to deal with the large range of information from the external environment, an organization has to employ attenuation devices that filter external information to absorb only what is compatible with the organization's processing capacity and pieces of information that are truly relevant to it. This is called variety balance (Espejo *et al*, 1996) understood as the proportional equity between demanded and really handled variety.

The intelligence function is effective only if the variety is handled. To do so, it is necessary to develop abilities to harvest, filter, select, absorb, interpret, compare, process and to transmit only crucial information (Espejo *et al*, 1996) to the organization's activities, which sets up the learning process (Senge, 2006). The dynamics of the intelligence function follows a flexible protocol close to the analytical steps of another systemic approach – Peter Checkland's Soft Systems Methodology (SSM) – (Checkland, 1981). This methodology was developed as an alternative approach to deal with real world problems that are obscure, unstructured and hard to quantify that traditional quantitative hard methods do not have the ability to solve (Espejo *et al*, 1996). Therefore, it can be applied to learn about organizations' interactions.

The integration of the VSM and the SSM methodologies, focusing on the role of the intelligence function, can create a model of action to prospect, select, treat and distribute information inside an organization, with a structured (but flexible) methodology that promotes efficacy and efficiency of all processes. This combination can be labeled Intelligence Systems Methodology (ISM), whose assumptions and dynamics are discussed in this paper. In such a systemic approach, the intelligence role becomes more effective reducing the risk of missing opportunities to organizational learning.

DEFINING ORGANIZATIONAL INTELLIGENCE: DESIGN AND ROLE

The term intelligence can be found in the academic management literature under several meanings related to a large range of relations between organizations and their environment. Traditionally, it refers to the survey of relevant information to companies', institutions' and other systems' or individuals' survival (Wilensky, 1967; Allee, 1997; March, 1999). The roles of this intelligence activity vary depending on the kind of organization it serves, since organizations have different objectives, principles, activities and cultures.

The definitions of the term intelligence have two identifiable approaches: the individual and the organizational. The individual approach focuses on the actors observing a person, a group or an institution learning process and talents. The term 'emotional intelligence', for example, is concerned with specific skills or attributes of a group, individual or process (Matthews et al, 2004). This kind of approach is the same applied by biology to cognition processes or to the individual consciousness state (Koch, 2004). The organizational approach does not limit the intelligence to the information cognitive processing and its collateral connections, but encompasses the relations between actors and environment looking to understand the behaviour of the latter. The definition of the term and the differences of all its meanings are well-presented in Akgün et al (2007). By their perspective, intelligence is more than exploitation, but also exploration (Akgün et al, 2007). To be intelligent is to be conscious of everything around that is concerned to our needs.

Intelligence, at least in the corporate structure, not only refers to the capacity of an organization's cognition on a specific field, but also to the quest for elements to advise managers. There is a common sense meaning constructed around the perception of intelligence as a resource linked to decision-making processes that support decision makers, boards, councils and advisors with information about the environment where the organization operates. Even if the decision is based on the available choices and edged by environmental rules (laws, dynamics and social–cultural background), these conditions are best viewed through the contribution of the intelligence action that prospects information about a problem situation elucidating obscured issues related to it. Intelligence enables decision makers to have an environment richer picture reducing the risk of errors in organizational interactions.

As described by March (1999), decisions are viewed as rational choices based on four primary elements of the rationality: knowledge of alternatives, knowledge of consequences, consistent preference ordering and decision rules. The intelligence action is closely connected to the first two and the last elements aiming to clarify environmental situations reducing ambiguity and inconsistency of decision making. Decision makers are widely distributed across the departments of an organization. They are the top agents of their subsystems.

Organizational intelligence is also related to knowledge management since it provides the relevant information needed to maintain operations knowledge up-to-date. As explained by Asimakou (2009, p. 83), the philosophy 'traditionally distinguishes three types of knowledge': knowing how (refers to the skills of how to do something), knowing that (resembles information) and knowing things (knowledge of familiarity). The intelligence role is usually related to the formation of the last two.

According to Wilensky (1967), organizational intelligence is the gathering, processing, interpreting and communicating relevant information needed the decision-making process. In the same vein, Glyn (1996) argues that intelligence is formed by information processing functions that permit the adaptation to the environment, considering its demands and forwarding them to the organization's development responsibility.

Despite the several meanings that intelligence theory applied to organizational management has acquired only two are relevant to this paper: the competitive and the organizational intelligences. The 'competitive intelligence' has been deeply studied since the 1970s and according to Dutka (1999, p. 4) 'is a process that involves collecting, analysing and acting on information about competitors and the competitive environment'. The 'organizational intelligence' is 'the capacity of an organization to mobilize all of its brain power, and focus that brain power on achieving the mission'

(Albrecht, 2002, p. 15). It is, thus, a wider concept that can embed the previous one as well.

Liebowitz (2004) points out another meaning of organizational intelligence that sees it as a 'collective assemblage' of all the intelligences of the organizational domain. It includes all knowledge obtained by all departments via individual and organizational learning processes. The challenge is exactly to transform individual learning into organizational learning.

Espejo *et al* (1996) consider organizational intelligence as part of a recursive structure, which composes the strategic management aiming to fit an organization in its environment. On the basis of Beer's VSM (Beer, 1979, 1981, 1985), Espejo defines strategic management as the composition of the three higher levels of VSM – Policy, Intelligence and Control, as shown in the Figure 6.1. This structure is responsible for the adaptation of an entire organization to its environment, being a process that includes internal changes to produce more effective responses to the external stimulus. Fitting to the external environment means a redesign of internal relations, frameworks and mental models to maintain the balance between control and intelligence functions, which depends on the role of the policy/normative functions.

The idea of balance between control and intelligence comes from the dependency of the internal system on the environmental dynamics. An organization could not survive without the interaction with its external environment, this relation being a mutual influence. Figure 6.2 shows the simplified schematic dynamics of the relations between the organization and its external environment along with its relevant elements. This model is the combination of the perceptions of Argyris (1999) and Jackson (1991) about the approaches of Beer (1981, 1985).

The organization receives the outcomes emanating from the environment about any earlier interaction that are attenuated in order to be absorbed by individuals and groups inside the organization. The outcomes are, mostly, information about the relations that were previously established with the external environment. In Figure 6.2, these

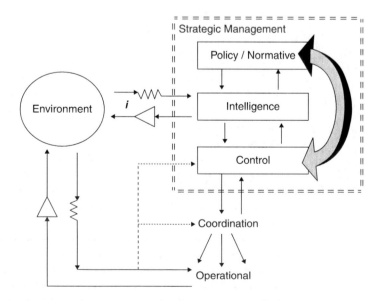

Figure 6.1 – Interactions among functions and the environment on an organization through the VSM

Source: Adapted from Beer (1985) and Espejo *et al* (1996).

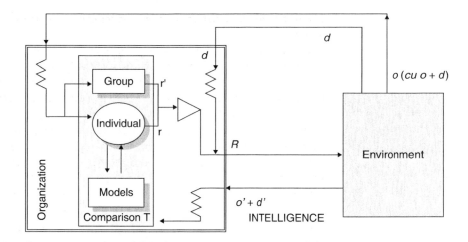

Figure 6.2 – Simplified interactions of internal organizational elements and the environment leading to organizational learning

Source: Adapted from Argyris (1999) and Jackson (1991).

outcomes are represented by *o*, and sometimes suffer disturbances emerging from the environmental relations. These disturbances, represented by *d*, could be comprehended as 'noises' in the communication processes, or unpredictable influences of unknown actors. When these disturbances appear along with the outcomes, it is hard to have a consistent picture about the effects of the previous interaction with the environment. Often, it is difficult to know if they are present or what their strength is. From this difficulty emerges the first challenge of the interaction process between organization and environment: to read the environmental feedback separating what is really a result of the organization's action from the disturbances originating in the environment.

These attenuated outcomes (with or without disturbances) are processed by groups and individuals responsible for the previous interaction or for the collection of the feedback from the environment. It is important to note that this is a small part of the intelligence role that is sometimes, perhaps in most cases, executed by other departments than the intelligence one. The feedback is interpreted by formulating mental models based on the collected information, which will create individual knowledge about the impacts of previous actions on the environment. This knowledge is based on the comparison of the feedback and the expected parameters designed before the earlier interaction. The expected parameter is named target (*T*), a mental projection about a desirable future outcome. It is the reference to the organization's responses to environmental outcomes. The parameter *T* is an objective to be reached in the next outcome and a guide to the formulation of individual, departmental and organizational responses. By the VSM logic, these responses are targets to be reached in order to complete the organization's mission. They are defined by the normative internal level (Beer, 1985) and designed by the strategic management interdepartmental board, thus influencing the composition of *T*.

The composition of *T* is not determined only by the board, but also by the expectations about the environmental dynamics. Therefore, *T* is defined both by the organization and its environment. In this sense, the second great organization's challenge is to analyse the environmental context to design a *T* that will be seen as reference for the actions of the internal organizational elements. This is the core of the intelligence function: to extract from the environment the appropriate information to develop a consistent T and responses R that approximate the processed outcomes (o) to T, which means a successful action.

In order to be successful in this endeavour enhancing the possibility of formulating an effective R, the intelligence function has to identify the disturbances. This identification amplifies the simple recognition of the disturbances (d) that distort organizational responses (R), it encompasses also the disturbance's progressive dynamics and the investigation about the causes and consequences of d, which can be called d'. In addition, the intelligence function must identify the outcomes (o) from the organization's actions and its competitors as well as collecting relevant information about the dynamics of the environment and its activities to delineate a perspective about the future (o').

Generally, the role of intelligence is not carried out by a specific department or team, rather it is distributed among several. Every organizational actor is directly related to activities in which the exchange of information with other agents is required.

THE BLACK BOX AND CHAOS

The complexity of a system is determined by the interaction of four elements: the number of components of the system, how they interact, their attributes and the degree of organization. The latter relates to the rules that guide the interactions and attributes inside the system. The proliferation of complexity happens with the expansion of the internal and external relations. In a complex system, the outcomes cannot be described with precision, since the increase of complexity makes the knowledge about all the stages of the processes and the prediction of outcomes more difficult and complicated.

Therefore, this kind of system presents a chaotic response to the inputs as the results of the interactions cannot be easily controlled. From the cybernetics point of view, systems like this are described as 'black boxes'.

According to Jackson (1991), organizations and their environments are close to being black boxes as managers and advisers can never fully comprehend the causes and consequences of processes or understand the entire behaviour of the system. He presents the 'Black Box technique', which is the manipulation of inputs to try to find regularities in the outputs in a restricted internal environment for some purposes. However, at a wider scope this process is long and inefficient and inadequate to face the dynamic context of the contemporary markets and environments.

The Black Box technique (Figure 6.3) is the mapping of the system's responses by feeding it with selected inputs. As the complexity of the system rises, the responses for the same input will change as time goes by. Far from having a well-delineated pattern, sometimes the outcomes are chaotic and unpredictable. Even if it is possible to foresee the major structure of an outcome, some specific components of the system's response can be very different from what was expected and difficult to be observed first time leading to disturbances in other inputs and making future outcomes unpredictable.

On the other hand, a fully understandable system is called a 'transparent box'. As complexity decreases the transparency of a system, the aim of intelligence is precisely to deliver relevant information to managers that can be used to transform 'black boxes' into more 'transparent boxes'. However, it is worth noting that there can be no full transparency in the systemic interactions among persons, organizations and environments.

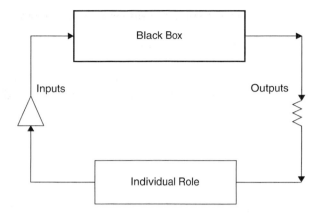

Figure 6.3 – The interaction model of the individual role proposed by Espejo *et al* (1996) and Jackson (1991)

Source: Espejo *et al* (1996).

In the real world, the intelligence role is limited, providing just a small quantity of information about the environment. Even the most efficient intelligence service can only inform about a small part of what really happens in the real world. The variety demanded to deal with the whole of the real interactions that influences the situations concerned to an actor or organization in the environment is always higher than the available variety capacity. This is why the interactions are always referenced by Beer (1985), Espejo *et al* (1996) and other authors combined with attenuators or amplifiers. An organization cannot cope with all demanded variety without attenuators, because its absorption capacity is less than the environment's production capacity. Even if an organization has the capacity to deal with all major environmental elements relevant to its activities, there are many other issues that influence these elements that make it impossible for an organization to control them completely.

In addition, there is another important aspect about the organization–environment relation that affects the intelligence role: the *Weltanschauung*. The *Weltanschauung* is the personal unique perception or worldview that underpins all information exchange among human beings about something. The acquisition of information via observation of reality happens through the patterns grounded in the observer's mental model that means that his or her experience influences the construction of new mental models.

Language, as an amalgamation of signs and codes with associated meanings, is a fundamental aspect of the *Weltanschauung* since each person may have a different meaning about a shared code. The convergent region of the meanings is what gives the sensation of understanding. However, as Culler (1983) as well as some linguistic authors such as Saussure (2000) and Orlandi (1998) point out, the communication is a particular kind of misunderstanding where differences of meanings do not matter as long as the core of the information can be comprehended. The differences of meanings in the communication processes intensify the complexity of organizational interactions amplifying the chaotic characteristics of the Black Box concept.

In contrast to the traditional systemic concept shown by Ashby (1964), the intelligence function must have a discriminative view of the Black Box separating the organization from the environment (Figure 6.4). The complexity of the chaotic relations between environmental actors needs to be exhaustively studied and attenuated despite there will always be some misunderstanding about the true reality. However,

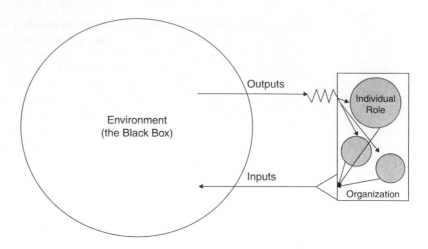

Figure 6.4 – ISM's Black Box position

Source: The Authors.

it is imperative that all the complexity of an organizational internal relation can be handled, which means that, in order to produce effective responses to environmental feedbacks, an organization needs to take into account the reports of the intelligence about the changes of parameters produced by the environment.

The use of the ISM has to take into account the low predictability of the environmental behaviour. Even if the information gathered under the methodology is enough to orientate decisions, it is necessary to have in mind that all information is just a representation or interpretation of something, not the thing itself. Therefore, the information that it is possible to cope with is always an attenuated representation of reality. This is not a new perception and most of the literature about systems modeling recognizes that models are only attenuations of reality never being fully reliable and that all predictions based on representations are only expectations not an unalterable perspective.

STIMULATED ACTION CYCLEE (SAC) – INTRODUCTION TO ISM

The activity of the intelligence function encompasses two continuous and simultaneous loops that report to the strategic management board. The first one encloses the processes of a permanent search in the behaviour of the environment, named in this paper 'Active Environmental Mapping' (AEM). The second loop – 'SAC' – depends on the interaction with other agents in the environment. To introduce the ISM, this study presents initially, for pedagogical purposes, the description of the stimulated action of the intelligence function according to the steps of the SSM. Nevertheless, the ISM is not only applicable under the SSM scheme for problem situations diagnosis, as it will be seen below. Even so, as Molineaux & Haslett (2007, p. 494) concluded, SSM is an 'inherently creative' methodology with 'significant advantages over the others' constituting an effective device to deal with 'human activity systems or soft systems' (Molineaux & Haslett, 2007, p. 482) that demand creative interactions.

In order to successfully interact with the environment, an organization needs to have a complete vision of its elements. The interaction can be described as the stimulation of the environmental processing, inputting information to outcome results which can be compatible to the organization's strategy, aiming to reach its objectives. This interaction is a kind of two-way flow communication established to one or many agents in a defined systemic environment. This concept has consonance with the mathematical theory of communication (Shannon & Weaver, 1964), but does not ignore the approach of Discourse Analysis proposed by authors as Michel Pêcheux and Michel Foucault (Gregolin, 2005) or the theories developed by Saussure (2000) and Bakhtin (1997).

The environment, as understood by Ashby (1964) and Wiener ([1948] 1965) and more recently Jackson (2000) and Espejo et al (1996), is the systemic arrangement of relations, agents, objects, devices and culture, limited or not by a specific territorial or thematic region, with particular characteristics and behaviour that can be transformed by the action of its components. The knowledge of environmental boundaries, peculiarities and agents is critical for an organization to reach its strategic objectives. The intelligence about the environment is entirely connected to the design of the organizational strategy.

The strategy is the schematic plan, guideline or pattern to be followed by the organization to successfully reach its objectives. Therefore, the strategic management cannot start to lead the organization in the way to its objectives without a complete vision of the operation context (environment where it operates). In the SSM approach, the organization's vision of the context can be represented by the 'rich picture', a 'cartoonlike representation of the problem situation' (Jackson, 1991, p. 154) that assists in formulating the root definitions of the relevant systems associated with the organization's context.

The rich picture is a tool that enables managers to realize a mental model about the real situation, defining its root definitions or the condensed representation of each context component (agents, objects or relations) in its most fundamental form. The role of the intelligence function, under the prism of the Checkland's SSM, should be associated primarily with the rich picture constitution, which represents the result of the methodology's second step. The search for environmental information can help to foment a more real world effective image or to design a richer picture about the context. The SSM processes are represented by Figure 6.5.

The SSM represents for the ISM the original guideline that coordinates the needed operations to pursue relevant information for the organization. According

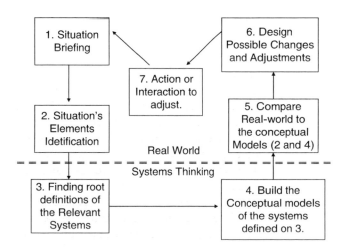

Figure 6.5 – Checkland's SSM summary. Adapted from Checkland (1981), Jackson (1991) and Donaires (2008)

to Checkland & Scholes (1990, p. 25), 'SSM is a systemic process of enquiry which also happens to make use of systems models. It thus subsumes the hard approach, which is a special case of it, one arising when there is local agreement on some system to be engineered'. The SSM was originally presented as a seven-stage process that is not necessarily developed in sequence. For pedagogical reasons, this paper represents the correlation of the SSM and the ISM in the original seven-stage process of the Checkland's methodology, but it is clearly understood that it is only a demonstration of a possible entire cycle of SAC-ISM operation, with no repetition or suppression of steps that might happen in other situations.

Assuming step one of the SSM as the starting point of the managerial process (actually, it is a permanent cycle, and finding the exact start of the process is quite difficult, sometimes impossible), all action starts with the perception of a situation (a problem or an opportunity). In this first stage, there are no formally defined elements about the situation, just the perception of its existence. Checkland (1981) considers the first stage as the primal contact with the context when there is not a clear idea of what is the problem. Figure 6.5 shows the first stage as a 'situation briefing' where the organization starts to contact with the context. If the situation is concerned the interaction with the environment, this briefing happens because of the receiving of o, o', d or d' (Figure 6.2) by the internal participants of the organization.

The SSM second step is dedicated to the description of the situation elements having as outcome a framework about what really happens in the environment

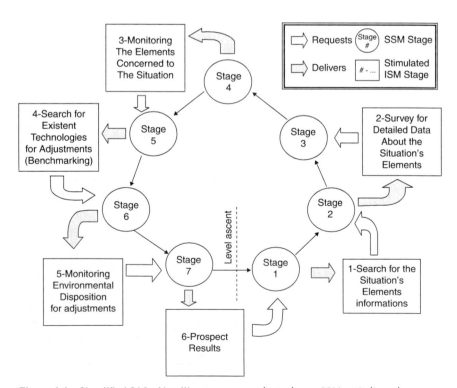

Figure 6.6 – Simplified SAC of intelligence systems (outer) over SSM cycle (inner)

Source: The Authors.

regarding the perceived problem or opportunity. To collect the needed information about the elements to create this rich picture of reality, the intelligence function has to prospect data for the demanded issues related to the problem. It starts a recursive cycle between the first and the second step that could be handled using the SSM. This is what this study intends to call ISM, the recursive intelligence secondary cycles acting to acquire relevant information to enable the main cycle of the situation treating.

The ISM assumes the existence of an inner cycle concerned with the management of the problem and outer cycles that refer to the intelligence role with several interactions over the resolution of main situation. Figure 6.6 illustrates the cycles of the intelligence function action along the SSM stages.

The first stage of the SSM generates the need for information about the perceived issue to delineate the situation's characteristics and identify its elements. To get on to the next step, the inner cycle requests the needed data from the intelligence function that starts the first stage of the ISM under the SAC (SAC-ISM). This stage refers to the search for information on the situation's elements to help in designing the rich picture of the real context.

The SAC-ISM stages are based in two kinds of double loop processes. The first is the search for information requested by the inner cycle of the situation's treatment. It comes to action in the first, second, fourth and sixth SAC-ISM stages, illustrated in Figure 6.7. The black arrows represent the flow of actions concerned with developing methods while the white ones indicate the cycle of action to realize what is prescribed by the developed methods to finally obtain the requested information. This double loop process is the ISM Survey Cycle, based on Senge's learning cycles (Senge, 2006) and on Dixon's observations about the organizational learning cycles (Dixon, 1999), combined with Espejo et al (1996).

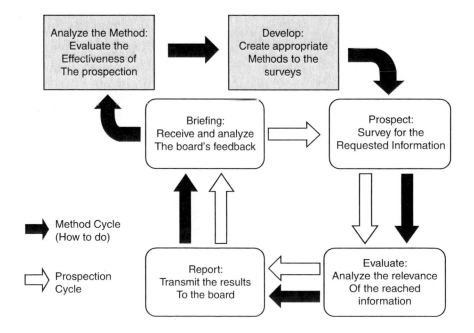

Figure 6.7 – Simplified ISM's survey cycle

Source: The Authors.

It is important to bear in mind that the ISM description given here is only intended to be a guideline not a mandatory scheme. There are several possible routes as may be seen from Figure 6.6. For example, as Checkland & Scholes (1990) show, it is possible in SSM theory to jump from Stage 3 to 5 or to go back to Stage 1. Each case is different and even at the return to a specific position in the inner cycle there is no regular rule, which strictly determines the ISM steps that have to be followed. The judgement of the user to employ the most suitable technique is essential for the good development of the stimulated action and active mapping cycles. However, it is not possible to illustrate all the possibilities, so this paper will keep its focus on the idealized model of the SAC as a six step outer cycle over the seven steps of SSM, always keeping in mind that this presentation is for explanation purposes and does not represent real world situation.

The survey cycle is started by the briefing about the needs of the ISM current stage that is the search for information to construct the rich picture about the reality. It is the search for data about the situation elements trying to explain its functions and behaviours. After the briefing, once the board's needs are properly analysed, the survey cycle initiates the development of the method to prospect the requested data. It is symbolized by the observation of the methods that were employed before in similar surveys and their utilization, creation or adaptation for the current task. If the cycle is in the second iteration or later, the method analysis depends on the board's feedback about the earlier search.

Once the survey method (sometimes a strategy made up of many methods) is delineated, the survey cycle passes to its practical action implementing what was designed in the earlier step. If the information is obtained, it has to be evaluated to diagnose its relevance to filling the board's request. If it fits to the requested patterns, the information is reported to the board following the specified format for this step. It is fundamental that the intelligence report be based on the language and values of the division that will receive the survey's results, to avoid any mistakes in interpretation. Once the intelligence report is ready, the organization has to focus on the next step of the situation treatment. However, if the information found is not sufficient or adequate to the needs of the current problem situation treatment stage, the board will feedback to the intelligence function and the survey cycle will restart from the briefing again.

If the intelligence report is approved by the management, the rich picture can finally be designed moving to the third stage of the SSM, where the root definitions of systems relevant to the situation are described and, subsequently, the organization's systemic context conceptual model. The passage from the second to the third step of SSM represents the change from the real world perspective to the systems thinking ideal structure view. The quest for the situation's root definitions is, in fact, the search for the expected framework, a model of systems interactivity that is desirable to reach the intended results. According to Ferrari *et al* (2002), the third SSM stage must identify the elements of the relevant systems as customers (those affected by the system's activity), actors (who implement the actions in the environment), transformation processes (how the system processes the inputs and the outcome results), *Weltanschauungen* (the worldviews associated with each component of the system), owners (who have the tools to operate the system and take possession of its benefits) and environmental restrictions (limitations and rules which restricted the actor's actions). These elements are known as the CATWOE test (Checkland & Scholes, 1990). In order to elaborate the root definitions, the organization employs the second stage of the SAC-ISM that will process the request by the same survey cycle used in the previous stage with the difference of having many cycles as many systems are identified by the intelligence report. In Checkland's SSM, the root definitions are based on a process of creative design of the systemic elements' purposes and premises. However, to undertake this process it is necessary to have a deep comprehension about the role of each element in the real world, which justifies the use of the SAC.

Once the intelligence system satisfactorily completes the search for information, the inner cycle returns to its operation moving to the fourth step of the SSM, to design 'how the outstanding systems should be for this situation' (Ferrari *et al*, 2002, p. 58). This is a conceptual stage where the intelligence has a break – or concentrates its activities in the AEM processes, which is explained later.

From the fourth to the fifth stage of the inner cycle, the SSM describes the comparison between the model established in the fourth stage and the rich picture acquired in the second stage. This comparison makes apparent the differences between the reality and the desirable model, which will enable managers to create devices to change the reality to the expected patterns. Nevertheless, to ensure that the rich picture did not change while the third and fourth steps were undergone, the intelligence function has to watch the environmental behaviour to alert the board about any alterations found. This is the third stage of the SAC-ISM whose operations are based on the ISM Monitoring Cycle shown in Figure 6.8, which is explained later, in the AEM section. If there are no perceived changes in the environment to justify a return to the second stage of the SSM, the situation's management goes on to the sixth step of the inner cycle, having identified the differences between the reality and the desired model. The sixth SSM stage deals with the design of actions and adjustments to approximate the

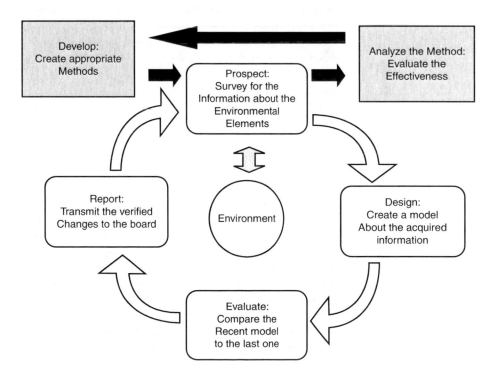

Figure 6.8 – Simplified ISM monitoring cycle

Source: The Authors.

reality to the model built in the fourth stage – the actual to the intended. It represents a new step for the SAC-ISM since the designed actions should use tools and principles already developed by other environmental actors reducing costs and time. The intelligence function is extremely important to search the leading edge (and, sometimes, traditional) devices that should be used to adjust the situation to the proposed model, but it is not the only way to reach it. Other functions can contribute to the process, or even lead it, when they have specific expertise on some issues related to the solution of the problems concerned.

The fourth stage of the SAC-ISM over the SSM deals with the search for existing techniques or devices to implement the necessary changes producing reports not only to the board, but also to the creative staff of the organization – if they are not part of the strategic management. This step is based on the Search Cycle (Figure 6.7).

Once the design of the plan (to approximate the existing to the idealized one) is done, the SSM moves to the seventh stage – the implementation of the designed plan. While implementation is taking place, managers need to have continuous feedback about the outcomes from each designed process. In this context, the ISM fifth stage emerges, which is the observation of the results and consequences of the implemented actions, via the continuous interaction with other system functions and direct observation of reality informing the board about any critical risk along the implementation. This monitoring process is a particular form of the ISM Monitoring Cycle (Figure 6.8), which includes the comparison of the outcomes and the board designed parameters.

Having implemented the adjustments, the SSM moves back to the first stage to restart the cycle again, in a continuous improvement of the organizational framework that, among other benefits, enhances knowledge via continuous learning. The intelligence function is requested again, to gather the full results of the first SSM cycle. The sixth SAC-ISM step is based in the Search Cycle (Figure 6.7) once more. The information sought has to include not only the evident outcomes, but the extended consequences of the actions from the last SSM stage including the generated disturbances and impressions of other environmental actors. When the needed elements are satisfactorily reported, the inner circle carries on its processes.

As the SSM is based on a concept of continuous improvement of the organizational actions, its cycles tend to be repeated with new contents each time, along the organization's lifetime. This is the assumption of the permanent role of the intelligence function with a projection that inspires the vision of a spiral evolution of the processes. Therefore, there are times when the stages can be skipped or repeated, as it is not a rigid cycle of seven steps. The use of SSM is preferred because of its flexibility. If it becomes a fixed cycle, as observed by Checkland (1981), it would be not useful in situations that escape the cyclic pattern.

Even when SSM is not the chosen methodology to diagnose and treat a situation (as it is not appropriate for all kinds of problems) ISM can be used as a guideline for the intelligence function's activity over the organization's interactions with the environment. ISM does not intend to tie the organization's actions to a rigid scheme. On the contrary, it tries to offer a flexible schedule to improve the visualization of the intelligence role in the organization's daily tasks, never losing the sight of the systemic arrangement of the coexistent elements in the environment. Up to now, we have discussed the intelligence function's action oriented by the stimulation of the organization, in other words, the intelligence by request. However, this is just half of the intelligence role. It is also important to pursue the environmental mapping continuously, not just when it is demanded. This is the focus of the second half of the intelligence role: AEM to the ISM.

AEM – THE ISM PERPETUAL DEVICE

As described by Tyson (1998), the organizations of the twenty-first century have to own perpetual strategies, with flexible structures and continuously changing processes. The change itself can be seen as a feature of the dynamic systems that could not be stopped. All attempts to break the environmental changes have other changes as a consequence. The organization has to be prepared to interact continuously with an unstoppable cycle of changes.

It is obviously a fallacious idea that only the intelligence function has the power to perceive changes in the environment. All organizational functions demand interaction, internal or external, and the actors involved are always changing. Those changes could be about *Weltanschauungen* transformation, new individual or group objectives, or several other issues. The most important is to keep in mind that a change often generates another change. In order to deal with dynamic sceneries and to generate its survival, it is essential that an organization be used to change itself. According to Deutsch (1956, p. 162), 'it is the change, more than the stability, we must explain' as stability is always temporary and change is an inevitable future context feature. Therefore, the continuous study of the processes related to transformations is essential for organizations.

As every function has the possibility of identifying changes in its domains, part of the intelligence role is enacted by each organizational element. Even if it is not formalized by reports, and never creates explicit knowledge about the daily situations, everyone in an organization has to acquire information about their domains of action to work. Part of the generated tacit knowledge is composed via the experiences of people in each organizational level when dealing with internal and external environments. Therefore, the intelligence function does not solely consist of people concerned in the strategic administration. In a recursive model, such as the VSM (Beer, 1985), the organizational actors have to assume the possibility of acting in many other different functions, not only their original ones, depending on the structure of the organization. The very first issue of the AEM model is 'tacit intelligence' or the process by which tacit knowledge is developed.

For the intelligence board – if the organization has one – every individual connected to the organization is a source of relevant information. Every person deals everyday with real world changes and this interaction contributes to individual learning and, when the right conditions exists, to the organizational learning (Senge, 2006). Therefore, practices of intelligence are always active in every organizational level even though they are not perceived. When individual learning brings new information concerning the organization's activity, it saves intelligence's resources by substituting its action. But only a small part of the environmental changes perceived by the individuals in their daily routines produce reports. The formalized registering and the internal dissemination of the information gathered about environmental changes are fundamental to the emergence of effective devices for strategic management as pointed out by Paraponaris & Simoni (2006) and Nonaka & Takeuchi (1995). Therefore, part of the organizational information about the environment is present only in the individuals' minds, which is called 'tacit intelligence' and has an important role to play in the organizational strategic management.

On the other hand, all the information that is reported and formalized represents the 'explicit intelligence' being the focus of the AEM. This intelligence encompasses what is registered, formalized and enabled to be transmitted as a support. This kind of intelligence, which is very important to the ISM concept, is that based on the production of a report, to offer analytical data that will help the decision processes. The production of reports from monitoring the environmental activities is the main concern of the AEM, a continuous process based on the Monitoring Cycle (Figure 6.6). As an active process, the AEM does not run on demand, on the contrary, it generates demands to the organizational strategic management. The AEM can be described as the ignition system of the organizational changes, as in the flowchart shown in Figure 6.9.

Just like the Monitoring Cycle used in the SAC, the AEM cycles are based on the design of models after observing the context. The steps of the AEM-ISM are continuous, the first one being the design of the observation method. After that, it is necessary to evaluate the method, by testing or analysing its effectiveness. The third step is the observation that aims to include all the elements, which are important to the organization's activity. Once the elements and their position in the environment are known, it is possible to design a model related to the perceptions of the reality. This model is stored in the memory of the process to be used for the comparisons in the next cycles. Therefore, it is possible to compare the recent model with previous ones (stored from earlier cycles), identifying possible differences or changes in the environment.

On the basis of the identified changes, the next step is to compose a report to the board alongside an evaluation of the effectiveness of the methods to be employed. If there are no identifiable changes, the flow starts again by the evaluation of the method. The constant evaluation and improvement of the methods are compatible

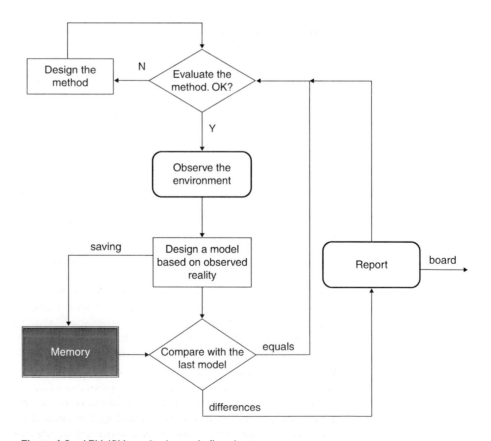

Figure 6.9 – AEM-ISM monitoring cycle flowchart

Source: The Authors.

with Senge's cycles of individual learning (Senge, 2006) and to Espejo *et al*'s (1996) discussions about the flexibility of the learning methods – learning how to learn (Senge's OADI model).

Throughout the AEM, both internal and external information are important, since the constitution of knowledge by the learning processes is only possible when the relations between the environmental elements and the organizational resources (agents and devices) are considered.

This method might look like a bureaucratic scheme with a waste of time between its steps. On the contrary, it is quite automatic and the processes are almost simultaneous, occurring at the speed of the cognitive processes of the actors. The AEM-ISM does not function as a formal protocol but as a guideline for the action of observation, which can be applicable to all kinds of watching tasks that demand reports with no responses to the environment. The responses are developed in another organizational level, usually the operational one (often executing responses designed by other levels), but not Beer's intelligence function (Beer, 1985).

In the internal environment, the information has to reach the individuals who are concerned with each issue. The correct transmission inside the organization depends on the internal knowledge sharing behaviour (Yi, 2009). Only by access to the relevant information, can the internal agents take more effective decisions.

THE ISM IMPORTANCE TO DECISION MAKING

Who decides in an organization?

The question seems like an attempt to refer to the power delegated to a specific centralized command actor. But according to the systemic approach, decision making is a process that every individual or group, component of an organization, may have to deal with. Every function has a range of decisions within its scope, because systems are based on recursions (Beer, 1981, 1985). It means that even in a reduced scope, every person in the organizational structure exercises a decision-making process to different degrees. What differentiates one decision from another is the importance attributed to its consequences. Generally, the strategic management board is accountable for the most important decisions.

The intelligence systems support all kinds of decisions contributing to the viable management of the organization. The channels of distribution of the information gathered are included in the concept of Management Information Systems (MIS), explained by Robson (1994) as a set of tools which links the intelligence systems to the other organizational actors supporting the decision makers. Jawedekar (2007) points out that the MIS is the organizational heart, 'pumping' information to 'oxygenate' the organization with news about the environment.

Designing a strategy is also a decision about the arrangement of possible future decisions expecting to create a specific effect with some specified consequences to the environment. As it is connected, a decision about a single system has implications for other structures and systems, emphasizing the importance of predicting at least a part of the effects of what is done. Systems thinking is anchored in the design of detailed descriptive models before implementing a decision, avoiding irreversible errors and reducing risks, according to Maani & Maharaj (2004). A systemic approach to the intelligence roles is necessary to complement systems thinking-based management, which highlights the importance of the ISM in creating full arguments for the decision-making process about organizational actions over the environment.

CONCLUSIONS

The intelligence systems are extremely necessary to organizational survival since they are accountable for gathering the relevant information to support actions over the environment, thus being an essential part of the management resources. According to systems thinking, especially that of Beer (1979, 1981, 1985), the intelligence function is performed recursively by diverse organizational actors within their specific domains of action.

Most of management science is based on modeling before implementing. Observing the intelligence systems through the lens of the VSM it is possible to idealize a methodology of action based on the SSM (Checkland, 1981) and the learning processes of Senge (2006). This specific methodology, designed to guide the intelligences processes, has been named in this paper as ISM.

The ISM stages aim to help the achievement of an effective performance of the intelligence systems, formalizing a soft approach to the development of the daily intelligence tasks with useful methods. It encompasses the stimulated actions and the active vigilance about the environment as two distinct and simultaneous actions of the same role.

Even with a methodological definition of the intelligence function, the decision makers have to keep in mind that the environmental behaviour depends on several factors and elements. The extreme complexity of dealing with so many actors, organizations and other subsystems, each one with its own interactions in the environment, has been named by the systems thinking authors as the Black Box concept. Can the intelligence function reduce the 'shadows' in the Black Box to transform it into a transparent one? That depends not only on the intelligence itself, but the organizational actors and decision maker positions, competencies and *Weltanschauungen* dealing with all that complexity.

The elaboration of the formal ISM description opens opportunities to report applications of the methodology to real situations. This paper is only a small step in the direction of designing a new basis for the intelligence action. It does not have the intention of describing all the possibilities and potentialities of the ISM application, but only to offer a new path for one specific issue of systems thinking: intelligence systems.

REFERENCES

Akgün AE, Byrne J and Heskin H (2007) Organizational intelligence: a structuration view. *Journal of Organizational Change Management* **20(3),** 272–289.

Albrecht K (2002) *The Power of Minds at Work: Organizational Intelligence in Action*. AMACOM, New York.

Allee V (1997) *The Knowledge Evolution: Expanding Organizational Intelligence*. Butterworth-Heinemann, New York.

Argyris C (1999) *On Organizational Learning*. Blackwell Publishing, New York.

Ashby WR (1964) *An Introduction to Cybernetics*. University of Michigan, Michigan.

Asimakou T (2009) The knowledge dimension of innovation management. *Knowledge Management Research & Practice* **7(1),** 82–90.

Bakhtin M (1997) *Estética da Criação Verbal*. Martins Fontes, São Paulo.

Beer S (1979) *The Heart of Enterprise*. John Wiley & Sons, Chichester.

Beer s (1981) *Brain of the Firm*. John Wiley & Sons, Chichester.

Beer s (1985) *Diagnosing the System for Organizations*. John Wiley & Sons, Chichester.

Checkland P (1981) *Systems Thinking, Systems Practice*. John Wiley & Sons, Chichester.

Checkland P and Scholes J (1990) *Soft Systems Methodology in Action*. John Wiley & Sons, Chichester.

Culler J (1983) *On Deconstruction*. Independent, London.

Deutsch KW (1956) *Towards an Unified Theory of Human Behavior*. Basic Books, New York.

Dixon NM (1999) *The Organizational Learning Cycle: How We Can Learn Collectively*. Gower Publishing, New York.

Donaires OS (2008) *Uma Abordagem Sistêmica ao Mapeamento e Melhoria do Processo de Desenvolvimento de Software. Anais do IV Congresso Brasileiro de Sistemas*. UNIFACEF, Franca.

Dutka AF (1999) *Competitive Intelligence for the Competitive Edge*. McGraw-Hill Professional, New York.

Espejo R, Schuhmann W, Schwaninger M and Bilello U (1996) *Organizational Transformation and Learning: A Cybernetic Approach to Management*. John Wiley & Sons, Chichester.

Ferrari FM, Fares CB and Martinelli DP (2002) The systemic approach of SSM: the case of a Brazilian company. *Systemic Practice and Action Research* **15(1),** 51–66.

Glyn MA (1996) Innovative genius: a framework for relating individual and organizational intelligences to innovation. *The Academy of Management Review* **21(4),** 1081–1111.

Gregolin R (2005) *Foucault e Pêcheux na análise do discurso: diálogos e duelos*. Editora Claraluz, São Carlos.

Jackson MC (1991) *Systems Methodology for Management Sciences*. Springer, New York.

Jackson MC (2000) *System Approaches to Management*. Springer, New York.

Jawedekar WS (2007) *Management Information Systems* 3rd edn, Tata Mc-Graw Hill, New York.

Koch C (2004) *The Quest for Consciousness: A Neurobiological Approach*. Robert And Company Publishers, New York.

Liebowitz J (2004) *Addressing the Human Capital Crisis in the Federal Government: A Knowledge Management Perspective*. Butterworth-Heinemann, Washington.

Maani KE and Maharaj V (2004) Links between systems thinking and complex decision making. *System Dynamics Review* **20(1),** 21–48.

March J (1999) *The Porsuit of Organizatinal Intelligence: Decisions and Learning in Organizations*. Blackwell Publishing, New York.

Matthews G, Zeidner M and Roberts RD (2004) *Emotional Intelligence: Science and Myth*. MIT Press, Cambridge.

Molineaux J and Haslett T (2007) The use of soft systems methodology to enhance group creativity. *Systemic Practice and Action Research* **20(6),** 477–496.

Nonaka i and Takeuchi H (1995) *The Knowledge Creating Company*. Oxford University Press, London.

Orlandi EP (1998) *A Linguagem e seu Funcionamento*. Pontes, São Paulo.

Paraponaris C and Simoni G (2006) Difusion des connaissances et outils de gestion. *Revue Française de Gestion* **32(166),** 69–94.

Robson W (1994) *Strategic Management and Information Systems: An Integrated Approach*. Pitman Publishing, London.

Saussure F (2000) *Curso de Lingüística Geral*. Cultrix, São Paulo.

Senge PM (2006) *The Fifth Discipline: The Art and Practice of the Learning Organization*. Doubleday-Currency, London.

Shannon CE and Weaver W (1964) *The Mathematical Theory of Communication*. University of Illinois Press, Chicago.

Tyson KWM (1998) Perpetual strategy: a 21st century essential. *Strategy and Leadership* **26(1),** 14–18.

Yi J (2009) A measure of knowledge sharing behavior: scale development and validation. *Knowledge Management Research & Practice* **7(1),** 65–81.

Wiener N ([1948] 1965) *Cybernetics: Or Control and Communication in the Animal and the Machine*. MIT Press, Massachussets.

Wilensky HL (1967) *Organizational Intelligence: Knowledge and Policy in Government and Industry*. Basic Books, New York.

Chapter 7

SECURING KNOWLEDGE IN ORGANIZATIONS

Scholarly and practitioner interest in the field of knowledge management continues to grow at an astounding rate. Knowledge management, as a discipline, has moved from a fad to a necessity if a company is to compete in today's marketplace. As postulated by the knowledge-based view of the firm, knowledge the organization possesses is the most salient source of sustainable competitive advantages (Kogut and Zander, 1992; Grant, 1996; Spender, 1996). The current literature on knowledge management has examined the questions of how, why, when, and where to leverage knowledge assets (see for example Davenport and Prusak, 1998; Alavi and Leidner, 2001; Desouza and Evaristo, 2004). While this line of thinking is apt for helping us gain an understanding of how to derive value out of knowledge assets by exploiting them to their full potential, it ignores a rather salient question: How can we secure our existing knowledge assets?

The value derivable from an asset is determined both by how it is used towards economic ends and also its scarcity in the marketplace. The current literature on knowledge management has focused exclusively on the former issue – leveraging knowledge for improving effectiveness, efficiency, and innovativeness of the organization. However, unless an asset possessed by an organization is rare and competitors have difficulty imitating it, the asset has limited value in terms of competition. Proponents of the resource-based view (Barney, 1991) have long argued that an asset must meet the characteristics of rare, valuable, non-imitable, and non-substitutable in order to be of salient value in terms of competition. If a resource does not meet the above characteristics, its exploitation is still important for organizational operations but it does not contribute towards competitive advantages. Consider the recent debate on the value of information technology (IT) in terms of strategic potency for an organization (Carr, 2004). As Carr remarks, IT, in its generic sense, has lost its value as a competitive weapon, as it is easily available to all in the marketplace. Unless an organization possess a "proprietary technology" (Carr, 2004), the chances are high that the mere possession of IT will not lead to strategic advantages.

Knowledge possessed by an organization consists of assets and routines. Knowledge assets represent codified pieces of knowledge that are valuable to the organization and are sources of competitive advantages. Routines, on the other hand, are knowledge in practice or knowledge that governs practices, processes, and methodologies in the organization. For example, for a restaurant, how the chef prepares the meat, marinates it, and serves it – the routine – might be a source of competitive advantage. Knowledge possessed by an organization must be protected and made scarce to the external world, in order for an organization to remain competitive.

The formula for making Coca-Cola is one of the mostly closely guarded trade secrets. If the Coca-Cola Company was to make this knowledge public, the chances are high that they would not be able to earn abnormal profits from the sale of Coke. The reason is simple: competitors would take advantage of such knowledge and cut at the Coke profits. Knowledge must be made proprietary to the organization and not a common good to all players in the marketplace. Thus if we all knew how the CIA gathers intelligence on threats, the value CIA offers to the US government would be diminished. We must point out that while "knowing" might help diminish value it does not destroy value completely, though "knowing+doing" can diminish value completely. If we not only knew how the CIA gathered intelligence but could duplicate their processes and functions, then we could extinguish the value of the CIA. Knowledge resources are the source of competitive advantages for organizations, and unless we have apt security measures in place we risk losing them to acts of theft, misuse, espionage, and disasters.

Securing knowledge assets is even more important given the current economic, social, and political conditions, such as the surge in terrorist activities. The problem of managing knowledge security gets compounded when we have to work in a distributed and heterogeneous setting. For instance, consider the case of cyber-terrorism (Desouza and Hensgen, 2003). Acts of cyber-terrorism can cripple an organization instantaneously by disrupting the flow of information and attacking the systems of the organization. Unless an organization has effective procedures in place to prevent unauthorized access to its information repositories and systems, the chances are high that they will be vulnerable to attacks of cyber-terrorism. What makes cyber-terrorism difficult to control is the fact that attacks can come from any location on the globe at any time and from almost any information channel. Distributed concerns are not restricted to the geographical dimension. With the current rise in alliances between organizations the need for security of knowledge takes on increased prominence. Organizations have accepted the fact that they must hone their core competencies, and forge alliances for securing their non-core needs (Hamel, 1991). Alliances call for sharing and relying on a business partner's knowledge (Hamel et al., 1989; Hamel, 1991). An organization not only must make sure that its internal controls and security protocols are functioning, but also must ensure that its business partners have adequate security protocols in place. As the old adage goes, the chain is only as strong as its weakest link. An organization must know how its knowledge will be used by its business partner, where will it be stored, and who will have access to it. Regardless of where a knowledge leak occurs, whether it be within the organization or at the business partner's location, the ramifications from the leak could be disastrous. With the recent surge of interest in offshore outsourcing efforts, it is even more salient to ensure the protection of intellectual assets (Fitzgerald, 2003). Fitzgerald (2003) documents cases associated with losses of intellectual property, such as software code, when an organization has poor intellectual property protection measures in place. A final point on distributedness that deserves attention is that the sophistication, ubiquity, and pervasive nature of technology can be a factor that compromises the knowledge security of an organization.

For knowledge communications and sharing, most of us use several devices which can range from the office phone and email to personal digital assistants, laptop computers, desktop computers, and so on. We work and communicate in multiple environments; hence we use these devices in multiple settings. The use of heterogeneous devices over heterogeneous environments makes the act of securing knowledge exponentially difficult. With the increase in hacking, sniffing, spoofing, spamming, spyware, worms, viruses, and other nuisances that intercept, harm, sabotage, and destroy electronic networks, digital communications are increasingly at risk. Moreover, heterogeneous environments call for additional efforts to ensure that knowledge assets are secured on multiple devices and that the operating parameters of multiple platforms are secure. However, it is not only communication over electronic networks is that at risk: a conversation between two executives on a train about a vital aspect of their company's strategy (knowledge) could put the firm in jeopardy were an industrial spy to be eavesdropping on them.

While private sector organizations have long taken knowledge security for granted, this is not the case in the intelligence and defense sectors of the government, especially those involved with issues of national security. We draw on our examinations of knowledge management practices conducted in organizations belonging to the defense and intelligence sectors (DIS) of the government. It is our belief that an exposure to these lessons will help private organizations improve their knowledge management security practices. Scholars can gain from a lively discussion on the security procedures and practices, and these mechanisms can then be put through rigorous scholarly investigations to gauge their effectiveness. Scholarly investigations and debates on the security management aspects of knowledge management will contribute to improving the state of the art.

We begin by remarks on our research methodology. Next, we detail our findings and their implications. In conclusion, we look at managerial and scholarly avenues for further investigations into security aspects of knowledge management.

METHODOLOGY

Data was gathered for this chapter from a wide assortment of sources, all of which were qualitative in nature (see Trauth, 2001). We gathered primary data from five DIS organizations, the primary goal of which is to protect the national security of their respective countries. Three of the organizations are based in the United States, one each in Asia and Europe. We conducted interviews with over thirty senior personnel at the various agencies, reviewed documents and manuals, engaged in on-site observations, and even elicited data using open-ended surveys (Eisenhardt, 1989). The data collected helped us gain an understanding for both the espoused security practices and those that were in use. The rich array of data collection methods provided us an optimal way to triangulate our findings and check for conformity and validity. Once analysis of data was completed, we presented our findings to members of the DIS organizations to receive feedback and seek their input on items that were still high in equivocality. We composed case studies (sometimes two or more from an organization) to document peculiar and unique practices in managing knowledge. In addition to conducting primary data collection we also reviewed the extant literature on security management in DIS organizations. We gathered unclassified material on knowledge management practices underway in the US Army, US Navy, Central Intelligence Agency, Department of Defense, Department of Energy, the Indian Navy, and the US Federal Bureau of Investigation (FBI). For example, we studied the cases involving security breaches of Aldrich Ames, Robert Hanssen, Harold James Nicholson, John M. Deutch, and others, to gain insights into security practices at the agencies. We commenced data collection and analysis, when it was found that additional data being collected was not adding to our understanding of the core concept (Eisenhardt, 1989).

SECURING KNOWLEDGE

We will now describe practices and procedures in place at DIS organizations that enable them to secure their knowledge resources. We segment practices by three focus areas – people, products, and processes. In order for an organization to have an optimal security program in place it must address the people, products, and process aspects of knowledge management; failure to protect all three will result in an incomplete program.

Securing knowledge – people

As one of our interviewees put it:

> In the defense business...you are obsessed with fighting an external enemy... the last thing on your mind is to fight scrupulous individuals within the agency...we must hence ensure that we have high standards to weed out the bad and only retain the best...we cannot afford the... garbage in garbage out syndrome...

DIS organizations are in fact obsessed with making sure that only people who meet the highest standards in terms of ethics, training, and knowledge are retained. This is the prime reason for the strict training and indoctrination processes associated with joining any of the armed services. By the same token, joining any intelligence agency is not a walk in the park. Now compare this with joining a private sector organization. At best, the most sophisticated private sector organization will resort to conducting employee background checks prior to hiring. Employees are allowed to be part of the organization and in many cases gain access to critical knowledge with minimal initial security controls and clearances, which leaves the organization vulnerable to acts of theft and knowledge misuse. During the course of our investigations we uncovered the following salient mechanisms whereby security of knowledge is enforced by people-based interventions.

Training and indoctrination

All DIS organizations have very strict training and indoctrination programs. All citizens that meet fixed criteria (such as age and educational requirements) have the right to join these organizations. Once an individual decides to exercise the right, they must apply to the DIS organization of choice and be pre-screened for training. Pre-screening, for the armed services, usually involves a basic interview and physical checkup. For organizations in the intelligence sectors, pre-screening is more complicated and may involve investigations into a number of aspects of the individual's life in addition to medical examinations and even evaluations via a polygraph. Regardless of screening procedure and agency, once candidates pass initial screening tests a rigorous training program is commissioned. It is during this training process that candidates are taught about the mission of their organizations and their roles and responsibilities. Knowledge is passed on to the candidates via in-class instructions and also field-based methods such as on-job training, simulations and physical exercises. Training regiments seek to mould the character of the citizen into one that meets the characteristics of a successful organizational member. One of the most important aspects of training, especially in the armed services, is the indoctrination of the code of conduct. Because these organizations are command-and-control-based and to a large extent are strictly hierarchical, it is essential that new members be acquainted with the right processes and procedures. For instance, in the case of the armed forces, there are entire training modules that seek to explicate the "code of conduct". The use of codes is as old as war itself. The Roman legions, for example, adhered to a code whereby if a man fell asleep while he was supposed to be on watch in time of war, he could expect to be stoned to death. In feudal Japan, Samurai warriors were not permitted to approach their opponent using stealth; rather they had to declare themselves openly before engaging the enemy. As noted by (French, 2003, p.3), "the code of the warrior defines not only how he should interact with his own warrior comrades but also how he should treat other members of his society, his enemies, and the people he conquers." The code explicates not only the highest standards of conduct but also how to use the knowledge provided in its intended manner. Failure to use the knowledge in its right spirit could lead to serious consequences and repercussions. One of the main aspects of a code is protection and allegiance to the organization. It is considered a serious crime if one was to defect to the adversary and also aid in the leakage of knowledge. In addition, to the code of conduct, trainees are subjected to learning via simulations. Members are thrown into real-life situations via simulations; for a marine cadet this might involve a simulated battle while for an intelligence agency trainee it might involve being captured by adversaries. By engaging in simulations, members learn how to conduct themselves in situations that are less than ideal and involve stress, fatigue, and emotional tolls. Their conduct is put to the test and is hardened to deal with adverse conditions. Hence, it is rare for DIS organizational members, once captured by adversaries, to leak knowledge of their missions, agencies, or nations. DIS agencies also follow a model whereby individuals are given "general knowledge" first; only after competency has been displayed and the individual has been vetted by the organization is "specialized knowledge" imparted. When one joins an air force, initial time is spent on learning the basics of a command-and-control regiment, physical conditioning, and also the background material of avionics. All of this can be considered as general knowledge as it is low on specificity to a given air force; whether you want to fly for the US Air Force or the Royal Air Force, such knowledge must be possessed. Only after competency has been achieved in the general knowledge areas and the organization has ensured the trainee's commitment to the organizational mission is specialized knowledge administered. Specialized knowledge can be defined as highly sensitive nuggets of insights that require security clearance to gain accessibility (see next point). To summarize, the training programs teach an organizational member what is acceptable behavior in terms of using the knowledge of the organization and it is this training that helps guard against theft from the insiders and the misuse of organizational knowledge.

Security clearances

Another key characteristic of managing the people aspect of security in DIS organizations is the concept of security clearances (Kaiser, 2003). DIS organizational members have a "status"; this can be rank status (private, lieutenant, captain, general, admiral, and so on) and/or a security clearance status (confidential, secret, and top secret). Rank status is used to identify what information and knowledge is pertinent to one's function in the field. A general or an admiral would have information needs different from a Lieutenant's. These are acquired statuses, that is, all enlisted personnel must follow a predefined process that governs how their ranks will change based on time in the service, skill development, and performance. No one entering the armed services will be given the rank of general or admiral on day one; this is acquired over time, effort, and experience. DIS organizations have very clear guidelines that articulate the roles, responsibilities, access, privileges, and accountability for each rank.

While rank status is earned, security clearances are given. Security clearances are given based on job functions. More specifically, the information access requirements of a job function govern the security clearances. In order to acquire a security clearance, individuals have to fill out a rather lengthy information sheet, either on computer or on paper, which is then used to conduct a thorough background investigation. Background investigations look into the history of the applicant over the previous five to ten years. Details such as criminal history, financial records, past employment, and travel are looked into; in addition investigators conduct interviews with friends, coworkers, educators, and neighbors.

To attain top secret clearance, each applicant goes through a security interview, mainly to see if they can handle classified materials in confidence. It is important to note that the investigative unit assembles only pertinent information and does not either grant or deny a security clearance. The decision to grant or deny a clearance is left to the applicant's agency, in most cases being taken by senior personnel with requisite authority. For example, in the United States, Department of Defense personnel seeking security clearances are investigated by members of the Defense Security Services (DSS) and the Office of Personnel Management (OPM); when investigations are complete, information is forwarded to the applicant's agency (for example the army, the navy, and so on) for a grant or deny decision. Similar procedures are also in place in the Indian armed forces.

Attaining a security clearance can take anywhere from six months to over a year, depending on applicant peculiarities. Each clearance is evaluated regularly; failure to adhere to prescribed codes of conduct and misuse of authority could result in its revocation. Security clearances are also required of DIS business partners such as contractors, researchers, and consultants before they are made privy to sensitive knowledge. These individuals must apply for security clearances with government and are given the same scrutiny as a regular DIS employee. Security clearances are apt investigating the agents who interact with sensitive knowledge. After all, in the DIS sector any knowledge that leaks to adversaries could be fatal in terms of national security. Security clearances are focused on ensuring that only authorized individuals have access to knowledge.

Counterintelligence

All DIS organizations have counterintelligence (CI) teams whose job is to catch culprits who steal, misuse, or vandalize knowledge. CI teams monitor activities to ensure that only authorized processes, activities, and behaviors are being conducted. These teams operate independently of the other functions of the organization and in continuum, that is they are not merely reactive, coming into existence after a breach has occurred. Their value is heavily tied into their ability to prevent a threat from materializing (Olson, 2001). Having CI teams serves as a deterrent to those who would otherwise contemplate conducting a security breach in two ways. First, because of their sheer presence, DIS members know that their actions are being monitored. Second, when breaches do occur, the CI teams can quickly intervene, mitigate the losses, and learn from these efforts to improve their capabilities. In recent times we there have been cases such as Aldrich Ames (CIA) and Robert Hanssen (FBI), made public as testimony to the CI efforts at the various agencies. As an interviewee noted, "While we do not have an Ames case every day, we do have signals of activities that might lead to such disasters...our job is to pre-empt these before they turn into an Ames." CI investigations range in scope and gravity. CI investigations can be used to alert a DIS employee that they are doing something wrong, knowingly or unknowingly. If the matter is not very serious, the employee can be counseled and asked to return to work. It is important for an organization to sense and act on signals of impeding failures before they materialize; case studies have shown that perpetrators of insider crimes are more likely to start out slowly by trying to cause small amounts of damage before committing their major catastrophic act. CI investigations can also be of grave magnitude, where an employee is the subject of an intensive investigation. As one of our interviewees put it succinctly, "Being subject to a CI investigation is worse than 100 IRS [Internal Revenue Service] audits...you are crippled and your assignments get crippled...sometimes you never recover from the time lost." In most cases, CI investigators do not let the employee know that they are being monitored. Valuable knowledge can be gained by monitoring the suspected individuals carefully. CI operations can be and are conducted on an agency's business partners to ensure that knowledge and information is used in appropriate manners. CI teams work closely with the security personnel at each agency to ensure that lessons learnt from operations can be used to bolster organizational security practices. While security personnel seek to prevent external threats from materializing, CI teams are focused on examining insider threats. To summarize, CI initiatives seek to monitor how authorized individuals utilize knowledge and information in pursuit of their task assignments.

Securing knowledge – product

Securing knowledge products takes an asset or information object view of the security problem. Documented knowledge is viewed as an asset and is subject to security procedures common to physical assets. Here we are concerned with the protection of explicit knowledge; most common knowledge is explicated in information documents. It is a known fact that DIS organizations have the most stringent security requirements and state-of-the-art information protection protocols (Pernul, 1995). We now describe some salient methods used in ensuring security of knowledge assets.

Documenting, documenting, documenting

DIS departments document almost everything; as one respondent noted, "Considering the amount of documenting that gets done...it is surprising we actually do any other work." The US Army, Navy, and Air Force have dedicated knowledge management portals and systems in place; these have replaced the traditional paper-based publication processes. As noted by Lausin *et al.* (2004), the US Army is one of the largest publishing houses in the world, in terms of volume of documentation. What makes documentation interesting is the importance placed on the act of documentation itself. In most private sector organizations, documentation of knowledge is an afterthought; not so in DIS organizations. DIS organizations, owing to both regulatory pressures and also their internal needs for knowledge sharing, realize the saliency of the documentation process. All DIS organizations we researched had teams in place whose sole responsibility was to document best practices and make them available as needed. Standardization of the documentation process is salient. In keeping with the theme of a hierarchical and standardized organization, knowledge documents are highly standardized in form, which enables quicker search, retrieval, and comprehension. In the case of the US Army, the manual AR 70-31, *Standards for Technical Reporting*, defines the manner in which technical information and knowledge are to be written up and covers intricacies such as issues of copyright, disposition information, and security information. In addition, reports like FM-101-5 specify details such as report and messaging formats, naming conventions, and so on Having a unified format greatly decreases the time taken to comprehend and act on the material presented. For instance, most knowledge documents clearly state the intended "objective" of the knowledge object. This is akin to an executive summary or an abstract; having this field as a mandatory requirement helps knowledge seekers sift through large repositories effectively and efficiently.

Documentation is not restricted to in-house work. DIS organizations also make use of the external literatures (academics, other government agencies, and public sources such as the internet) and use them to build the knowledge bases. Moreover, experts are regularly brought in from academia and industry to routinely help DIS organizations gain knowledge in areas where they lack competencies. This openness in seeking out experts and getting counsel on matters is something to be admired. Research and intelligence wings of DIS organizations such as the Office of Naval Intelligence or the Army Intelligence Agency, and their counterparts the Office of Naval Research and the US Army Research Laboratory, spend billions of dollars each year in science and technology efforts. Funding is handled through a competitive bidding process which ensures, all else being equal, that the best and brightest knowledge workers are given time to push their innovative capacities and create inventions that will further organizational missions. Like everything else, these also get documented and added to the knowledge repositories. In summary, the obsession with documentation processes, activities, and events helps DIS organizations to build sustainable and viable knowledge repositories.

Tagging knowledge documents

DIS organizations like most government organizations are notorious for their efforts in tagging assets. Every asset, whether a desk, lamp, chair, personal computer, and so on, is tagged with an identification number. Tagging is not restricted to physical assets; information documents are also tagged for identification. Each finished document, whether in the form of a report, working paper, investigative report, manual, notice, circular, memo, directives, or any other variant is marked with an identification number. This identification number can range from something as simple as a working paper report number to a more complex indexing code. Tagging of information objects helps the organization track each document, its movement, and its utilization. Moreover, it helps ensure traceability and connectivity among information objects. Traceability can be defined as

> an ability by which one may track a product batch and its history through the whole, or part, of a production chain from harvest through transport, storage, processing, distribution and sales, or internally in one of the steps in the chain, for example the production step. (Moe, 1998)

Creation of new information documents calls for integrating and connecting the new with the existing documents in the knowledge base. This is done through the processes of cross-referencing. For example, if there is an update to an investigate report, the updated report will refer to its predecessor and also note that it replaces the predecessor.

Tagging information documents enables one to conduct an audit and inventory of knowledge objects. As covered in the previous point, DIS organizations have strict guidelines that govern how a document is created; similar standards apply to tagging of information documents. One of the most interesting points, in terms of tagging, has to do with the destruction of information documents. In most private sector enterprises, employees are free to contribute their knowledge to a portal and also remove it from the portal (Davenport and Prusak, 1998). This is not the case in DIS organizations. Once an information document is created and tagged it becomes the property of the organization and is no more under the direct control of the knowledge creator. The knowledge creator cannot arbitrarily decide to delete the document from the knowledge base. Much the same applies to the removal of obsolete physical assets belonging to the government; information documents need to be inspected, assessed, and then removed with explicit permission from a supervisory authority. Moreover, the removal procedure ensures that the document will be destroyed and disposed of properly to ensure no security breaches occur; a history of information documents is always maintained for archival purposes.

Securing knowledge devices

Today, most computing is done on mobile and portable devices such as laptops, personal digital assistants, mobile phones, and so on. It is important to ensure these knowledge devices are tagged and secured. They need to be viewed as assets of the organization and appropriate security procedures must be in place to secure them. There have been many cases in the DIS sector where knowledge has been compromised owing to poor security of knowledge devices. In 1990, a senior British military officer had his laptop computer stolen from the back seat of his car while it was parked. The laptop contained files which documented the Allies' plans for the Gulf War. In another instance, a British spy lost a security services laptop after drinking too much and losing track of it. The computer contained details of British secret agents working abroad. More recently, there have been several security breaches at the Los Alamos National Laboratory in the United States (Linzer, 2004). Los Alamos National Laboratory is the home of highly sensitive nuclear research work, much of which is pertinent to issues of national security such as research on nuclear weaponry and advanced military systems. The lab has experienced some horrific security breaches such as missing portable computer disks containing sensitive material, over a dozen occurrences of classified information being sent on unsecured email systems, missing computer disk drives, and unsecured entrances to sensitive work areas.

It is important for an organization to have appropriate protocols in place to ensure that information processing devices are tagged and secured. Several DIS organizations have embraced the use of radio frequency identification (RFID) tags to help in tagging devices. RFID tags have the capability to emit real-time information that can help in monitoring the location, state, and status of the device. Organizations should have comprehensive asset management systems to keep track of particulars such as the serial number of each device, restrictions on its usage, and also details of the owner. Using an asset management system it will be easy to conduct routine audits of devices to ensure that each is secured, is being used in the manner intended, and is accounted for. An asset management system may help ensure that no device is taken into a hostile or unsecured environment. The defense contractor Northrop Grumman prevents any of its employees from carrying laptops into a countries that are politically unstable, have weak security and protection measures, or may have hostile adversaries. For example, when traveling to countries such as Colombia or Yemen, where it is common for executives to be taken hostage, an organization should be particularly careful to ensure that sensitive knowledge is not taken into such locations. Security personnel can use an asset management system to identify devices and ensure that sensitive devices are not moved outside acceptable locations and are not tampered with. In addition to the protection of knowledge devices, an organization must also ensure that unauthorized devices are not brought onto the organization's premises. For example, the use of mobile phones that are capable of taking photographs should not be allowed on organization premises, as they can be used to copy sensitive material.

Segmenting knowledge documents.   Tagging helps in tracking knowledge documents, segmenting helps in classification of the knowledge documents. Just as employees receive clearances, as discussed in the previous section, documents are segmented by security clearances and markings. Each document is marked by a notation such as confidential, classified, secret, or top secret. This ensures that the knowledge presented in the document is controlled in terms of who can have access to it. Only organizational members who possess the necessary security clearances can be privy to material that is of a given sensitive level. As seen earlier, getting a security clearance calls for an investigation into the individual's background, motives, and behaviors. We must note that an individual possessing a security clearance is not automatically privy to all knowledge objects classified at that level. For example, if a DIS contractor has a top secret clearance, that does not mean they will have access to a nation's nuclear secrets. Security clearances can be looked at as the bare minimum qualifications that are required. The nature of the individual's assignments, needs, and other peculiarities will determine if knowledge will be made available. This is a rather salient point, as it ensures that information documents are used in their intended manner for specific tasks. Only if a person has a business to know particular sensitive information is it made available. Sensitive information is made available for fixed time durations under specific guidelines dictating its usage, for example, a need-to-know basis. DIS organizations compartmentalize knowledge to projects and efforts that need them. Compartmentalizing knowledge requirements avoids issues of overload and also protects the sensitivity of knowledge artifacts.

One caveat is essential here: an organization should not use classification schemes indiscriminately. Currently some DIS organizations are suffering from the over-classification of knowledge documents. Classification of non-sensitive material will impair knowledge transfer mechanisms and will in many cases result in knowledge stuck in silos. Moreover, owing to the added burden of accessing classified material, an employee may opt to recreate existing knowledge rather than go through the bureaucratic process to access existing knowledge. Over-use of classification schemes can harm a viable knowledge management program; hence one must be judicious in the choosing knowledge documents for classification.

Segmenting of knowledge objects is a missing capability in current knowledge management agendas (Desouza, 2004). Unless knowledge objects can be segmented we will not be able to gauge the different value propositions they offer. The loss of an unclassified document though costly may not be serious. However the loss of a top secret document is serious and recovery efforts must follow to ensure that it is not used in an unintended manner. Segmenting of knowledge assets helps an organization focus its security management efforts. Not all knowledge objects are of equal importance; hence they do not deserve equal attention. We must focus energies on items that have a greater value than others and ensure security for highly sensitive material first, before beginning to address trivial matters. Unless we segment information and knowledge objects we risk being overwhelmed by the sheer number of objects and losing sight of their significance.

Securing knowledge – the process

Knowledge is of little use to an organization if it is not engaged in work practices. DIS organizations face the same difficulties as their private sector peers when leveraging knowledge and managing the process of knowledge generation and application. The intelligence failures associated with the events of 9/11 are testament to this: knowledge was present in the various security agencies but it was not engaged in an appropriate manner so as to destroy the threat. However, compared with the private sector, DIS organizations have certain peculiarities that ensure the security of knowledge while it is being processed. These security measures are rare, if not absent, in the private enterprise.

Security of the knowledge process

The process of knowledge generation and application must be protected from unauthorized disclosure or snooping, loss or destruction, and unauthorized modifications. The significance of a secure knowledge management process cannot be overstated in DIS organizations. Security for the knowledge process must encompass of four items – identification, authentication, authorization, and integrity.

An agent must identify themselves before getting access to the knowledge process. Identification mechanisms enable a user, a device, or a process to present credentials to a system. In the armed services, identification takes the form of seeing the badge and the stripes worn by the person you are engaging in conversation with. Civilian DIS personnel also must follow strict identification protocols. Security at and around DIS sites are tight and heavily monitored. It is interesting to note that there are restricted quarters within a given DIS location; hence one may be able to access the general area of the DIS center but not the sensitive areas. Authentication schemes are plentiful in the DIS arena, ranging from the use of ID badges, biometric sensors, voice recognition, and traditional passwords. There are three ways to authenticate an agent – (1) by something the agent knows (passwords), (2) by something the agent has (ID cards), and (3) by something the agent is (biometrics) (Schneier, 2004). Generally, two or more such credential sets are used for access to classified information. While we do not want to downplay the need for sophisticated authentication schemes, we feel that a more important point is the pragmatics of using the schemes. Authentication schemes and protocols are most strictly enforced in DIS organizations. One of our interviewees, who had worked on security projects in both the private and DIS organizations remarked:

> Even if we were to make the knowledge of our authentication schemes public...you know the underlying science of how we do them...the algorithms, designs, and specifications...it would be of no use to the private sector...private enterprises will sacrifice authentication protocols in the pursuit of work...if I need your password to finish this project and I call you...you will give it to me...that behavior would get you terminated and subject to an investigation in the defense department...authentication schemes are to authenticate you and only you.

Violating authentication procedures is a serious crime in the DIS sector.

Once the agent is authenticated, we must be able to gauge the actions and behaviors they are authorized to conduct. This is handled using the security clearances protocols discussed earlier in the chapter. Necessary authorizations are accorded to authorized personnel only, to access the information and knowledge on an as-required basis.

Integrity is concerned with protecting the state of knowledge while it is being processed and operated on, especially from malicious and accidental acts of modification. While, the concept of integrity deals more with "explicit knowledge" captured in information documents, it is equally pertinent to the exchange of tacit knowledge. The concept of integrity in the context of information objects has been aptly discussed in the extant literature of database and information security (see for example Pascal, 2000), so we will not reiterate this here. The concept of integrity in tacit knowledge exchanges is unfortunately less discussed. Consider for example the case, of gathering intelligence by agencies such as MI6, the CIA, the RAW (India), and others. In its purest form, intelligence can be likened to "information" (Shannon and Weaver, 1949); only after the information has been synthesized, evaluated, and assessed do we get to "knowledge." Information is neutral; knowledge is not (Hayek, 1945; Nonaka, 1991). Knowledge can be defined as a subjective evaluation of information. The fact that knowledge is not neutral but can be twisted and turned to make any claim that suits an agent is what makes the intelligence business a tricky one. What is significant for one person may not be the same for another, what is credible to one may not be credible to another, and so on. This is owing to the tacit nature of knowledge and knowledge processing. Given these tacit subtleties, DIS organizations have strict guidelines in place to ensure that integrity is maintained while evaluating and processing knowledge. By example, the intelligence organizations have strict guidelines that prevent the use of intelligence for political purposes (Snider, 1997); intelligence is to be used exclusively for informing. The job of the intelligence sector is to inform the legislative and executive branches of government to the best of their ability; they leave the interpretation, evaluation, and decision making to the branches of government. As discussed earlier, there are standards in place which govern the preparation of knowledge for distribution. These procedures govern the process of integrity by clearly articulating how knowledge should be explicated, the way assumptions should be stated, and how information that conflicts with the central thesis should be documented. DIS organizations take great care in ensuring that the context in which the knowledge object was created is secured and not tampered with while knowledge is moved and applied in organizations. Knowledge may lose it relevance if it is taken out of its original context. The use of clear language is salient when communicating. DIS organizations have clear terms and definitions of concepts. Hence the ambiguity associated with knowledge transferred is low; when one uses the term MIA, that means Missing in Action, not Ministry of Intelligence and Analysis. The use of abbreviations and auxiliary terms is also clearly specified. The clear language helps to ensure integrity in what is being communicated from source to destinations. DIS organizations, especially the armed services, have a tendency to "repeat instructions" back to the source and seek confirmation before actions are conducted. This is a mechanical process, but it helps to ensure knowledge is received clearly and understood in the right context. The concepts of accountability and the separation of duties have significant bearings on ensuring the integrity of the knowledge management process. Very rarely can an individual both create and apply a knowledge nugget without oversight and approval in some manner. Knowledge when created is put through an approval and rigorous process of discussion before it can be considered as applicable to a situation. This process prevents unauthorized knowledge from being used for decision-making. Taken together, these processes and practices ensure that the process of knowledge creation and application is secured.

Security of knowledge channels

Knowledge is communicated via channels. Channels can range from a telephone line or email to face-to-face dialogues. Regardless of channel, DIS organizations have stringent security measures in place to ensure that only authorized knowledge is communicated over an authorized channel. Classified material cannot be sent over an insecure communication channel and vice versa. Failure to ensure that appropriate channels are used could jeopardize the security of the knowledge, ultimately affecting the value of the knowledge (Lloyd and Spruill, 2001). A classic case-study describing the issues involved with security of systems and channels is John M. Deutch's mishandling of classified information. Deutch was Director of Central Intelligence

(DCI) in the United States from May 1995 to December 1996. Upon his departure from the DCI position, it was discovered that classified material was present on his home personal computer. Even though the computer was government-owned, it was designated exclusively for unclassified use (Snider and Seikaly, 2000). CIA personnel services retrieved sensitive material such as top secret communications intelligence, information on covert actions, and information on the National Reconnaissance Program Budget from Deutch's unclassified computer, which was connected to the internet via modems and hence a prime target for hacker attacks. Moreover, Deutch had used his government email addresses and aliases for unclassified communications over the internet and postings on websites. Out of all the people one might expect to engage in such sloppy work the last should be the DCI. To counter cases such as this one, a DIS organization must have effective security protocols in place. Various defense departments have devised complex text scanning algorithms, which screen network traffic to ensure that no classified information moves via insecure and unauthorized communication channels. The Office of the Under Secretary of Defense Acquisition, Technology and Logistics of the US Department of Defense uses a natural-language-based text scanning algorithm that has the capacity to scan 25,000 messages per hour and sift through email attachments in PDF, HTML, ZIP, and over 200 other formats (Lloyd and Spruill, 2001). The scanning algorithm works in two stages: (1) the sensitivity module flags documents that should be sent to the software analysis mode for analysis, and (2) once a document has been flagged as sensitive, the analysis module then needs to determine if the document contains classified information. The algorithms have inbuilt learning mechanisms to reduce the occurrences of false positives (an unclassified email is flagged as classified) and false negatives (email should have been flagged as a potentially containing classified information but is not) during the detection process. All false positive and false negative errors are inspected manually by network security personnel. Most DIS organizations have strict guidelines on how sensitive face-to-face conversations should be conducted. Communication channels are monitored regularly to ensure that they are safe for the secure transmission of knowledge, there are private soundproof rooms for engaging in sensitive discussions, and personnel are instructed to be aware of their surroundings before conversing on sensitive items.

In addition to securing knowledge channels, DIS organizations also pay attention to the storage and processing devices. In most DIS organizations, sensitive material is not permitted to be taken out of premises. Strict rules govern the copying, duplication, and storage of sensitive material. For instance, in highly sensitive arenas most computer terminals lack disk drives for the storage of data. If data must be copied, there are centralized copy stations which are closely monitored and regulated.

Protocols must also be in place to ensure the security of knowledge while in transit between government agencies and branches of government. DIS organizations are in existence to serve the needs of the executive branches of government and in doing so serve the citizens (Snider, 1997). As such, it is important to ensure that a process is in place to route sensitive material from the DIS sectors to the executive and legislative branches of government. Procedures are in place to protect the sensitive nature of knowledge. For example, in the United States, there are closed and open hearings on intelligence. Sensitive material is stripped away before intelligence is made public. Some units of the government, for example in the Senate Intelligence Committee (in the US), have access to sensitive material to which not all members of the government may be privy. Congress is to all intents a passive consumer of intelligence (Snider, 1997). The various sectors of the government differ in their ability to work with information that is of a classified and sensitive nature; few in Congress have the experience to deal with issues of national security. Hence, it is important that rather than simply transfer intelligence or knowledge we also assign personnel who are skilled and experienced in explaining it to the recipient. Failure to do this properly could result in knowledge being misused. As a rule, the more people to whom a sensitive material is made available, the greater is the potential for a leak or security breach.

DIS organizations have extensive backup and alternative channel arrangements. If the primary communication channel is compromised there are backups that get activated. This is an apt measure to ensure consistency in terms of security and protection. Failure to have backups will result in chaos and confusion during times of crises. During 9/11 when the towers in New York and the Pentagon in Washington, DC, were struck, the US president was moved to a backup command and control center where he could communicate with aides and monitor developing events. Backup channels must be tested on a regular basis and simulations must be conducted to test organizational response to crises.

Leadership

Many works have long touted the role of senior leadership as a critical enabler of knowledge management. However, they do little to explicate how leadership should influence the knowledge management process. Having been privileged to see the work in several DIS organizations, we can provide some answers as to the role leadership can play. First, mandatory usage of knowledge management systems should be ordered by leadership. Knowledge management systems are not optional tools; they are critical components of work practices, decision-making, and task assignments. The US Army, for example, has made it mandatory for all personnel to have an account on the knowledge portal Army Knowledge Online (AKO) (Lausin *et al.*, 2003). Knowledge management should be made as important as getting an employee ID card; failure to strictly enforce this can result in wasted expenditures on knowledge management programs. Second, leadership must seek to integrate the different functions of the organization. If one takes a DIS organization, whether it is a Department of Defense or an MI6, a single thing stands out: you have a collection of "experts" who must maximize synergies in order to succeed in missions. Failure is not an option. Leaders focus on ensuring direction and foresight. This is done by clear, frequent, and open communication with their staff members on a regular basis. Leaders communicate with their subordinates, who then must relay information to their own subordinates, and so on until the message is passed to all. It is interesting to observe the care with which the message is passed without any noise or alternation, this being a facet of having a command-and-control structure. Leaders also focus on ensuring goal conformity. The organizational missions are put at the forefront and all are asked to rally behind them. This calls for putting aside personal or individual agendas for the betterment of the whole. Leaders hold people accountable for their actions. Accountability in terms of knowledge management has received very little scholarly attention to date. Just as we would hold an employee accountable for stealing office property, we must begin to hold people accountable for the intangibles. Stealing a computer is not significant; rather it is the stealing of the information and knowledge that resides in the computer that might to do the most harm. It is important to ensure the people are held accountable in how they utilize organizational knowledge in the pursuit of tasks and assignments.

Security practices are in place to ensure that an organization behaves appropriately to control its agents. As postulated by control theories (Ouchi, 1979; Eisenhardt, 1985), there are two salient control mechanisms – behavior and outcome. Behavior mechanisms call for the organization to define the appropriate steps and procedures for task performances and then evaluate agents in terms of adherence to these

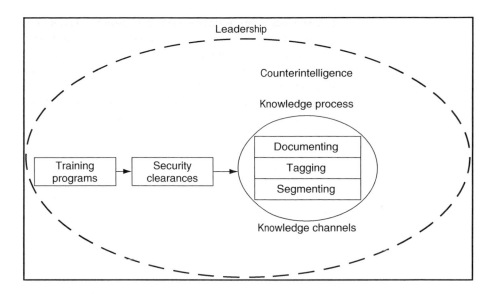

Figure 7.1 – A knowledge security process model

standards. Employing an outcome mechanism involves having the organization define the task outputs and targets to be achieved. It is left to the agents to decide how to meet the targets. Agents are evaluated according in terms of outcome achievement. In current organizations, one might argue, that there is a bias towards outcome-based control mechanisms, especially when it comes to security. Put another way, the ends are seen as justifying the means. Employees routinely share passwords, employ workarounds to evade security measures, most of the times in good faith, in an effort to meet task requirements. It is our contention that organizations need to pay attention to devising appropriate incentives to ensure behavior-based control mechanisms are in place, especially in terms of ensuring the security of knowledge assets. Without appropriate incentives, it will be difficult to ensure that security practices are followed in an effective manner. Hence it is critical for the senior leadership of the organization to show their support in terms of adhering to corporate security policies and not encourage achieving tasks at the cost of organizational security.

Figure 7.1 depicts a process model for understanding security mechanisms in defense organizations. The mechanisms of training and security clearances are used to prevent unqualified individuals from interacting with the core knowledge of the organization. The mechanisms of documenting, segmenting, and tagging deal with the security of knowledge artifacts, while the security of the knowledge management process and channels deal with the tacit components of communication and leveraging knowledge. Counterintelligence activities supervise the entire knowledge management agenda of the organization. Finally, leadership asserts its influence and provides the foresight for building a secure knowledge organization.

CONCLUSION: MANAGERIAL AND RESEARCH IMPLICATIONS

Before discussing the research and managerial implications, we must address and qualify some of the work presented in this chapter. First, while we have painted a very rosy picture of knowledge management security efforts in DIS organizations, we do want to acknowledge that the efforts are not perfect. Even with some of the most stringent security protocols in place, security breaches do occur. Second, the presentation of core concepts above is not exhaustive; limited by the length of the chapter, we have focused our energies on those concepts we have felt are most salient. Third, the findings here need to be viewed with caution as they are preliminary in nature; the findings are from DIS organizations and hence we cannot claim that they are generalizable to all situations and practices. Qualifications aside, we feel the work presented in this chapter opens up a forum for discussion on the concept of security as applied to knowledge management.

For scholarly minds, our chapter presents several avenues for future research. First, the security procedures outlined above can gain from a wider debate that examines their applicability in the private sector arena. Research energies should also be directed towards examining the effectiveness, success, and outcomes of the security measures outlined here. It would be interesting to develop a model akin to the capability maturity model for software engineering, which addresses how to build a mature security program. Security of knowledge management can be linked to other constructs in the management literatures such as trust, and system usage. Future research can also examine the antecedents and consequences of effective knowledge management security programs. Security as a concept can have bearings on other facets of knowledge management system design and development, and may also inform system usage behavior.

For practitioners, our chapter has highlighted critical interventions that may help illuminate security practices in organizations. While we do understand that some of the suggestions below are costly, we firmly believe that the benefits outweigh the costs. During the course of our research we have seen a number of security breaches that could have been avoided with better security controls. As food for thought, consider the following disguised scenarios:

> An employee was having lunch at a neighborhood tavern. During his lunch, he decided to read through the company's unreleased memo regarding the coming downsizing of the workforce. During the course of the lunch, he received an urgent call from his secretary and had to leave abruptly. He did not take the memo with him. The memo led to a full-page article in the local newspaper the very next day, and employees heard their fates from a report in the newspaper instead of hearing it from company personnel.

> An employee allowed her children to use a laptop issued for work purposes. During the course of surfing the internet, one child managed to damage corporate files and also to email them to unknown aliases on the internet.

> An employee's password to the company's network was compromised. Only after one month was it detected that two individuals were accessing the network using the same logon information. The organization could never find who breached the security nor what information and knowledge was compromised.

We suggest several guidelines on how to improve organizational security:

- Conduct an organizational knowledge audit (Desouza and Awazu, 2004). The knowledge audit must be systematic and holistic. Key issues in conducting a knowledge audit include – (1) identification of knowledge assets, (2) identifying knowledge assets creators, owners, hoarders, distributors, and users, (3) valuing knowledge assets, (4) assessing threats to these knowledge assets and the personnel interaction with the assets, and (5) assessing the implications of knowledge assets to the competencies and competitive advantages of the organization.

- Ensure that employees are trained effectively on the organizational mission, goals, and accepted behaviors. Training is not a one-time deal; training must be conducted at regular intervals so as to keep employees updated to changes in policies and procedures.
- Do not allow access to critical knowledge unless a security clearance is conducted and the employee has gone through training and indoctrination efforts.
- Develop counterintelligence teams to monitor, check, and enforce security practices.
- Ensure that business partners have an effective security program. A business partner's security program must be as good as the one in your organization if not better. Do not sacrifice security for cost savings as eventually they will lead to more organizational headaches.
- Have procedures in place to secure knowledge devices and communication equipments. Only authorized personnel should know the location of these devices and how to interact with them.
- Secure and manage communication channels effectively. We suggest creating exclusive communication channels for the handling of sensitive knowledge.
- Monitor the movement of knowledge within and especially around the organization. We must remember that even with technologies such as VPN that allow employees to securely tap into their organizational resources from offsite locations, we must still be concerned with what knowledge and information is stored on mobile devices such as PDAs and laptops. Losing these devices could be costly as knowledge can be retrieved from them.
- Authentication schemes must be improved upon in terms of both technology and also human implementation. Employees must be trained and counseled on the dangers of sharing authentication schemes with others and the risks to the organization.
- Enforcement must be clear and serious for breaches of security. Regardless of rank, status, and tenure within the organization all members must be held accountable for any breaches in security that may result from their negligence.
- Leadership must show foresight, determination, and resolution in security efforts for knowledge management. They must lead by actions and not by words alone.
- Upgrades and updates to security procedures must occur in a proactive rather than a reactive manner, that is a security update should expose any security breaches or holes instead of reactively fixing the security flaws.

In conclusion, the world we live in today, and the one that awaits us in the future, can be characterized as insecure and uncertain. Organizations must employ in protecting and managing their most valuable resource – *knowledge*. Researchers, futurists, forecasters, and practitioners must lead the effort to make security a critical aspect of knowledge management agendas.

REFERENCES

Alavi, M. and Leidner, D. (2001). "Review: Knowledge Management and Knowledge Management Systems: Conceptual Foundations and Research Issues," *MIS Quarterly*, 25(1), 107–136.

Barney, J.B. (1991). "Firm Resources and Sustained Competitive Advantage," *Journal of Management*, 17(1), 99–120.

Carr, N.G. (2004). *Does IT Matter?* Boston, MA: Harvard Business School Press.

Davenport, T.H. and Prusak, T. (1998). *Working Knowledge: How Organizations Manage What They Know*. Boston, MA: Harvard Business School Press.

Desouza, K.C. (2004). "Segmenting and Destroying Knowledge," in S. Crainer and D. Dearlove (eds), *The Financial Times Handbook of Management*, London: Financial Times/Pitman Publishing, pp. 601–603.

Desouza, K.C. and Awazu, Y. (2004). "Securing Knowledge Assets," *J@pan.Inc*, 58(August), 22–25.

Desouza, K.C. and Evaristo, J.R. (2004). "Managing Knowledge in Distributed Projects," *Communications of the ACM*, 47(4), 87–91.

Desouza, K.C. and Hensgen, T. (2004). "A Semiotic Emergent Framework to Address the Reality of Cyber Terrorism," *Technology Forecasting and Social Change*, 70(4), 385–396.

Eisenhardt, K.M. (1985). "Control: Organizational and Economic Approaches," *Management Science*, 31(2), 134–149.

Eisenhardt, K.M. (1989). "Building Theories from Case Study Research," *Academy of Management Review*, 14(4), 532–550.

Fitzgerald, M. (2003). "At Risks Offshore," *CIO Magazine*, November 15, 2003.

French, S. (2003). *Code of the Warrior: Exploring Warrior Values Past and Present*. Lanham, MD: Rowman & Littlefield.

Grant, R.M. (1996). "Prospering in Dynamically-Competitive Environments: Organizational Capability as Knowledge Integration", *Organization Science*, 7(4), 375–387.

Hamel, G. (1991). "Competition for Competence and Inter-Partner Learning with International Strategic Alliances," *Strategic Management Journal*, 12, 83–103.

Hamel, G., Doz, Y. and Prahalad, C. (1989). "Collaborate with Your Competitors and Win," *Harvard Business Review*, 67 (1), 133–139.

Hayek, F.A. von (1945). "The Use of Knowledge in Society," *American Economic Review*, 35 (September) (4), 519–30.

Kaiser, F.M. (2003). "Access to Classified Information: Seeking Security Clearances for State and Local Officials and Personnel," *Government Information Quarterly*, 20(3), 213–232.

Kogut, B. and Zander, U. (1992). "Knowledge of the Firm, Combinative Capabilities and the Replication Technology," *Organization Science*, 3(3), 383–397.

Lausin, A., Desouza, K.C. and Kraft, G.D. (2003). "Knowledge Management in the US Army," *Knowledge and Process Management*, 10(4), 218–230.

Linzer, D. (2004). "Lab Security Breaches Criticized," *Washington Post*, July 21, 2004, p. A11.

Lloyd, D. and Spruill, N. (2001). "Security Screening and Knowledge Management in the Department of Defense," in *Proceedings of the Federal Committee on Statistical Methodology (FCSM) Research Conference*, November 14–16, 2001, Arlington, Virginia.

Moe, T. (1998). "Perspectives on Traceability in Food Manufacture," *Food and Science Technology*, 9, 211–214.

Nonaka, I. (1991). "Knowledge-Creating Company," *Harvard Business Review*, 69(6), 96–104.

Olson, J.M. (2001). "The Ten Commandments of Counter Intelligence," *Studies in Intelligence*, 11, Fall-Winter, 81–87.

Ouchi, W.G. (1979). "A Conceptual Framework for the Design of Organizational Control Mechanisms," *Management Science*, 25(9), 833–848.

Pascal, F. (2000). *Practical Issues in Database Management: A Reference for the Thinking Practitioner*. Reading, MA: Addison-Wesley.

Pernul, G. (1995). "Information Systems Security: Scope, State-of-the-Art, and Evaluation of Techniques," *International Journal of Information Management*, 15(3), 165–180.

Schneier, B. (2004). "Sensible Authentication," *ACM Queue*, 1(10), 74–78.

Shannon, C. and Weaver, W. (1949). *The Mathematical Theory of Communications*. Urbana, IL: University of Illinois Press.

Snider, B.L. (1997). *Sharing Secrets with Lawmakers: Congress as a User of Intelligence*, Monograph. Langley, Virginia: Center for the Study of Intelligence, Central Intelligence Agency.

Snider, B.L. and Seikaly, D.S. (2000). *Improper Handling of Classified Information by John M. Deutch*, Report of Investigation (1998-0028-IG). Langley, Virginia: Central Intelligence Agency, February 18, 2000.

Spender, J.C. (1996). "Making Knowledge the Basis of a Dynamic Theory of the Firm," *Strategic Management Journal*, 17, Winter Special Issue, 45–62.

Trauth, E.M. (ed.) (2001). *Qualitative Research in IS: Issues and Trends*. Hershey, PA: Idea Group.

Chapter

KNOWLEDGE OF THE NATURAL AND THE SOCIAL: HOW ARE THEY DIFFERENT AND WHAT DO THEY HAVE IN COMMON?

ABSTRACT

Knowledge of the natural and the social are irreducibly different yet have much in common. The differences lie at the levels of complexity they engage, modes of explanation they adopt, investigation aims they allow and whether they assert a 'double hermeneutic' effect to the behaviour of the studied objects. Knowledge are in common in that they are all construed out of available resources, justified based on the consequences of acting upon them, settled until better alternatives emerge, and serving as walking sticks for beating unknown paths in human life. Because of this, there can be no hierarchy of knowledge or unity of methodology, and dialogical encounters guided by situational ethics, not professional deafness driven by onto-logical/instrumental fallacies, are a viable strategy for morally and practically wise actions, including knowledge management projects.

INTRODUCTION

Human life can be seen as consisting of 'projects' of many kinds: growing up, falling in love, launching a product, restructuring an organisation, revitalising a regional economy, doing experiments in a laboratory, serving customers in the marketplace, applying funding from the government, having fun on 'Facebook', fighting wars, negotiating for peace, managing knowledge, and on and on.

Involved in projects, we are not alone. We associate in various ways with many 'others': friends and rivals, computers and machines, contracts and protocols, mission statements and quality circles, etc. Some (e.g., Latour, 2005) call these 'actors', human and non-human, in that they together, acting as 'networks', make us do certain things in certain ways. We are at once resourceful and bounded. Look at the kids: one generation ago, they played together in the street, today they chat via mobile phones or game on a Nintendo, each sitting in his/her own bedroom, with significant consequences to the kids themselves, to families, communities, industries and society. The same 'resourceful and bounded' logic applies to our projects, just in more complex ways.

We do projects with our capacity to act in specific situations, which we call knowledge. Furthermore, we value and seek efficiency in the production of things, including production of knowledge. To this end, we created an intellectual division of labour between natural and social sciences, specialised respectively in *Naturwissenschaften* or *Geisteswissenschaften* (Dilthey (1833–1911), cf.: Czarniawska, 2003, p. 128). We still, to a great extent, research, theorise and educate under this division. Meanwhile, the call becomes louder and louder for combining knowledge of 'the natural' and 'the social', apparently because experiences in the real world keep telling us that human life projects, including knowledge management (KM) ones, do not fit with the great divide very well (Ackoff (1919–2009), 1973, p. 667; Zhu, 2008, pp. 118–121).

Yet efforts in integration proved frustrating. Some blame the 'pretence of knowledge' – the error of pretending that the methods for studying the natural can be indiscriminately applied to investigating the social (Hayek (1899–1992), 1989); some others point to 'incommensurability' – there can be no shared ontological, epistemological and methodological grounds among 'paradigms' – despite Kuhn (1922–1996) (1962) applying this notion chiefly on the cyclical process of 'puzzle solving' and 'revolutionary change'; which leads further others to promote an isolationist strategy – abandoning any attempt of communication, let alone integration, altogether (Burrell & Morgan, 1979). Recently, the double-condemnation becomes more the desperate: intellectual division of labour is criticised as the political hubris of academia at the first instance, whereas the subsequent searching for integration is rejected as an impossible dream of a 'perfect language' (Eco, 1995). Divide or combine? We found ourselves in a no-win situation: whatever we choose, according to the double condemnation, we are doomed to fail.

What is going on, what went wrong and where is the way forward? Does it still make sense to hold on to the dichotomy of 'the natural' and 'the social'? Has 'nature' no history, is 'society' unnatural? Is there one method for studying the natural while another for the social? Or should there be a methodological unity across studying the natural and the social? Should we accept Rorty (1931– 2007) (1991) that the sooner the better we get rid of the idea of 'different methods appropriate to the natures of different objects' (p. 110)? Shall we follow Czarniawska (2003) in choosing a 'vocabulary' for projects based purely on 'ethico-political' judgements (p. 129)? Is division or integration the only option?

These are big questions. To bring these questions closer to KM projects, it may be useful to begin with a small step to explore a finer understanding of the differences and commonalities between knowledge of the natural and the social. This step is useful because, if differences are real, then a variety of skill sets, methods and strategies are necessary and 'pretence of knowledge' should have no place; if commonalities do exist, furthermore, then situated conversation and practical collaboration are feasible and can be purposefully pursued.

With this paper, I would attempt such a tentative step. Particularly, I intend to do three things. We shall begin with looking at differences between knowledge of the natural and the social, by drawing mainly on Boulding (1910–1993), Elster, Merton (1910–2003), Dreyfus, Ghoshal (1948–2004), Stacey, Brown and Duguid. We then explore commonalities, by incorporating insights from Peirce (1839–1914), James (1842–1910), Dewey (1859–1952), Wittgenstein (1899–1951), Bourdieu (1930–2002), Foucault (1926–1984), Latour, Rorty (1931–2007) and many others.

Finally, we indicate implications of the differences and commonalities for human life and KM projects, by referring chiefly to Aristotle (ca. 384–322 BC), Hayek (1899–1992), Habermas (1929–2007), Ackoff (1919–2009), Mintzberg, Baert and Flyvbjerg.

Two alerts may be useful before we proceed. First, the theories and perspectives introduced below are not meant to be exhaustive, but inevitably selective, merely as an indicative starting-point for a long inquiry. This may disappoint some readers because many important figures and relevant ideas are missing. Owing to the limited space of a journal paper and particularly my limited knowledge, I can only offer my apology to these readers and invite them to join the inquiry, to make their own contributions. More daunting, then, is perhaps the highly risky enterprise of bringing together writers with quite different, some would regard incompatible, traditions and viewpoints, for example, from Boulding to Latour, from Merton to Habermas, from pragmatism to actor-network-theory, not least because there exist huge diversities and obvious tensions *internal* to these traditions and theories. It is not news that there are today as many pragmatisms as many pragmatists, as many constructivisms as constructivists. We are told, for example, that there were 'hard' and 'soft' pragmatisms well before Rorty launched his brand of 'neo-pragmatism' (see, e.g., Mounce, 1997; Rescher, 2005), and that, within actor-network-theory, Latour, just to name one, appears to have 'his own agenda' (Hacking, 1999, p. 40) and, as time goes by, 'has come to sound more and more like an instrumentalist' (Kukla, 2000, p. 27). Given all this, in this paper I still choose to be open and inclusive, refuse to be mapped into familiar habits of thought. With this paper I do not claim to be loyal to any doctrine or consistent with any theory in its totality – whether there is such totality and whether it is a good thing is another debatable issue – save the pragmatist spirit that is tolerant of and reaches out to different schools of thought as long as they have contributions to make in enlarging humankind's potential – in the context of this paper help to enrich our understanding or alert us about controversies (for introduction to such a pragmatist spirit see, e.g., Ormerod, 2006).

Now let our journey 'begin' – or we should say 'continue' given the relevant contributions already published in *Knowledge Management Research and Practice* such as those of Mingers (2008) and Müller-Merbach (from vol. 2 (2004) to vol. 6 (2008), 19 issues). Indeed, as inquirers, we are always already in a flow (see Nonaka *et al.*, 2008).

DIFFERENCES

Between knowledge of the natural and the social, differences can be highlighted under the following headings.

Hierarchy of complexity

Boulding (1910–1993) (1956) proposed arranging theoretical systems in a 'hierarchy of complexity'. To Boulding, humankind faces problems with different levels of complexity, which he called 'empirical fields'. Boulding was particularly interested in nine levels of complexity, namely, (1) static (e.g., patterns of electrons around a nucleus), (2) simple dynamic (e.g., the solar system, a clock), (3) cybernetic (systems moving to the maintenance of given equilibrium), (4) open (e.g., a cell self-maintaining and self-reproducing), (5) genetic-societal (e.g., a plant, with differentiated and mutually dependent parts, towards blueprinted growth), (6) animal (systems characterised by increased mobility, teleological behaviour and self-awareness), (7) human (a person, possessing self consciousness, knowing that she/he knows), (8) social (concerning the content and meaning of image, message, role, value and emotion), and (9) transcendental (the 'inescapable unknowables') (Figure 8.1).

According to Boulding, on the one hand, 'each level incorporates all those below it, much valuable information and insights can be obtained by applying low-level systems to high-level subject matter'. Hence, the study of the social (upper end of the hierarchy) 'is almost certain to be better off' if we are able to skilfully employ techniques and skills originally designed for and accumulated during the studies of the natural (lower end of the hierarchy).

On the other hand, and this is Boulding's dedicated emphasis and intended contribution:

> Perhaps one of the most valuable uses of the above scheme is to prevent us from accepting as final a level of theoretical analysis which is below the level of the empirical world which we are investigating. ... We should not be wholly surprised, therefore, if our simpler systems [at lower levels], for all their importance and validity, occasionally let us down [at higher levels]. (Boulding, 1956, p. 207)

Particularly, Boulding took great pains to expose the 'unwillingness of science'

> to admit the very low level of its successes in systematisation, and its tendency to shut the door on problems and subject matters which do not fit easily into simple mechanical schemes. (p. 208)

Formulated 50 years ago, the nine particular levels chosen by Boulding may not fit very well with our concerns today. The completeness of the scheme is also in question: where is mathematics, for example? Furthermore, it appears ambiguous in

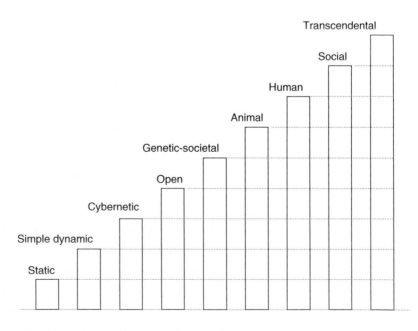

Figure 8.1 – Hierarchy of complexity of theoretical systems

Source: based on Boulding (1956).

Boulding whether the notion 'hierarchy of complexity' is confined to 'abstractions in our theories' or 'the nature of things', or both.

These are unsettling points. However, this should not distract us from the enduring value of Boulding's thesis that we are dealing with problems of different levels, or kinds, of complexity. To create a democracy is not the same as making a desk; to understand human action is not like studying the behaviour of ants and birds (Stacey, 2007). They trigger different 'cognitive interests' (Habermas (1929–2007), 1972) and 'aims' (Baert, 2005), and demand different kinds of skills, methods and strategies (Flyvbjerg, 2001).

Modes of explanation

Also useful for exploring differences in knowledge is Elster's (1983) scheme. Beginning with philosophy of science, the scheme first distinguishes natural sciences from humanities, and then differentiates these into the studies of inorganic and organic matters, social sciences and aesthetic fields. The scheme further suggests that the difference between these inquiries lies in the modes of explanation (Figure 8.2).

Seen via this scheme, for the sciences of inorganic matter, the only acceptable mode of explanation is the causal mode. For the sciences of the organic matter, however, both functional and causal explanations are needed, with the former explaining the features and behaviours of organisms, while the latter supplies an overarching causal mechanism of natural selection and reproduction of the fittest.

Significantly, somehow converging with Boulding, Elster posits, when studying the social, causal and functional explanations may still have a role to play, but only in limited circumstances. This is because human actions are usually guided by 'intentionality' which is related to interest, value and morality. This can serve to clear much hidden confusion. While it is widely accepted nowadays that both organic and human systems need to, and do, 'adapt', for example, what tends to be under-addressed is the qualitative difference:

> Intentional beings can employ such strategies as 'one step backward, two steps forward', which are realised only by accident in biological evolution. (Elster, 1983, p. 36)

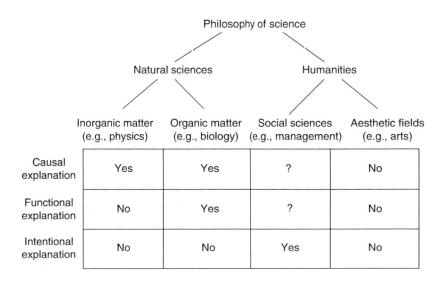

	Inorganic matter (e.g., physics)	Organic matter (e.g., biology)	Social sciences (e.g., management)	Aesthetic fields (e.g., arts)
Causal explanation	Yes	Yes	?	No
Functional explanation	No	Yes	?	No
Intentional explanation	No	No	Yes	No

Figure 8.2 – Different modes of explanation for different sciences

Source: Elster (1983), adopted from (Ghoshal, 2005, p. 78).

Elster's taxonomy may not satisfy everyone – one may ask, for example, where is engineering? In the way we learn from Boulding, we shall suggest, while Elster's thesis is unable to serve all purposes, it insightfully draws our attention to matters that differentiate the natural and the social as well as our knowledge of them.

Organisation capacity of the social

So far, I have treated 'the natural *vs* the social' and 'non- human *vs* human' as if the two differentiations can be used as substitutes for each other. Can this be justified? I note that Czarniawska (2003), in introducing actor-network-theory, draws our attention to what it is meant by 'social':

> Etymologically it comes from *socius*, an ally, a companion, which can be another person but also a dog or a computer. (p. 130)

I appreciate the insight that 'another person' and 'a dog' and 'a computer' all have effects in the production of order surrounding us – *in this sense* they all can be seen as 'actors'. I nevertheless still chose to believe in significant differences between people and dogs and computers, *in another sense*.

This 'another sense' can be linked to a debate in the recent complexity studies. The debate is about whether humans have unique organisational capability in comparison with animals and computer programs. Upon this, Brown & Duguid (2001) have this to say:

> Humans and insects show many intriguing similarities, but these should not mask their important differences. In particular, most champions of complicated adaptive systems, particularly those of artificial life, say relatively little about the importance to human behaviour of *deliberate social organisation*. To pursue the analogies from entromology or artificial life much further, we would need to know what might happen if insects decided to form a committee, bats to pass a law or artificial agents to organise a strike or join a firm. (p. 46; *emphasis* added)

It deserves notice that influential proponents of actor-network-theory, who insistently highlight 'generalised symmetry' between human and non-human actors, submit explicitly that 'it is *not* our intention to say that scallops have voting power and will exercise it, or that door-closers are entitled to social benefits and burial rites' (Callon & Latour, 1992, p. 359; *emphasis* added). In the context of this paper, my reading is that Callon and Latour's scallops and door-closers resemble Brown and Duguid's insects, bats and artificial agents – they are different from human actors after all in matters of voting power, social benefits and burial rites.

It is *in this sense*, I would still believe that the differences between humans and dogs and computers are too significant to ignore. And it is based on this difference, that is, 'deliberate social organisation' or the lack of it, I would conceptualise human relations and interactions as 'the social' while treat dogs and computers as 'the natural'. It is, accordingly, in this sense that I justify treating 'the natural *vs* the social' and 'non-human *vs* human' as interchangeable in the context of this paper. For other purposes, of course one can rightly argue that humans and dogs can be studied in similar ways, as part of nature, for example in brain science and biology. Furthermore, it does not follow that a dog and a computer are the same kind of things simply because both can for certain purposes be seen as different from humans – such a quick-jump implication is not taken in this paper.

Double hermeneutic

The natural and the social differ further in their 'reaction', or the lack of it, to our knowledge about them. For this we turn to the thesis of 'double hermeneutic'. Simply put, the thesis suggests that, while natural sciences do not alter the behaviour of the studied subject, social sciences do (Gergen, 1973; cf.: Ghoshal (1948–2004), 2005, p. 77).

Our knowledge about subatomic particles and moving planets – right or wrong – does not change the behaviours of the particles and planets. Kepler (1571–1630), Newton (1642–1727), Einstein (1875–1955) and Prigogine (1917–2003) did not make such changes. We may, based on new knowledge, redesign a machine and subsequently change its behaviour; nevertheless, the machine will not change its behaviour if our new design remains on paper. The natural answer back to what we do upon, not what we think about, them.

However, our knowledge of the social – if it gains sufficient currency – changes the behaviour of humans. Marx (1818–1883), or we may say his knowledge, profoundly changed the way people see and act in their relations, with painful or joyful consequences – depending on who you are, and agency theory in strategic management continues to make managers act in accordance with the 'opportunism' doctrine – like it or not (see Ghoshal, 2005). As studies reported, economics students were significantly more likely to defect in 'prisoner's-dilemma' scenarios than other students (cf.: Wicks & Freeman, 1998). The more you 'know' how the prisoners behave, the more you behave like them, in more situations! Watch: are bankers not currently, with the blessing from governments, creating even bigger banks given the public outcry 'too big to fail'?

This phenomenon has drawn attention from a wide spectrum of paradigms in philosophy:

> We are faced, in the social sciences, with a full and complicated interaction between observer and observed, between subject and object. (Popper (1902–1994), 1964, p. 14)

> Only men [and women] can reconstitute themselves in accordance with the newly acquired knowledge of their own situation. (Lichtman, 1967, p. 143)

> ... sociological 'truths' have come ... to influence the way people see themselves and their societies and, thus, have been consequential for the behaviour that emerges from such conceptions. ... What people believe about the way the world works can contribute to making it work that way. (Bell & Mau, 1970, pp. 208, 220)

> The technical language and theoretical propositions of the natural sciences are insulated from the world with which they are concerned because that world does not answer back. But social theory cannot be insulated from its 'object-world', which is a subject-world. (Giddens, 1982, p. 13)

> [Self-fulfilling prophecies occur when] an initially false but widely shared prediction, expectation, or belief is fulfilled in practice not because it was at the outset true, but because enough people took it to be true and, by acting accordingly, produced the outcome that would otherwise not have occurred. (Merton (1910–2003), 1982, p. 203)

> If men [and women] define situations are real they are real in their consequences. (Schutz (1899–1959), 1964, p. 348)

The citations can go on and on. Like these inquirers, who may profoundly disagree on almost everything else, I believe that double hermeneutic characterises the link between knowledge and behaviour only in the social, not the natural, unless evidence displays that insects do form committees, bats pass laws and artificial agents organise strikes because Brown and Duguid question their ability to do so. George Orwell's (1903–1950) (1989) *Animal Farm* is in fact about humans not animals.

Rules vs contexts

Studying the natural, submitted Habermas (1929–2007) (1972, 1984a, b), we aim at prediction and control. Accordingly, mainly in the English-speaking world, ideal knowledge in natural sciences, often mistaken as 'science' in general, has been explicit, universal, abstract, discrete, systematic, complete and predictive (for a critique of such a view on knowledge see, e.g., Flyvbjerg, 2001, ch. 3). These features are in principle possible because behaviours of the natural appear rule-based. Stones fall to the ground based on the same rule regardless of where and when over the globe. Even when they behave 'differently', for example, in a fast-diving aircraft, we can still explain and predict the change of behaviour based on rule(s). Hence, natural sciences as a form of knowledge, relying on rule-based rationality, have been serving particular human purpose reasonably well – so long as we set up the right conditions for the rules to work (Cartwright, 1999).

The social is different, however, in that the majority of human activities cannot be reduced to rules – we are not able to duplicate the 'right' social conditions. We already got a hint from 'double hermeneutic': should a rule or a set of rules in the social be generalised, a self-destroying effect would make them non-rules or have-been rules. Bourdieu (1930–2002) puts it this way: 'practice has a logic which is not that of logic' (cf.: Flyvbjerg, 2001, p. 38). This is because human actions are based on judgements and experiences which cannot be formulated into theoretical formula, that is, formal rules. This is in principle so; more resources and efforts (e.g., bigger software, wider websites, cleverer study designs) will not make knowledge of the social more predictive.

This is not to say that no human behaviour is rule-based, just that rule-based activities have little to do with strategy or innovation, and that rule-based thinking has to be balanced by sensitivity toward contexts and experiences. In their phenomenological study, Dreyfus & Dreyfus (1986) conceptualise five levels in human learning and performing:

- novice,
- advanced beginner,
- competent performer,
- proficient performer,
- expert.

There is, Dreyfus note, a qualitative jump from the first three to the fourth and fifth levels: the former are logical, rule-based while the later intuitive and experientially based. Sophisticated human skills and innovative actions have no general rules but depend on contexts. To put it another way, in the place of rules in the study of the natural, there are contexts in that of the social. While in studying the natural we, ideally at least, control contexts 'out' for the sake of repeatability and universality, in studying the social we must bring contexts 'in' so as to understand the situated working of meaning, values, interests and intentionality. Furthermore, in the social, context-dependence does not mean more complex rules in bigger numbers; it means open-ended, non-repeatable, contingent relations between contexts and actions and interpretations, which strips formal rules of almost their entire significance and prediction its possibility (Flyvbjerg, 2001, p. 43).

This explains why Herbert Simon (1916–2001) and his Carnegie colleagues' rule-based decision-making model yields good results when it is applied to well-defined tasks and situations, for example, routines, while less so in complex tasks and messy situations. This also explains, I would suggest, why the powerful computer programmes sitting in Wall Street had not been able to detect, let alone to solve, the recent 2007–2009 'subprime crisis': because they are rule-based 'agents', insensitive to contextual experimentations, that is, the subprime lenders' ethics and 'innovative' manoeuvre. Indeed, it is far from irrational to suspect that it was the if-then computer programmes in the trading halls and rule-based decisions in the boardrooms in New York, London and Zurich that contributed to the crisis. Rule-based rationality, in the lack of proper checking, pushed smart and experienced bankers to purchase risky financial products they did not understand (for case analysis see, e.g., *Economist*, 2007; *Financial Times*, 2007). *Fortune* magazine reports:

> Shocking, because a pack of the highest-paid executives on the planet, lauded as the best minds in business and backed by cadres of math whizzes and computer geeks, managed to lose tens of billions of dollars on exotic instruments built on the shaky foundation of subprime mortgages. (*Fortune*, 2007, p. 40)

Rule-based rationality, models and techniques, for example, agent-simulation tools and web-building skills, which have been proved powerful in studying the natural, are not problematic in themselves even in studying the social. They have a place, but also limits. They become problematic when we elevate them from being necessary and supportive to being sufficient and central, regard them as the first choice and the last resort, taking them as *the* solution for all problems, to the near exclusion of other possibilities (Flyvbjerg, 2001, ch. 2).

Differences summarised

Common to the hierarchy of complexity (Boulding), modes of explanation (Elster), deliberate social organisation (Brown and Duguid), double hermeneutic (Merton and many others) and rule- *vs* context-dependence (Dreyfus and Flyvbjerg) is the emphasis that the problems facing humankind, the phenomena we are investigating, the knowledge we generate and the impacts of our knowledge to the studied objects all can be qualitatively different and, accordingly, they demand different attitudes, expectations, methods, skills and strategies of investigation.

COMMONALITIES

Despite all the differences, the closer we look, the more blurred the distinction between natural and social sciences, or between 'science' and 'non-science' (see Baert, 2005; Bernstein, 1985; and, particularly, Rorty, 1991). Is this so? What do knowledge of the natural and the social have in common, then?

Construed out of available resources

Knowledge, of both the natural and the social, does not come from nothing but is always built upon what are available at the time of our inquiry, or so the pragmatists would posit, conceptual, theoretical, technical, material and social. While we have freedom to choose and create, we do not do so arbitrarily in a vacuum. The present effectively limits the possible preferences; we are not free to think or do anything we want (Putnam, 1996).

Remember Latour's (2005) idea we cite at the beginning of this article that we are contingently yet inevitably resourceful and bounded? Articles and books, computers and microscopes, timetables and laboratory layouts, company visions and customer complaints, funding bodies and evaluation committees, corporate sponsors and journal editors, of one kind or another, faulty or true, enlightening or misleading, honest or mean, alive or dead, now and then, in-here and out-there, all are actors that make us see, talk and do certain things in certain ways.

Let us have a look at just two of the resources: our beliefs and language. According to Quine (1908–2000) (1953), our beliefs are circular, self-referential and holistic; that is, beliefs form a web in which the justification of any particular belief is established on the basis of its coherence with the whole set of beliefs. If 'one for all and all for one' can be found anywhere, it is here. Hence, new pieces of evidence are incorporated in existing webs of beliefs, and inquirers reweave the web in the light of the new beliefs acquired (Guignon & Hiley, 2003, p. 9).

In other words, taking action and creating knowledge, we have to accept the irreducible contingency of our investigative resources (Williams, 2003, p. 69). While beliefs should be empirically based, facts are not belief-free. Broadly understood, science, like other forms of knowledge, is a language game with a set of assumptions, beliefs and prescriptions one accepts before playing the game.

> The hardness of fact [in science] ... is simply the hardness of the previous agreements within a community about the consequences of a certain event. (Rorty, 1985, p. 3)

Einstein's (1879–1955) theory of gravity is a revolutionary paradigm-shift against Newton's (1642–1727), yet Einstein relied on Newton's belief in mass, energy and movement to move beyond Newton, to construe a new belief. It is Newton's belief that makes Einstein's possible. So too is postmodernism: we, including those self-claimed postmodernists, are still using established beliefs of the modern for making sense of the post-modern. Our presuppositions are a *sine qua non* for any understanding (Gadamer (1900–2002), 1975). At any stage of inquiry, we can only work with whatever beliefs and theories and criteria we have at hand. Not ideal? – perhaps. Regrettable? – up to you. Can anyone escape from this? – I doubt it.

In studying the natural as well as the social, data or facts do not recommend, prove or impose themselves upon us; instead, they are picked up and interpreted in the light of the concepts we already hold. Sellars (1963), like Wittgenstein (1889–1951) before him, claims that 'all awareness is a linguistic affair' – one must already possess a fairly wide range of concepts before one can have sensory experience in the epistemically relevant sense (Guignon & Hiley, 2003, p. 10). Inquirers cannot escape using a conceptual system; we detect data and make sense of them against the background of the conceptions and assumptions at the time. Surely, a physicist and a biologist and a social scientist have different concepts of different sorts of things, but they all have one thing in common: they rely on some sort of concepts which cannot be otherwise but linguistically construed.

This is the situated and conditional 'nature' of human inquiries, of both the natural and the social. We cannot step outside history, there can be no atemporal foundations (Rorty, 1980).

Justified based on consequences

'This may be true in theory, but it does not apply in practice', Kant (1724–1804) ironically stated (cf.: Müller-Merbach, 2007, p. 313) (this is part of a tactic Kant used to challenge theorists who do not engage practice and practitioners who do not value theory). Let us borrow Kant's statement and put it into the context of this paper: in a world limited in resources and plentiful in suffering, does such truth make sense? Supposed you know a truth but that truth turns out to be not working – it does not help you solve problems in living experience, do you still consider it a truth? If you still do, then what does truth mean, is still worthwhile talking about it?

Then, what is knowledge and what is it good for? Is knowledge something on the shelf, an object, a mirror, in your possession, which shows you more or less accurately the way things are, which you can hold on or share with other people? Or is it something alive, active, a form of action, a form of change, a form of process, always in the making, enables you to accomplish what you want to achieve in specific situations, to make real something you value, to bring favoured changes to the world?

The logical problem of the static, passive 'mirror' image, that is, what the pragmatists call the 'spectator view of knowledge' (Baert, 2005, ch. 6), is that, while reality might be independently there, a corresponding truth is not. This is because we have never been, are not, and will never likely be, able to access reality 'as it is'. As Rorty (1931–2007) puts it, 'we shall not see reality plain, unmasked, naked to our gaze' (1982, p. 154). In the same spirit, Davidson (1917–2003) (1980, 1984) submits that while causality may not be in question, descriptions and explanations are. Without accessing reality 'as it is', we are not able to determine whether our 'mirror' is accurate or not. In the spirit of Wittgenstein (1889–1951) that of what we cannot know we must remain silent (1922, p. 151), we do not have much to say if truth means accurately copying the world, capturing the way things are (Rorty, 1980). In this, the conversation between Picasso (1881–1973) and a rich man appears enlightening:

> 'Mr. Picasso, I'd like to ask you something. Why don't you paint the people the way they are?' And Picasso asks, 'How should I do that? How does that work? What are people like? Can you give me an example?' So the rich man opens his wallet and pulls out a little picture and says, 'See, here you can see what my wife looks like.' Fascinated, Picasso takes the picture, turns it over and says, 'So, that's your wife. She's so small. And so flat!'. (von Foerster, 2002, p. 100)

If we are not so small or flat, what can we do – how are we to justify our knowledge claim, then? A viable alternative is to put our beliefs into action and look at the consequences. If the consequences show that a belief enables us to accomplish what we want to achieve, we consider it justified and accept the knowledge claim. This is indeed what we humans have been doing in our wise moments. We accept Newton's theory because it produces intended results (Mintzberg, 2001); we learn to appreciate Deng Xiaoping's wisdom because it dramatically changed and is still changing the world (Zhu, 2007). This we may call a pragmatist 'action theory of knowledge', in contrast with a 'correspondence theory of truth' (for the latter see, e.g., Mingers, 2008, p. 68; in this journal). Did Newton (1642–1727) and Deng Xiaoping (1902–1997) capture the Truth, or truths? We do not know and it is not interesting.

While entrenched epistemological disputes can go on and on, consequence-disciplined managers, public administrators and police makers need to, as they usually wisely do, de-emphases such debates for getting jobs done under specific conditions (Wicks & Freeman, 1998). In promoting an action theory of knowledge, William James (1842–1910) (1907) suggested that we should seek truth in action, forget metaphysical accounts of the nature of truth and look at how we actually shape and solve situated problems. John Dewey (1859–1952) (1930) saw knowledge as a way of meeting our desires, a way of dealing with life's demands. Knowledge is not about faithfully copying but satisfactorily coping. Richard Rorty (1931–2007) (1980) contended that knowledge is not mirrors that passively reflect the essence of reality, but tools that may prove useful for certain situated purposes, engage us actively with the world, bring something forth via our life projects. Inquirers should focus on how humans do in making practical differences, rather than on what they found through theorising. To these pragmatist writers – let us put aside the differences and tensions between them for the moment – the mandate of science is not to find truth, the existence of which is perpetually in dispute during the last several thousand years, but to facilitate human problem-solving, which we can engage actively and experience the consequences.

Understood as such, knowing as one among many human activities is characterised by all of the contingency, ambiguity, ambivalence, fragility, instability, fallibility and finitude. Knowledge should be justified and adjusted on the basis of visible, substantial, practical differences. It might be useful to retain the notion of truth, in so far as it is defined in terms of practical consequences ('Does it help in getting our job done?'), not as an 'elevator word' that always raises the abstract level of discourse (Hacking, 1999, 21ff.), confines us to metaphysical essence ('Is it faithfully representing reality?') or philosophical foundations ('Is it confirming to the principle?').

(Un)settled through competition

Action consequences and practical differences, like 'data' or 'facts', do not speak for themselves, they beget interpretations, and interpretations are usually plural. Indeed, Aristotle (ca. 384–322 BC) and Galileo (1564– 1642), Einstein (1879–1955) and Bohr (1885–1962), Keynes (1883–1946) and Hayek (1899–1992), Habermas (1929–2007) and Foucault (1926–1984), also Ansoff and Mintzberg as well as Porter and Prahalad, interpret 'consequences' and 'differences' differently. Given that there are no atemporal-universal master keys or final courts to settle for better interpretations, what can we do? Accepting any interpretation as good as the next one? (This applies to metaphors, paradigms, and so on).

Anti-foundationalism though, pragmatism is no relativistic. While there are always multiple language-games available, Putnam (1996) points out:

> Not only are there better and worse performances within a language game, but it is quite clear that Wittgenstein thinks that there are better and worse language games. (p. 37)

Rejecting foundationalism and relativism, Charles Sanders Peirce (1839–1914) introduced us to the notion of intersubjectivity and the method of abduction. In Peirce, intersubjectivity does not imply consensus. Instead, it means that justifying knowledge is not a matter of ascertaining a special relation between ideas and objects, but participate in a community where the members exchange interpretations with one another (Guignon & Hiley, 2003, p. 10). Hence, 'justification reaches bedrock when it has reached the actual practices of a particular community' (Rorty, 1980, p. 178). Rorty (1991) called this 'mild ethnocentrism' – grounding knowledge claims is circumscribed by the practices of a particular cultural group at a particular point in history.

'Abduction', usually interpreted as the method of 'inference to the best explanation' (see, e.g., O'Here, 1989; Sklar, 1995), is not concerned with a theory conforming to the conventional demands of formal logic, deduction or induction; rather,

> So long as a proposition provides a profitable leading, we retain it, deploy it, and improve it. But when it begins to frustrate discovery, and alternative propositions become more attractive, we abandon our original proposition, and call it a false. But we need never insist that our propositions copy reality, or remain wholly consistent with one another – if they produce results, we keep them. (Powell, 2001, p. 884)

Indeed, we accept and keep the natural selection theory of evolution not because we consider Darwin proved correct, but because his interpretation has no serious rivals, so far (Popper (1902–1994), 1976). Wittgenstein (1899–1951) puts it this way: 'What a Copernicus [1473–1543] or a Darwin [1809–1882] really achieved was not the discovery of a true theory, but of a fertile new point of view' (1977, p. 18).

Our settled interpretations – those to which we currently see no viable alternatives – together with our involuntary observations and practical interests, function as severe constraints on what we can accept as justified (Williams, 2003, p. 69). And our interpretations, and hence knowledge claims, remain settled until other, still better interpretations emerge from fair, sustained and rigours competitions among plausible rivals. Referring to Peirce, Habermas (1984a, b) contends that knowledge is temporal, that is, fallible, to be preserved until a better argument comes along through undistorted communication and forces the community to take a different view.

Is there not a tension between justification based on practical consequences and justification via abductive inference to the best explanation? The answer is yes if competitions between rival knowledge claims are for theory's sake, about truth that 'works' in theory but not in practice, about differences that don't make a difference (Wicks & Freeman, 1998). The answer is no, however, if competitions are pragmatically governed, located in concrete situations, focused on the emergent present, around specific problems that face researchers, managers and decision-makers, producing challenging inputs to ongoing dialogues and actions (Flyvbjerg, 2001, ch. 7).

Reading Habermas in this light, it is with the 'forces' of practical consequences that better arguments utilise their 'teeth' to pursue a community to take a different view. Thus, practical consequences and better arguments do not necessarily antagonise each other. In pragmatically oriented research and practice they invite each other and work hand-in-hand, push falliable knowledge forward along human inquiry (Putnam, 1996).

Justification as social practice

Human inquiry, including science, is conditioned by culture, history and tradition (Kuhn (1922–1996), 1962). To know something, one must have a belief and that belief must be justified, which in turn means that one can say something, by presenting, proposing, responding, explaining, defending, and so forth, on behalf of that belief, that will pass muster among members of a community (Gutting, 2003, p. 44). And communities by definition have distinctive cultures, histories, traditions and norms. Hence, justification is always 'a matter of social practice' (Rorty, 1980, p. 186), involving ethics and value (Habermas, 1984a, b), politics and power (Foucault, 1979).

According to Rorty (1931–2007), cultures and communities are not dead things to discover, accept or pass on, but contingent matters to make and remake by participants:

> Our identification with our community – our society, our political tradition, our intellectual heritage – is heightened when we see this community as *ours*, rather than *nature's*, *shaped* rather than *found*, one among many men have made. (Rorty, 1982, p. 166; *emphasis* original)

In other words, men, also women, could always have made cultures and communities alternatively. In doing sciences, both natural and social, there is no 'God's-eye view' telling us what to do. That is, values, like truth, are not foundational or atemporal but contingent and situational – it is always *our* choice, *our* doing, *our* making, at least partly. In the face of ever present multiplicities and possibilities, it is our ethical judgement and political act that make the difference. Hegel's (1770– 1831) 'history' logic is a dead one. It is we living people as inquirers and citizens who continuously re-interpret, re-negotiate, re-make our lifeworlds which we share and belong to, and we do this based on what Flyvbjerg (2001, p. 130) calls Aristotelian 'situational ethics'.

What follows is that we cannot escape the responsibility to make ethical judgements and take political stands. Science may not be political, scientists are. Bruno's (1548–1600) belief is not meant to be political, his body and the fire burned him dead certainly were. Monkeys and mice in the laboratory are innocent, scientists who do the experiments upon them are not. Owing to 'self-fulfilling' effects, this is more so to social sciences and social scientists (Ghoshal (1948–2004), 2005). The 'historical necessity' Hegel is dead, long live the 'open-ended process' Hegel: once upon a time a strict communist regime, China has today been made by its people into perhaps the most capitalistic 'community' on earth. They had Confucius (551–478 BC), Mao Zedong (1893–1976) and Deng Xiaoping (1902–1997), they apparently made their choice; and the practical consequences so far appear to justify their choice (Zhu, 2007).

Given, on the one hand, that there is no historical necessity or foundational principles and, on the other, that different groups typically have different interests, how do we, then, make choices? We make choices, according to Foucault (1926–1984), by exercising power and involving in conflicts and struggles. To Foucault, power, as well as conflicts and struggles, is not something one can choose to be for or against, pick up or throw away, obtain or share, but a process, in various forms of domination and resistance, that we cannot live without, we cannot do science without, we cannot know without. Knowledge and power directly imply one another.

> Perhaps, too, we should abandon a whole tradition that allows us to imagine that knowledge can exist only where the power relations are suspended and that knowledge can develop only outside its injunctions, its demands and its interest. (Foucault, 1979, p. 27)

This is so because power, as understood by Foucault, can be constructively useful:

> We must cease once and for all to describe the effects of power in negative terms: it 'excludes', it 'represses', it 'censors', it 'abstracts', it 'masks', it 'conceals'. ... [Rather,] power produces, it produces reality; it produces domains of objects and rituals of truth. (Foucault, 1979, p. 194)

If we see knowledge as situational, if we consider history as open-ended, if we accept that we could always have made choice alternatively, then it is reasonable, indeed quite insightful, that Foucault drew our attention to how power actually works, how conflicts actually operate, how struggles actually proceed, how certain knowledge and methods actually get legitimised while others marginalised, why certain practices and arrangements are promoted while others rejected, in specific, particular, concrete situations. If this makes sense, then it is necessary, in every human life project, to ask such questions as: who gains, and who loses? Through what kinds of power relations? What possibilities are available to change existing power relations? (Flyvbjerg, 2001, ch. 7).

It is hubris to dismiss that Foucault's concern is irrelevant to science, or relevant merely to social, not natural, sciences. Let's have a look at perhaps the most 'scientific' field of inquiry.

In a 2007 book *The Trouble with Physics*, Lee Simon, himself a career physicist, analyses how the discipline has, since the late 1970s, experienced 'the strangest and most frustrating period in the history of physics since Kepler (1571–1630) and Galileo (1564–1642) began the practice of our craft 400 years ago'. The reason for this, Simon presents, is that a particular theory, 'string theory', had been regarded as the only way forward. One prominent string theorist is reported claiming that 'there are no alternatives'. This happened despite, if Simon is correct, the theory can never be proved or disproved to be true. Nevertheless, working on string theory has now become the ticket to a professorship. In the US, 'theorists who pursue approaches to fundamental physics other than string theory have almost no career opportunities'. 'In the past 15 years', while more than a thousand scientists working in the best conditions on string theory, 'there have been a total of three assistant professors appointed to US research universities who work on approaches to quantum gravity other than string theory, and these appointments were all to a single research group'. Simon voices his 'resistance':

> This hurts science, because it chokes off the investigation of alternative directions, some of them very promising. ... I am extremely concerned about a trend in which only one direction of research is well supported while other promising approaches are starved. (Simon, 2007; cf.: FT Magazine, 2007, p. 21)

Is it not time to bring Foucault in? Perhaps the whole mankind is the loser: an at-least-30-years opportunity cost. And, if Foucault's questions are useful for physics, why not other sciences?

A walking stick for beating an unknown path

Every action takes place in a situation, or more precisely a 'problematic situation' (Dewey, 1938). Action that is appropriate to a situation is, as we posited in foregoing sections, conditioned by available resources, but – and this is the other side of the coin – not reduced to these resources. Action, particularly innovative and strategic action, requires that we explore unconventional paths, and that kind of paths are almost always characterised by ambiguity, instability, fragility, uncertainty, unpredictability and risk. This is what the pragmatist thinker, Joas (1996), who follows Dewey, would like to share with us; he calls his thesis 'situated creativity'.

The Spanish poet Machado (1875–1939) puts it beautifully: 'Life is a path that you beat while you walk it'. Only on looking back can you see the path that you have beaten; ahead there is only uncharted terrain. Every step forward is a step into uncertainty (de Geus, 1996, p. 81). As to knowledge and ethics, the Taoist Zhuangzi (ca. 369–286 BC) had this to say:

> *Tao* is made in the walking of it. (*Zhuangzi*, 4/22/33; tr. Ames & Rosemont, 1998, p. 29)

For beating unknown paths, can roadmaps help? It depends. For Dewey (1859–1952), a map cannot be made *a priori*, but only after one has traversed much of the territory, and it is never finished (cf.: Myers, 2004, p. 49). To some, misleadingly, roadmaps are simply another, fashionable name for rule-based procedures. These latter kind of popular roadmaps are dead things, an atemporal metaphor, gearing us toward predictions by those who believe they hold 'God's-eye view'. Based on such roadmaps, 'knowing' is easily deteriorated into ritualistic acts in which 'knowledge', rather than being a source of inspiration or novelty, is merely a medium through which what is already 'known' gets reproduced (Rorty, cf.: Baert, 2005, p. 138). A roadmap matches well with Hegel (1770–1831) and Marx's (1818–1883) attempts at 'world history', perhaps supplies us with some psychological comfort, but no sense of George Herbert Mead's (1863–1931) (1938) 'emergent present' and 'incurable contingency of the future'. Roadmaps are useful for the routine, not the novel, helpful for Dreyfus & Dreyfus's (1986) 'novice' and 'beginners', not 'proficient performers' or 'experts'.

Knowledge is, to the pragmatists, better conceived as walking sticks (Ghoshal, 2005, p. 81). A walking stick prompts action, generates hope, guiding us toward unknown paths. It implies no certainty, nor comfort, only distance from our present to the unknown future. With a rule-based roadmap, there is an implication of a pre-defined destination or a pre-set goal. With a walking stick, there is none. The future is not closed, but made by people, depending on how we actually beat our paths (Sztompka, 1991). And achievable goals cannot be pre-set, either externally fixed or self-imposed. Goals emerge, get revised, realised or abandoned as our capacity to set goals increases during action (Dewey, cf.: Joas, 1996, pp. 153–164). A walking stick always reminds inquirers that our presuppositions and expectations are merely a temporary starting-point; they can be typically affected by the unknown path that we embark upon. Without fixing a destination, knowledge as walking sticks allows people to explore alternatives and experience what is not present, enlarges human's potentialities (Dewey, 1930).

Here, we are not talking about uncertainty of the studied objects, but of the inquiry process, that is, the creating of knowledge, the practice of sciences, the conducting of projects. The unpredictability of studied objects, for example, 'double hermeneutic', differentiates the natural and the social, as we discussed in the last section. The point of uncertainty and unpredictability in the inquiry process which we stress right now, on the other hand, underscores a commonality: there can be no atemporal, universal, general procedure, formula or algorithm for the production of knowledge, knowledge of both the natural and the social.

Einstein (1879–1955) is reported to have commented upon the laws of physics he had constructed thus:

> ... to these elementary laws there leads no logical path, but only intuition, supported by being sympathetically in touch with experience. (cf. Flyvbjerg, 2001, p. 75)

If metaphors matter, which metaphor captures Einstein's spirit better, a roadmap or a walking stick? And, if there is no logical path for finding logic in physics, why should we dream one for other sciences?

Commonalities summarised

Knowledge of the natural and the social are in common in that all are construed out of available resources, conditioned by history, justified socially upon the consequences of acting upon them, settled until better, competitive alternatives emerge and serving as walking sticks that help humankind beating unknown paths in their lives and projects.

IMPLICATIONS

If the above discussion about differences and commonalities makes sense, then the following implications can be drawn.

Knowledge: beyond hierarchy and unity

It is ill-conceived a hierarchy between natural and social sciences, between 'science' and 'non-science'. Seen from a pragmatist perspective, they are different forms of knowledge that we create for coping with life problems. Furthermore, knowledge, that is, our capacity to act in specific situations, is not cognitive matter alone. Science and politics and aesthetics interweave with each other (Law, 2004, p. 156). There is no ground to rank knowledge: which is more true, essential or valuable in our life projects – Newton's (1642–1727) theory (logic), Confucius's (551–479 BC) teaching (ethics), or Picasso's (1881–1973) painting (beauty)?

It is misleading to compare natural and social sciences in terms of a particular set of qualities and to set such qualities as the general ideal for all knowledge, qualities such as being explicit, universal, repeatable and predictive. Such comparison and quality-setting are attempts, perhaps not intentionally, to reduce human life into one-dimensional fantasy. Given the differences we discussed above, it is self-defeating to pretend that knowledge of the social can be as 'scientific' as the natural (Hayek, 1989), it is pointless to approximate all knowledge to 'science' (Flyvbjerg, 2001), it is hopeless to search for an integration of natural and social sciences (Baert, 2005). Indeed, if there is no single methodology (Rorty, 1982) or mode of explanation (Elster, 1983) even among studies of the natural, for example, between physics and biology, how can there be a unified methodology across studies of the natural and the social?

Different knowledge have their respective strengths and weakness, they serve different purposes. While natural sciences, together with technology and engineering, are good at helping us sending men and women to the moon, running more cars on the road, curing diseases and killing each other more efficiently, they are weak in answering Tolstoy's (1828–1910) question, indeed humankind's most basic and important question: 'What shall we do and how shall we live?' (Wicks & Freeman, 1998, p. 127). This becomes all the clearer when we experienced the frustration and tears at the Kyoto, Bali and Copenhagen summits (*Economist*, 2007, p. 10; *The Sunday Times*, 2009). The problem goes deeper: by focusing on prediction, control, efficiency and rule-based rationality, by regarding natural sciences, or 'science', as the ultimate ideal for knowledge, we distract ourselves from Tolstoy's question, reduce ourselves to dogs and computers.

Where natural sciences are weak, social sciences are strong (Flyvbjerg, 2001). Knowledge of the social is good for raising value-rational questions (Weber (1864–1920), 1947), focusing attention on power and politics (Foucault (1926–1984), 1979), bringing ethics and purpose back (MacIntyre, 1981), making dialogues part of public sphere (Habermas (1929–2007), 1984a, b), dialogues about problems and risks we face and how things may be done differently (Dewey (1859–1952), 1930).

This has direct and immediate implications for our day-in-day-out practice, including KM projects. Time and again, we witness organisation initiatives, such as 'knowledge creation' and 'social innovation', being translated into agent-simulation and web-building exercises. These techniques and expertise become regarded not as supporting tools but guiding principles; IT support has become KM itself (for this point see, e.g., Müller-Merbach, 2008, p. 355). Ethics, interest, value, purpose, power and on-the-spot learning, which uniquely make us human, are either fitted-in as add-on features, bent into programming rules, or excluded because they are difficult to model. In doing so, to put it in Boulding's metaphor, we shut the 'door' on 'human life and society in all its complexity and richness' (Boulding, 1956, p. 205). Shutting the 'door', our partial strengths become the source of our undoing, our technical competence become the problem instead of solution, 'we have made a mess of things' (Hayek, 1989, p. 3) – just look at the mad-cow disease and the toxic financial products.

While the notion of hierarchy of knowledge is misleading and harmful, the notion of hierarchy of complexity is challenging and helpful. To overcome reductionism and 'scientistic attitude' (Hayek, 1989, p. 3), it is useful to hold the notion of hierarchy of complexity in a way that we enter each, yes each, project through Boulding's 'door', to appreciate the complexity and richness that are distinctively social and human, to engage Tolstoy's question, and then move to see what other level complexities may involve, what supporting roles rule-based rationality and associated techniques can play. Furthermore, the 'door' should be opened not just for a particular group of experts, it should be made wide enough to allow all students of Confucius, Newton and Picasso to join in.

Method: beyond ontological vs instrumental fallacies

This brings us to the issue of method choice. Rorty (1931–2007) took great pains to reject 'ontological fallacy' – the erroneous assumption that methodological questions can be reduced to matters of ontology, that references to ontological differences, for example, 'natural' or 'social', would be sufficient to settle methodological disputes.

As an alternative, Rorty stressed purposes. According to Rorty (1982, pp. 196–197), it is practical aims (cum Dewey), not the nature of things or phenomena (cum Popper), that make the difference: if we want to predict and control (cum Habermas), 'naturalist' approaches (cum Newton) will do; if we want to treat humans as moral beings (cum Confucius) and tackle issues of power (cum Foucault), then surely 'anti-naturalist' (*sic*) approaches are called for. Rorty (1980, pp. 315–322) also stressed timing (cum Kuhn): 'puzzle-solving' within a 'normal science' requires 'epistemology' whereas in periods of 'revolutionary change' 'hermeneutics' prevails.

While Rorty is right, in my view, that there is no one-to-one relationship between a method and a domain of inquiry, that differences between the natural and the social alone can never be sufficient to ground questions of methodology, he appeared to be committing 'instrumental fallacy' – the equally erroneous assumption that the choice of a methodological path can be reduced to a matter of merely cognitive aims (for this point see Flyvbjerg, 2001, p. 29; Baert, 2005, p. 141). Cognitive interests and practical aims, although critically important, will not make the differences disappear between the natural and the social, the knowledge about them, and the methods we cope with them. And this is Rorty's blind spot: to Rorty, there is no difference between the way we argue about morals and politics and the way we argue about 'there are twelve chairs in this room' (Williams, 2003, p. 78).

This is why, I shall appreciate, when differentiating human cognitive interests as well as validity claims, Habermas (2003) wisely backed them up with distinctions between 'three worlds': the realms of external nature, of internal nature, and of society. The distinctiveness of the 'social world' makes it necessary to pursue cognitive aims other than those we attach to the 'natural world', for example, critique of society, self- and mutual-understanding. When we reduce cognitive aims and investigation methods into the empirical-analytical kind alone, we become part of the problem. Habermas is wise because he kept open Boulding's 'door', he differentiated humans from dogs and computers, and he thus was able to maintain heterogeneous knowledge and methods.

In contrast to Habermas, Rorty appeared to have failed to appreciate the significance of a paradoxical balance between 'the domain of study' and 'practical aims'. Rorty, while rightly questioning the privilege of 'science' as the master narrative, had 'tended to treat technoscience as a type of literature, thus more or less inverting the old positivist-scientific model that attempted to establish a hegemony for science' (Hickman, 2004, p. 498). Rorty merely turned the totalising game upside-down; Rorty's is still a project Rouse (1996) calls 'wholesale legitimation'.

To move beyond what Rorty rightly rejected as well as what he wrongly committed, it is imperative to uphold a balanced understanding that method choice is not simply a matter of aims, nor of 'the nature of things'. On the one hand, questions of methods always entail questions of aims and, as such, the methods used depend at least in part on what our projects want to achieve. On the other hand, while methodology choice is in so far dependent on our aims, it remains a *bounded* one, bounded by the differences between the phenomena we are investigating, by what they allow us to accomplish (Baert, 2005, ch. 7). This is so if hierarchy of complexity, modes of explanation, human intentionality, deliberate organising, double hermeneutic and context-dependence in and of the social, which we discussed in previous sections, ever make sense.

For bringing the issue closer to practice, Aristotle's (ca. 384–322 BC) differentiation between *episteme*, *techne* and *phronesis* is useful (see Tsoukas & Cummings, 1997; Flyvbjerg, 2001). Taking a risk of being simplistic, we can relate *episteme* with the modern scientific ideal as expressed in natural sciences, interpret *techne* as instrumental rationality that focuses on having jobs done via artfully applying *episteme* knowledge, and appreciate *phronesis* as situational ethics that ensures *techne* utilisation of *episteme* knowledge is governed by value-rationality. The significance of *phronesis*, in the context of this paper, is that it reminds us the relevance of morally practical purpose, connects such purpose with value and interest, and brings issues of ethics and power back into the debate and application of methods.

To be ethically, not merely instrumentally, wise, we need to engage in each specific project, including KM ones, the following practical questions: which methods, techniques and tools, what they are good for, in what way(s) they serve our purposes, what purposes, how our purposes are decided, what knowledge we are to manage, manage for whose interest, who to involve in the decisions and why, can there be alternative purposes and methods, how to envisage, create and make alternatives a reality? Avoiding these questions does not make them unimportant, it is a sign that we have already accepted answers that are problematic and potentially dangerous. Just to take one example: suppose you are a life-insurance company executive, how are you to utilise our knowledge of people's – your customers' – genes, what method(s) are appropriate for this? (Zhu, 2008, pp. 117–118).

Conversation: beyond division and integration

In the previous sections, we talked about fair, sustained and rigours competition, about 'inference to the best explanation', about 'the force of better arguments'. This, I admit, assumes that conversation between knowledge claims, interpretations, paradigms – take the word you like – is possible. But is this not another dead dream, idealist but naïïve in this politically murky world?

Fifty years ago, Boulding (1910–1993) expressed his worry about 'the spread of specialised deafness':

> Science, that is to say, is what can be talked about profitably by scientists in their role as scientists. The crisis of science today arises because of the increasing difficulty of such profitable talk among scientists as a whole. Specialisation has outrun Trade, communication between the disciples becomes increasingly difficult, and the Republic of Learning is breaking up into isolated subcultures with only tenuous lines of communication between them – a situation which threatens intellectual civil war. (Boulding, 1956, p. 198)

Today, Boulding's worry becomes reality. 'Paradigm incommensurability' is institutionalised as an unquestionable truth, and specialised deafness is not considered an illness but praised as a prudent strategy (e.g., Burrell & Morgan, 1979). Insofar as conversation is concerned, the present appears gloomy.

But, if we truly believe that 'history' is made not given, if we take that the future is open not fixed, if we keep in heart that it is our imagination, choice and action that make the difference, then we have reason to be hopeful. The reason for being hopeful is that differences and diversity do not necessarily lead to professional isolation or closure, that paradigms might be incommensurable at one level, but not necessarily so at others.

When we talk about (in)commensurability and 'levels', I do not indicate an 'ahistorical metavocabulary in terms of which to formulate algorithms for theory choice' (Rorty, 1991, p. 48), nor a 'neutral guideline' to adopt 'prior to an open conversation between peers' (Baert, 2005, p. 168). I mean something else, which I explain below.

There can be disagreements about conceptual schemes (e.g., paradigms), suggests Davidson (1984), only if there is a wider background of agreement in terms of which those disagreements can be specified (cf.: Guignon & Hiley, 2003, p. 19). That is, certain commensurability is the pre-requisite for talking about incommensurability. Indeed, without accepting their two dimensions as the wider, if not higher, conceptual background, we can hardly make sense of Burrell & Morgan's (1979) supposed incommensurability between diverse social theories and organisational analysis. When I began my study in Britain 20 years ago, I had immense difficulty in appreciating Burrell and Morgan's incommensurability thesis because, I recognise now, the polarising scheme of subjectivity-vs-objectivity and radical-change-vs-stable-order was so alien, indeed so incommensurable, to me as an outsider at that time; and students from China and Japan keep telling me today that this remains true to them. It is, at the same time, worth noting that, because of exposures to Western ideologies in their early life and education, students from ex-colonies of the West are more ready to follow, reject or engage with Burrell and Morgan's thesis.

In other words, only when we have established some sort of shared vocabulary, can we think and talk about differences. Difference is a relational concept, so is diversity; without comparison based on some sort of agreed yardstick, we are not able to specify differences, nor to appreciate diversity. To put it another way, incommensurability at one level without commensurability at other levels is illogical, contrary to empirical experiences, is merely an article of faith, manufactured and defended for hidden purposes. 'Incommensurability' and the associated dimensions, boxes, schemes and paradigms are all part of a particular language game, no more and no less.

If Foucault is correct, and I think he is, that truth and power imply each other, then it is not so difficult to understand that the 'truth' of paradigm incommensurability, as well as the impossibility of conversation, is itself a product of power, struggle and conflict, vested with sectional interests. Incommensurability is not exceptional: it is a historical thing, it is our making. Once upon a time, the thesis of incommensurability (cum Kuhn) was a useful tool for challenging a specific domination, it now becomes the excuse for professional deafness; it is now hurting sciences and humanity (cum Boulding).

The decision over conversation is hence less an intellectual but more a moral and political one. We do not engage in conversations because we do not want to and we pretend we are not able to, for this we make total incommensurability a reality. Fuller (2002) arrives at a similar conclusion: 'paradigmatic differences' are less metaphysical 'but themselves artefacts of an institutionalised communication breakdown between kindred intellectual factions, which in principle can be either maximised or minimised' (pp. 51–52).

If we could maximise it, we can minimise it; if we made it, we can unmake it. We can be hopeful that, if we are willing to, we can appreciate differences and diversity while at the same time promote practically relevant conversation. In the end, division of labour is beneficial only when exchange happens (Boulding, 1956). Exchange, of course, demands specific investments and induces costs; for example, it requires new attitudes and skills, which take time and resources to nurture. But this is a price worth paying because disengagement is not an option: everybody will be worse-off in an all-specialisation-no-exchange system (Mahoney, 1993).

Reaching out for exchange is everyone's business, not just for 'naïve positivists' but also 'sophisticated anti-positivists'. As we saw from Rorty earlier, it would be equally disastrous to turn the positivistic hierarchy of knowledge upside-down by electing the privilege of interpretivism or whatever. If the following here-and-now observation is accurate, it deserves our reflection:

> It is more common for positivists to explore alternative paradigms than for interpretivist/critical researchers to go 'back to basic' and study positivism. (Kelemen & Hassard, 2003, p. 77)

Hierarchy of knowledge is unjustified, bad for inquiry and dangerous to practice – period, full stop.

Participating in conversation, style matters (Bernstein, 1991). There are 'adversarial' or 'confrontational' styles where in

> Assertions of the opposite school are targeted and criticised with the aim of demolishing them. The views of members of opposing academic tribes are shown to be false, incoherent or insignificant. Those engaged in this form of debate do not attempt to learn from other view points, nor do they use the opportunity of academic exchange to reflect upon and question some of their own presuppositions. Foundationalists build and defend intellectual fortresses while destroying rival constructions. (Baert, 2005, p. 154)

But there are alternatives, for example 'dialogical encounter' in which participants

> trust rather to the multitude and variety of its arguments than to the conclusiveness of any one. Its reasoning should not form a chain which is no stronger than its weakest link, but a cable whose fibres may be ever so slender, provided they are sufficiently numerous and intimately connected. (Peirce, 1868, 5.265, p. 157).

> People do not wish to score points by exploiting the weakness of others; they try to listen to them by understanding them in the strongest way. They strengthen their arguments so as to make them most credible and to learn from them. ... The ultimate aim is not to defend or refine a particular system but to use academic conversation to enhance our imaginative faculties (Baert, 2005, p. 154).

Whether academics have the will for conversation, whatever styles they adopt, whether they act as links of a chain or fibres of a cable, practitioners have to, as they usually do, encounter various knowledge honestly. This is because, while academics can hide behind separated disciplines and insulated paradigms, practitioners cannot. If they do, they will be punished by day-in-day-out complexity. 'Nature is not organised the way our knowledge of it is' (Ackoff, 1973, p. 667). Problems in the real world, unlike those in philosophers' study, are never separated along discipline or paradigm lines, never divided out-there awaiting us to 'integrate' them. They are inherently interrelated and reciprocal, or so pragmatists would posit (Zhu, 2008, pp. 118–121). As Latour suggests,

> The ozone hole is too social and too narrated to be truly natural; the strategy of industrial firms and heads of state is too full of chemical reactions to be reduced to power and interest; the discourse of the ecosphere is too real and too social to boil down to meaning effects. *Is it our fault if the networks are simultaneously real, like nature, narrated, like discourse, and collective, like society?* (Latour, 1993, p. 6; *emphasis* original)

What is true to Latour's ozone hole is also true to our life projects. At this 'level', that is, in specific practical situations, pragmatist sensibility is indispensable, commensurability between the incommensurables prevails and dialogical encounters, not specialised deafness or confrontational assertions, are the best way forward.

KM is not immune from the division-integration controversy. It is suggested in *Harvard Business Review* (Hansen *et al.*, 1999) that managers must choose either a computer-based 'codification strategy' or a people- network-based 'personalisation strategy' – 'pursuing both at the same time can quickly undermine your business'. In a contrasting spirit, in this journal Zhu (2008) interprets the HP 'Eureka project' as the success of a KM strategy that connects technology, trust and power. Either-or choice on the one hand and situated encounters on the other, thoughtful managers can find much food-for-thought from the two cases, from the division- integration debate.

CONCLUSION

There are irreducible differences and significant commonalities across knowledge of the natural and the social, an appreciation of which exposes the illusiveness of hierarchy of knowledge, the impossibility of theory-oriented knowledge integration and the necessity of practice-governed dialogical encounters. Knowledge serve humankind best when we understand their respective strengths and weaknesses, when we take them as useful tools for coping with specific problems, when our judgement and action are guided by situational ethics. For this to happen, we need to bring value and purpose back in, we need to engage in power and politics, we need to enlarge our resource pool: technological, intellectual, social, emotional, political. For KM projects in particular, we need to handle information, opinion and knowledge properly (Müller-Merbach, 2008), we need to manage knowledge, knowing and knower with appropriate strategies (Zhu, 2008). Given the interpenetration and reciprocality in and of KM problems, we need to invite Confucius, Newton and Picasso into our projects, invite them as equals. We humans are more than dogs and computers; our value, intentionality, skill, political will for making-do and association with other actors, that is, our capacity to act in specific situations, matter. (In)commensurability and conversation are of our making, the future is wide open, the path is under our feet, and the choice is in our hands. All this is, from a pragmatist point of view, as true to KM as to other human life projects.

REFERENCES

Ackoff R (1973) Science in the systems age: beyond IE, OR, and MS. *Operations Research* **21(3)**, 661–671.

Ames RT and Rosemont H (1998) *The Analects of Confucius: A Philosophical Translation*. Ballantine Books, New York.

Baert P (2005) *Philosophy of the Social Sciences: Towards Pragmatism*. Polity Press, Cambridge.

Bell W and Mau JA (1970) Images of the future: theory and research strategies. In *Theoretical Sociology* (Mckinney JC and Tiryakian EA, Eds), pp 205–234, Appleton Century Croft, New York.

Bernstein RJ (1985) *Beyond Objectivism and Subjectivism: Science, Hermeneutics, and Praxis*. University of Pennsylvania Press, Philadelphia, PA.

Bernstein RJ (1991) *The New Constellation: The Ethical-political Horizons of Modernity/Postmodernity*. Polity Press, Cambridge.

Boulding K (1956) General systems theory – the skeleton of science. *Management Science* **2(3)**, 197–208.

Brown JS and Duguid P (2001) Structure and spontaneity: knowledge and organisation. In *Managing Industrial Knowledge* (Nonaka I and Teece D, Eds), pp 44–67, Sage, London.

Burrell G and Morgan G (1979) *Sociological Paradigms and Organisational Analysis*. Heinemann, London.

Callon M and Latour B (1992) Don't throw the baby out with the bath school. In *Science as Practice and Culture* (Pickering A, Ed), pp 343–368, University of Chicago Press, Chicago.

Cartwright N (1999) *The Dappled World: A Study of the Boundaries of Science*. Cambridge University Press, Cambridge.

Czarniawska B (2003) Social constructionism and organisation studies. In *Debating Organisation* (Westwood R and Clegg S, Eds), pp 128–139, Blackwell, Oxford.

Davidson D (1980) *Essays on Actions and Event*. Oxford University Press, New York.

Davidson D (1984) *Inquiries into Truth and Interpretation*. Oxford University Press, New York.

De Geus A (1996) Strategy and learning. *Reflections* **1(1)**, 75–81.

Dewey J (1930) *The Quest for Certainty: A Study of the Relationship between Knowledge and Action*. Allen & Unwin, London.

Dewey J (1938) *Logic: The Theory of Inquiry*. Holt, Rinehart & Winston, New York.

Dreyfus H and Dreyfus S (1986) *Mind over Machine: The Power of Human Intuition and Expertise in the era of the Computer*. Free Press, New York.

Eco U (1995) The Search for the Perfect Language. Blackwell, Oxford.

Economist (2007) The bank that failed. 22 September, p. 15.

Elster J (1983) *Explaining Technical Change*. Cambridge University Press, Cambridge.

Financial Times (2007) Questions and answers on a sadly predictable debt crisis. 5 September.

Flyvbjerg B (2001) *Making Social Science Matter: Why Social Inquiry Fails and How It can Succeed Again*. Cambridge University Press, Cambridge.

Fortune (2007) Wall Street's money machine breaks down, 26 November, p. 40.

Foucault M (1979) *Discipline and Punish*. Vintage Books, New York.

FT Magazine (2007) The trouble with physics, 17/18 February, p. 21.

Fuller S (2002) *Knowledge Management Foundations*. Butterworth-Heinemann, Boston, MA.

Gadamer H-G (1975) *Truth and Method*. Sheed & Ward, London.

Gergen KJ (1973) Social psychology as history. *Journal of Personality and Social Psychology* **26(2)**, 309–320.

Ghoshal S (2005) Bad management theories are destroying good management practices. *Academy of Management Learning & Education* **4(1)**, 75–91.

Giddens A (1982) *Profiles and Critiques in Social Theory*. University of California Press, Berkeley, CA.

Guignon C and Hiley DR (2003) Introduction: Richard Rorty and contemporary philosophy. In *Richard Rorty* (Guignon C and Hiley DR, Eds), pp 1–40, Cambridge University Press, Cambridge.

Gutting G (2003) Rorty's critique of epistemology. In *Richard Rorty* (Guignon C and Hiley DR, Eds), pp 41–60, Cambridge University Press, Cambridge.

Habermas J (1972) *Knowledge and Human Interests*. Polity Press, Cambridge.

Habermas J (1984a) *The Theory of Communicative Action*, vol. I. Beacon Press, Boston, MA.

Habermas J (1984b) *The Theory of Communicative Action*, vol. II. Beacon Press, Boston, MA.

Habermas J (2003) *Truth and Justification*. MIT Press, Cambridge, MA.

Hacking I (1999) *The Social Construction of What?* Harvard University Press, Cambridge, MA.

Hansen MT, Nohria N and Tierney T (1999) What's your strategy for managing knowledge? *Harvard Business Review* **77(2),** 106–116.

Hayek FA (1989) The pretence of knowledge. *American Economic Review* **79(6),** 3–7.

Hickman LA (2004) On Hugh T. Miller on 'Why old pragmatism needs an upgrade'. *Administration & Society* **36(4),** 496–499.

James W (1907) *Pragmatism: A New Name for Some Old Ways of Thinking*. Longmans, New York.

Joas H (1996) *The Creativity of Action*. University of Chicago Press, Chicago, IL.

Kelemen M and Hassard J (2003) Paradigm plurality: exploring past, present, and future trends. In *Debating Organisation* (Westwood R and Clegg S, Eds), pp 73–82, Blackwell, Oxford.

Kuhn T (1962) *The Structure of Scientific Revolutions*. University of Chicago Press, Chicago, IL.

Kukla A (2000) *Social Constructivism and the Philosophy of Science*. Routledge, London.

Latour B (1993) *We Have Never been Modern*. Harvard University Press, Cambridge, MA.

Latour B (2005) *Reassembling the Social: An Introduction to Actor-network-theory*. Oxford University Press, Oxford.

Law J (2004) *After Method: Mess in Social Science Research*. Routledge, London.

Lichtman R (1967) Indeterminacy in the social science. *Inquiry* **10(1–4),** 139–150.

Macintyre A (1981) *After Virtue: A Study in Moral Theory*. Duckworth, London.

Mahoney JT (1993) Strategic management and determinism: sustaining the conversation. *Journal of Management Studies* **30(1),** 173–191.

Mead GH (1938) *Philosophy of the Act*. University of Chicago Press, Chicago, IL.

Merton RK (1982) *Social Research and the Practicing Professions*. Abt Books, Cambridge, MA.

Mingers J (2008) Management knowledge and knowledge management: realism and forms of truth. *Knowledge Management Research and Practice* **6(1),** 62–76.

Mintzberg H (2001) Thoughts on schools. In *Rethinking Strategy* (VOLBERDA HW and ELFRING T, Eds), pp 41–42, Sage, London.

Mounce HO (1997) *The Two Pragmatisms*. Routledge, London.

Müller-Merbach H (2007) Mutual interdependence between theory and practice: Kant's lesson. *Knowledge Management Research and Practice* **5 (4),** 313–314.

Müller-Merbach H (2008) Knowledge management: a program for education and leadership. *Knowledge Management Research and Practice* **6(4),** 350–356.

Myers WT (2004) Pragmatist metaphysics: a defence. *Transactions of the Charles S. Peirce Society* **XL(1),** 39–52.

Nonaka I, Toyama R and Hirata T (2008) *Managing Flow: A Process Theory of the Knowledge-based Firm*. Palgrave Macmillan, Basingstoke, UK.

O'Hear A (1989) *An Introduction to the Philosophy of Science*. Oxford University Press, Oxford.

Ormerod RJ (2006) The history and ideas of pragmatism. *Journal of the Operational Research Society* **57(8),** 892–909.

Orwell G (1989) *Animal Farm: A Fairy Story*. Penguin, London.

Peirce CS (1868) In *Collected Papers of Charles Sanders Peirce* (Hartshorne C and Weiss P, Eds) (1931–1935), Harvard University Press, Cambridge, MA.

Popper KR (1964) *The Poverty of Historicism*. Harper & Row, New York.

Popper KR (1976) *Unended Quest: An Intellectual Autobiography*. William Collins Sons, Glasgow.

Powell TC (2001) Competitive advantage: logical and philosophical consideration. *Strategic Management Journal* **22(9),** 875–888.

Putnam H (1996) *Pragmatism: An Open Question*. Blackwell, Oxford.

Quine WVO (1953) *From a Logical Point of View*. Harvard University Press, Cambridge, MA.

Rescher N (2005) Pragmatism at the crossroads. *Transactions of the Charles S. Peirce Society* **XLI(2),** 355–365.

Rorty R (1980) *Philosophy and the Mirror of Nature*. Blackwell, Oxford.

Rorty R (1982) *Consequences of Pragmatism*. University of Minnesota Press, New York.

Rorty R (1985) Texts and lumps. *New Literary History* **17(1),** 1–15.

Rorty R (1991) *Objectivity, Relativism and Truth*. Cambridge University Press, Cambridge.

Rouse J (1996) *Engaging Science: How to Understand its Practices Philosophically*. Cornell University Press, Ithaca, NY.

Schutz A (1964) *Collected Papers I: The Problem of Social Reality*. Nijhoff, Hague.

Sellars W (1963) *Science, Perception and Reality*. Routledge, London.

Simon L (2007) *The Trouble of Physics*. Penguin, London.

Sklar L (1995) Philosophy of science. In *The Cambridge Dictionary of Philosophy* (AUDI R, Ed), pp 611–615, Cambridge University Press, Cambridge.

Stacey RD (2007) *Strategic Management and Organisational Dynamics: The Challenge of Complexity*. FT Prentice-Hall, London.

Sztompka P (1991) *Society in Action: The Theory of Social Becoming*. Polity Press, Cambridge.

THE SUNDAY TIMES (2009) Hot air in our time, 20 December.

Tsoukas H and Cummings S (1997) Marginalization and recovery: the emergence of Aristotelian themes in organization studies. *Organisation Studies* **18(4),** 655–683.

Von Foerster H (2002) *Understanding Systems: Conversations on Epistemology and Ethics*. Kluwer Academic/Plenum Publishers, New York.

Weber M (1947) *The Theory of Social and Economic Organisation*. Free Press, New York.

Wicks AC and Freeman RE (1998) Organisation studies and the new pragmatism: positivism, anti-positivism, and the search for ethics. *Organisation Science* **9(2),** 123–140.

Williams M (2003) Rorty on knowledge and truth. In *Richard Rorty* (Guignon C and Hiley DR, Eds), pp 61–80, Cambridge University Press, Cambridge.

Wittgenstein L (1922) *Tractatus Logico-Philosophicus*. Routedge and Kegan Paul, London.

Wittgenstein L (1977) *Culture and Value*. University of Chicago Press, Chicago, IL.

Zhu Z (2007) Reform without a theory: why does it work in China? *Organisation Studies* **28(10),** 1503–1522.

Zhu Z (2008) Knowledge, knowing, knower: what is to be managed and does it matter? *Knowledge Management Research and Practice* **6(2),** 112–123.

COMMUNITIES OF PRACTICE: FACILITATING SOCIAL LEARNING WHILE FRUSTRATING ORGANIZATIONAL LEARNING

INTRODUCING ORGANIZATIONAL LEARNING AND COMMUNITIES OF PRACTICE

Despite its almost fifty years of existence, the literature on organizational learning is still growing. Over the years, the topic has been approached from various angles. Some scholars have been mostly interested in learning processes as adaptation with typically organizational routines as its outcomes (for example Simon and March, 1958; March and Olsen, 1976; Cyert and March, 1963; Levitt and March, 1988). Others focus mainly on the cognitive rather than the behavioural aspects that typify the learning of organizations (for example Hedberg, 1981; Argyris and Schön, 1978). With the advent in the 1980s of Management Information Systems, IS scholars joined the organizational learning debate by introducing an information processing perspective to learning (for example Huber, 1991; Duncan and Weiss, 1979; Walsh and Ungson, 1991), stimulating people to think of ways to technically support learning processes and storage and retrieval of organizational knowledge bases. At the start of the 1990s, yet another perspective was introduced within the literature on organizational learning. This time the topic gained attention from ethnographers studying organizational behaviour. Based on theories derived from Vygotsky and Piaget, the idea was introduced that learning is essentially social. The learner as (peripheral) member of a community participates in actual practice and as such gradually learns how to think and act as a community member (Lave and Wenger, 1991). The focus on COPs as the core social unit where learning in organizations takes place, has gained almost total acceptance within the OL discipline. By participating together, communities emerge whose members have learned tacitly how to interpret knowledge, how to behave as an insider, etc.

The concept of communities of practice inspired many authors to think of it as a tool or social mechanism to support learning processes (for example Davenport and Prusak, 1998; Wenger, 1998; Boland and Tenkasi, 1995; Dougherty, 2001; Brown and Duguid, 1991). Probably the most often-cited article that relates learning with COP is Brown and Duguid's article in *Organization Science* (1991). Their argument is that COPs are social structures that are able to blend learning, working and innovating during day-to-day work activities. In his book *Communities of Practice: Learning, Meaning and Identity,* Etienne Wenger (1998) provides more theoretical depth while linking the two concepts. Central to his work is a 'social theory of learning'. Learning occurs through active participation in practices of communities while at the same time identities in relation to these communities are constructed. Learning thus refers both to action and belonging by members of (multiple) COPs. Wenger's work and the work of Brown and Duguid can be considered breakthroughs in later academic and practice-oriented debates about learning, knowledge, and management.

Communities contribute to this social learning as they provide the most suitable setting for learning to take shape. Collections of individuals bound by informal relationships share knowledge in action, and voluntary and informal learning happens. In general, the argument goes that COPs stimulate social learning by providing a suitable 'non-canonical', non-hierarchical, informal and flexible surrounding that is considered a fruitful breeding ground for learning.

After a decade of enthusiasm for COPs' role in promoting organizational learning, it might be time to become more critical about this mutual relationship. In fact, in this chapter we will argue that although we know a lot about COPs' contribution to learning *within* organizations, not much is known about their role in contributing to learning by organizations or 'organizational learning'.

Those who see learning as a social practice resulting in shared, situated knowledge usually consider the concept of organizational learning as learning *within* organizations. What is typical is that they tend to downplay the role of COPs in supporting *organizational* learning defined as the learning *by* organizations.

The distinction between learning within and learning by organizations is an important one. Learning by organizations refers to the process of institutionalization in which knowledge gains acceptance by members of the organization and is taken for granted. Organizational learning in that sense refers to the process in which shared knowledge becomes subsidiary knowledge (Polanyi, 1966). To understand what makes learning dinstinctly organizational, it helps to shift the attention from the product 'organization' to the process of 'organizing' (Weick, 1979). Organizing implies generalizing or institutionalizing knowledge. During organizing, institutionalized knowledge is used by individuals in their day-to-day activities while at the same time they create new and rearrange existing institutional knowledge. When this organizing process occurs at the level of the organization, we refer to organizational learning. Depending on various conditions, such as history, size, the multidisciplinarity of professions etc., this process of institutionalization can take years. When organizing processes occur at the level of the group or community, we refer to learning within organizations and focus on learning processes that take place within the context of an organization but do not necessarily influence the organization. This learning within organizations can be mainly individual learning, but can also have a more collective nature, which is the case with community learning.

We will argue that COPs' contribution to *support organizational learning* is much more complex in comparison to their often-praised role in supporting social *learning within organizations*. This distinction between learning within and learning by sheds a less optimistic light on the contribution of COPs. With the use of ideas on social construction and institutionalization of knowledge as well as Polanyi's ideas on focal and subsidiary awareness, more theoretical underpinnings will be given to the idea that COPs facilitate social learning but at the same time frustrate organizational learning.

ORGANIZATIONAL LEARNING AND LEARNING WITHIN ORGANIZATIONS

Despite the still-growing literature on organizational learning, there remains a need for more scientific understanding on how to explicate actual organizational learning processes (Thatchenkery, 1996). Perhaps the most important cause of this confusion lies in the combination 'organization' and 'learning' on top of the fact that both terms are highly conceptual. Because of the conceptual nature of these terms, it is difficult to see organizations as well as to see learning taking place (Yanow, 2000). Researchers have problems *seeing* organizations and likewise seeing the learning of organizations. If organizations cannot be observed, than it will be difficult to theorize about them, let alone about the process of organizational learning (Sandelands and Srivatsan, 1993; Yanow, 2000). Learning only becomes apparent after the fact, when something has been learned. Learning is usually approached as an 'achievement' verb, focussing on learning as changes or confirmation of existing knowledge (Sandelands and Drazin, 1989). This means that the same word 'learning' refers to both an outcome and a process, concealing rather than revealing the dynamics of learning. In combination with the problem of perceiving organizations (Sandelands and Srivatsan, 1993), this is probably one of the most important reasons that although scholars talk about OL, the practical illustrations deal with learning by individuals and groups. Many well-known OL researchers, such as March and Olsen and Argyris and Schön, treat organizational learning as individual learning within an organizational context (Weick and Westley, 1996). For example, Aryris and Schön as well as March and Olsen state that the organization learns that when individuals adapt their cognitions and behaviour to the feedback signals as environmental reactions to individual actions. Although March and Olsen acknowledge that organizational learning is usually not based on the outcome of individual learning ('audience learning'), they in fact refer to management learning as representatives of the organization. Supplementing top management as the visible representative of organization, is a tendency of many OL scholars (for example Senge, 1992) again mixing up organizational learning with learning within organizations.

Weick and Westley (1996), as well as Yanow (2000) and Cook and Yanow (1993), have tried to address this problem by introducing a cultural perspective on learning. They argue that by treating organizations as culture, we are better able to see learning happening. These and other scholars argue that communities of practice are a suitable perspective to open up our eyes for the cultural approach to learning. Based on cultural-interpretive research methods, learning is studied within, for example, communities of system analysts (Ciborra and Lanzara, 1994), maintenance engineers (Orr, 1996), midwives (Jordan, 1989), flight crews and ground staff (Weick and Roberts, 1993), claim processors (Wenger, 1998), IT consultants (Teigland and Wasko, 2000), flutemakers (Cook and Yanow, 1993), and technicians (Barley, 1996). The interpretive ethnographic methods try to reveal how the 'social world is constituted by the local production of meaningful action' (Suchman, 1987: 58). The focus is not so much on the outcome or the achievement of learning but on the process of learning as it has actually taken shape as part of the day-to-day activities of communities. In the course of their day-to-day interactions, people learn to become a practitioner, such as a photocopier repairman or an experienced midwife. Learning within these communities takes place through the communication of tacit knowledge. Or as Yanow (2000: 255) puts it 'in interaction with and through the actifacts, leaving their embodied meanings unspoken'. This learning is very much tacit. In terms of Polanyi, practitioners learn to become a community member while focussing on something else.

This cultural approach has contributed significantly to the debate on organizational learning. As mentioned earlier, this approach to organizational learning has put COPs as suitable vehicles for learning to the forefront. This can be considered a very welcome contribution. Because of its use of learning as a 'process verb' the approach provides more insight into *how* learning takes place. Further, it departs from the individual bias within the literature on organizational learning (Huysman, 2000a) by directing the attention on (tacit) learning of collectives and in specific on community learning. Combined, the approach provides a valuable framework to analyse the actual process of learning by communities. Its downside is, however, that although these and other scholars talk about 'organizational learning' they in fact continue the tradition within the OL literature by approaching OL as learning within organizations. In the rest of this chapter we will make the argument that in the case of community learning, group-level learning is facilitated but organizational learning is frustrated. This statement will be based on the theory of social construction and institutionalization of knowledge (Berger and Luckmann, 1966) combined with some ideas on focal and subsidiary knowledge introduced by Polanyi.

A SOCIAL CONSTRUCTIVIST APPROACH TO ORGANIZATIONAL LEARNING

A social constructivist approach to OL will show that organizational learning is different from social (community) learning in that the former needs objectification of the outcome of the latter. Social constructivist approaches to organizational learning emphasize the process through which an organization constructs knowledge or reconstructs existing knowledge. Through knowledge sharing, individual knowledge may become shared knowledge. This shared knowledge might become taken-for-granted, tacit organizational knowledge that will – often as subsidiary knowledge – influence subsequent action. In other words: organizational learning can be looked upon as a process that occurs as a result of the actions of the organization's members, while these same actions are simultaneously influenced by collectively accepted knowledge. As a result of this duality between, on the one hand, the actions of individuals and, on the other, the deterministic or formative influences of existing organizational factors, organizational learning can be viewed as a process of institutionalization (Berger and Luckmann, 1966).

The term 'institutions' is used to describe social practices that are regularly and continuously repeated, are sanctioned and maintained by social norms and have a major significance in the social structure (Abercrombie *et a.*, 1984). Institutionalization is the process through which social practices become sufficiently regular and continuous as to be described as institutions. This concept is widely used in sociology, though often without precise specification. Different schools of sociology treat the concept of institutionalization in different ways. For example, functionalists tend to see institutions as fulfilling the needs of individuals or society (for example, Durkheim, 1978; Parsons, 1960) while phenomenologists may concentrate on the way in which people create or adapt institutions rather than merely respond to them (Berger and Luckmann, 1966; Schutz, 1971). Scott (1987) distinguishes different 'institutional schools': two dealing with the process of institutionalization and two with institutions as systems. Institutionalization can be conceived of as 'a process of instilling value'. Selznick, for example, argues that 'institutionalisation is to infuse with value beyond the technical requirement of the task at hand' (Selznick, 1957: 17) which may lead to an unplanned and unintended nature of institutions. Institutionalization can also be conceived of as 'a process of creating reality'. Social order is founded on a shared social reality, which is created by social interaction. In this chapter Selznick's conception of institutionalization is used. The process of institutionalization requires that 'types of behavior in types of situations are connected to types of actors' (Berger and Luckmann, 1966).

With organizational knowledge, reference is made to knowledge as in rules, procedures, strategies, activities, technologies, conditions, paradigms, terms of reference, etc. around which organizations are constructed and through which they operate (Levitt and March, 1988). Organizational knowledge refers to knowledge that is being generated, developed and transmitted by individuals and that individuals use when acting as organizational members. This is organizational knowledge in the weak sense (Tsoukas and Vladimirou, 2001). In a strong sense, knowledge becomes organizational when 'individuals draw and act upon a corpus of generalizations in the form of generic rules produced by the organization' (Tsoukas and Vladimirou, 2001: 979).

Berger and Luckmann (1966) describe the process of institutionalization as consisting of three phases or 'moments': 'externalization, objectification, and internalization'. These three moments refer to the two interpretations of institutionalization: constructing a social structure which members use to act upon. Externalizing refers to the process through which personal knowledge is exchanged with others. Objectifying refers to the process through which society becomes an objective reality. During internalizing, 'the objectified social world is retrojected into consciousness in the course of socialization'.

As such, the authors point to a dialectical relationship between action and structure: 'the relationship between man, the producer, and the social world, his product, is and remains a dialectical one. That is, man (not, of course, in isolation but in his collectivity) and his social world interact with each other. The product acts back upon the producer' (Berger and Luckmann, 1966: 78).[1]

These three moments have proven relevant when analysing organizational learning processes (Huysman, 2000b; Pentland, 1998). Relating these processes of institutionalization with organizational learning, provides an image of organizational learning as consisting of these three consecutive moments:

- *externalizing* individual knowledge in such a way that individually held knowledge becomes shared;
- *objectifying* shared knowledge into organizational knowledge so that shared knowledge is eventually taken for granted and becomes part of the subsidiary knowledge of the organization;
- *internalizing* the organizational knowledge among members of the organization, such that organizational knowledge forms subsidiary knowledge of organizational member.

It should be noted that after the publication of the popular book by Nonaka and Takeuchi (1995) it is no longer possible to talk unequivocally about externalization and internalization processes. The popularity of their analysis stems to a large extent from the (creative) use of Polanyi's concepts of tacit and explicit knowledge. When Nonaka and Takeuchi use the term 'externalization', they mean the process of converting tacit knowledge into explicit knowledge; and when they use the term 'internalization' they are referring to the transfer from explicit to implicit knowledge. We depart from this conception of tacit and explicit and go back to the original work of Polanyi by combining it with Berger and Luckman's notion of institutionalization.

We follow Polanyi's argument in positing that tacit knowledge is not something that can be converted into explicit knowledge (Tsoukas and Vladimirou, 2001). Polanyi distinguishes two levels of awareness: focal and subsidiary awareness that contribute to the personal knowledge. One of Polanyi's examples to demonstrate the distinction and the dependency of both is the blind man using his stick to explore a hole in the floor. But we can also use a more contemporary example of children using a joystick to play computer games. The child focusses on the character in the game on the screen while being only subsidiarily aware of how she holds on to the joystick to do so. In the words of Polanyi, the child has dwelled into the tools, making it feel as if it is an extension of his own body. A person who has never played a computer game has not yet assimilated the tool, which means that by holding the joystick it receives focal awareness of the tool. By repeating actions, experiences are transformed into subsidiary awareness. Polanyi relates explicit knowledge to focal awareness and implicit knowledge to subsidiary awareness. Implicit knowledge proceeds and forms the source of explicit knowledge. Explicit knowledge consists of entities and objects that are within the focal awareness. When we are not focussed on these entities, there is no longer any explicit knowledge. Instead, we will then depend on our imaginations and associations to recall the experience and make it explicit again.

This original conception of tacit and explicit knowledge is important in understanding the role of COPs in contributing to learning, at both the social and the organizational levels. Individuals in organizations often use and create organizational knowledge without being fully aware that they are doing so. In the words of Tsoukas and Vladimirou (2001: 983):

> Organizational knowledge is the capability members of an organization have developed to draw distinctions in the process of carrying out their work, in particular concrete contexts, by enacting sets of generalizations (prepositional statements) whose application depends on historically evolved collective understandings and experiences. The more prepositional statements and collective understandings become instrumentalized (in Polanyi's sense of the term); and the more new experiences are reflectively processed (both individual and collectively) and then gradually driven into subsidiary awareness, the more organizational members dwell in all of them, and the more able they become to concentrate on new experiences (through focal awareness MH), on the operational plane.

Figure 9.1 provides a theoretical model of learning as the process of institutionalization, in which the three subprocesses or moments are conceptually unravelled. Due to the possible confusion with the terminology, we have employed the following terms in relation to organizational learning:

- externalization: *exchanging knowledge (for reuse or renewal)*
- objectification: *collective acceptance of knowledge*
- internalization: *acquiring organizational knowledge.*

COPs seem to be well suited to support two of the three processes that make up organizational learning: internalization and externalization. In fact, COP writers that connect the concept with learning usually focus on these two processes (for example, Lave and Wenger, 1991; Brown and Duguid, 1991; Botkin, 1999). The question of whether COPs also contribute to learning at the level of the organization, depends on the role of COPs in supporting the process of objectification. In the following sections, we will discuss this relationship between COP and learning within and by organizations in more detail.

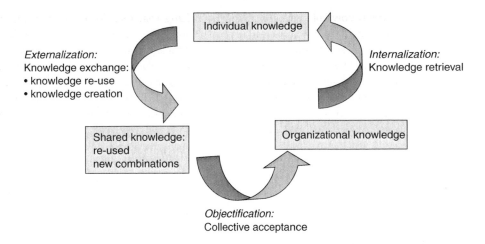

Figure 9.1 – Processes of institutionalization in relation to organizational learning

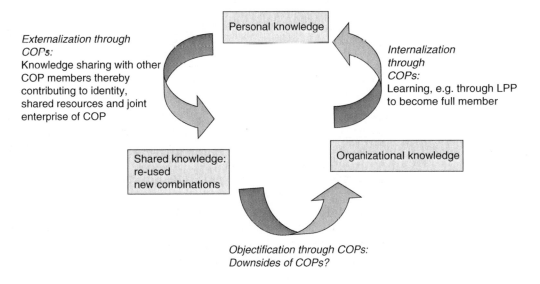

Figure 9.2 – COPs' contribution to OL as institutionalization

COMMUNITIES OF PRACTICE AND LEARNING AS INSTITUTIONALIZATION

In the rest of this chapter, an attempt is made to conceptually unravel the relationship between organizational learning and COP. This will be done by using a theoretical framework based on the notion of learning as the process of institutionalization.

Figure 9.2 illustrates the contribution of COP in supporting the process of learning as a process of institutionalizing knowledge.

COPs can be appropriate structures to support this process of internalization. Through internalization, individuals acquire organizational knowledge. It is through internalization that individuals become members of the organization. In fact, internalization means the process through which one becomes an 'insider'. A powerful way to support competence learning by newcomers is by letting people work together.

There is a growing band of authors who argue that learning should be considered as being inextricably bound up with working (for example, Brown and Duguid, 1991; Gherardi, 2000; Nicoloni and Meznar, 1995; Yanow, 2000). For example, Lave and Wenger (1991) introduced the concept of 'legitimate peripheral participation' as a method of learning by actively participating as opposed to learning outside the relevant task environment such as accumulating information from manuals.

Participating in COPs, or at least in their periphery, is often seen as one of the key mechanisms through which individuals socialize and learn 'collective knowledge'. Referring to Lave and Wenger, Brown and Duguid (1991: 50) put it as follows:

> Learners need legitimate access to the periphery of communication – to computer mail, to formal and informal meetings, to telephone conversations, etc. and, of course to war stories. They pick up invaluable know how – not just information but also manner and technique – from being on the periphery of competent practitioners going about their business.

Next to learning to become competent in a new organization, learning in COPs also happens for the purpose of knowledge re-use or knowledge renewal. This process of *externalization* supported by COPs is often seen as important to support knowledge sharing and knowledge management. Many organizations nowadays are experimenting with the concept of COP to enable the knowledge transfer between – often geographically dispersed – organizational members (Botkin, 1999; Leonard and Sensiper, 1998; Sole and Huysman, 2001). The idea is that by building or supporting COPs, people are more inclined to share knowledge with each other, which otherwise would either be lost or duplicated. It is in particular the communication of tacit knowledge for which COPs are believed to offer a suitable environment. Tacit knowledge in COPs is communicated through explicit knowledge. Communication within COPs is usually 'done' in interaction with and through artefacts, leaving their embodied meanings unspoken (Yanow, 2000: 255). A way to support the transfer of this knowledge in communities is for example by telling stories and swapping anecdotes (Sims, 2000) between old-timers and newcomers.

Just because knowledge is exchanged does not mean that the shared knowledge has already been collectively accepted. Shared knowledge only turns into organizational knowledge when the organization's members accept it as such. Collective acceptance as a process is, in other words, the link between individual learning and organizational learning.

This process of collective acceptance or objectification usually does not take place consciously and can be a long, drawn-out process. By collectively accepting local knowledge the collective – often gradually – starts to accept existing shared knowledge as being part of the organization. This process is not so much one of sharing knowledge but more one of sedimentation. Von Krogh *et al.* (2000) refers to this process in the context of knowledge creation as 'globalizing local knowledge'. For example, a group of technicians might have learned a new way of fixing a machine. This new operational knowledge remains local knowledge until it is accepted by the organization, for example - as expressed in organizational stories, in manuals and in the training of newcomers. This process of objectification usually takes much longer than is the case with the two other sub-institutionalization processes discussed above (Berger and Luckmann, 1966; Dixon, 2000; Douglas, 1987). Ignoring the importance of collective acceptance can be a serious obstacle to organizational learning. In fact, most organizations tend to ignore the outcomes of local learning processes or have problems collectively accepting these outcomes (Huysman and De Wit, 2002).

Below two general tendencies inherent to communities are discussed that might obstruct the objectification of local knowledge and therefore hinder learning by organizations. These are the tendency of COPs to be less visible and consequentially be ignored by management, and the tendency of COPs to be unconscious of their own (tacit) knowledge that has been learned over time. We will discuss these two negative tendencies below.

COPs FRUSTRATING ORGANIZATIONAL LEARNING

Tsoukas and Chia (2002) argued that although there are ongoing changes in organizations, this should not be taken to mean that organizations constantly change. The same argument applies to learning: although there is a lot of learning going on in organizations, this does not mean that the organization as a whole learns. A lot of learning within organizations remains unrecognized. Non-learning or inflexibility in an organization is often the result of managers not paying attention to learning processes that take place within communities (Brown and Duguid, 1991). During their day-to-day activities, COPs continuously create new knowledge as a solution to daily problems. They create new ways of working, give new interpretations to their situation and discuss existing practices. In other words, whereas internalization and externalization practices can be highly innovative, the problem often lies in inflexible objectifying processes, as local knowledge is often not transformed into new organizational knowledge.

More often than not, collective acceptance occurs when knowledge sharing processes are ratified through the endorsement of dominant coalitions within an organization (Simon and March, 1958). Dominant coalitions are formed by, for example, management, a critical mass, reference groups, old-timers, or charismatic personalities. Dominant coalitions can have a negative impact on the result of learning processes. For example, management – as an important member of a dominant coalition – might be oblivious to what is actually going on within the organization. 'Whether local changes are amplified and become institutionalised depends on the "structural context," created to a large extent... by senior managers' (Tsoukas and Chia, 2002: 579). By not accepting existing knowledge as being important to the organization as a whole, management hinders the construction of organizational learning, as a result of which the learning process of the organization will eventually become out of step with the learning process of individuals within the organization (Brown and Duguid, 1991).

The next illustration provides an example of the power enjoyed by dominant coalitions, consisting of management and old-timers, who were able to frustrate the collective acceptance process and thus organizational learning as a whole.

A group of information system (IS) designers worked in the computer department of a large organization for a number of years. They all had records of long service within the company, where they had previously been employed as computer programmers. The company was using a number of routines that had been introduced by these employees over the years. For example, employees worked mainly on their own, there was little contact with the clients, almost every designer used his or her own particular style of IS design and there was a heavy bias towards technical details. The fact that their clients were unhappy with these routines was never explicitly discussed. This complacency was reinforced because the department enjoyed a monopoly position within the organization.

At the beginning of the 1990s, the demand for information systems doubled, which resulted in a drastic expansion in the number of personnel. Twenty new system designers were brought in from outside the organization; all of who had enjoyed a professional training in IS design and had often worked for a substantial length of time for software houses. These newcomers brought knowledge and skills with them that radically differed from the organization's existing in-house knowledge and skills. However, despite the fact that knowledge was exchanged, the existing collective routines and practices did not change. A critical mass consisting of 'old-timers' and management did not adapt to the new practices that most of them even did not recognize. Over time, the majority of the newcomers eventually adapted to the established routines. Although they realized that clients were unhappy with the methods and knowledge that were being used, they learned not to express their opinions in public and definitely not to report them to management (Huysman, 2000).

Consequently, despite the potential for the organization to learn new (IS designers') routines, inflexibility was the result. The community of old-timers formed such a powerful coalition that it hindered the transformation of newly shared knowledge into organizational knowledge.

Next to being not recognized by existing dominant coalitions such as management, organizational learning is hindered by the fact that COPs are often unaware of their own learning and, consequently, of the potential new knowledge that might be the result of this situated learning. Ciborra and Lanzara (1994), for example, describe the case of system designers at a computer company who were unaware of their innovative ways of working that developed over time. Because their personal activities are so much integrated in their day-to-day context, they became blind to changes in their 'formative context'. This subsidiary knowledge that community members share will only become recognized by the members when explicit focus on certain knowledge requires bringing this knowledge into focal awareness. It is only in such cases that tacitly shared knowledge of which COP members are not aware become explicit and might be communicated to others across the COP borders.

There are various ways to support the process of objectification so that knowledge becomes accepted by the organization as a whole.

Top management can support objectification through their explicit acknowledgement of the importance of COPs (Huysman and De Wit, 2002; Brown and Duguid, 1991, 2000; Cohen and Prusak, 2000). Recognizing the importance of communities and networks requires an awareness of where valuable communities are located and what holds them together (Wenger, 2000). According to Wenger, this requires a new set of responsibilities that are a long way from the technical emphasis of knowledge management. It requires an 'anthropological nose' (Wenger, 2000: 19). COPs cannot be managed nor structured, but instead calls for new – if you like 'soft' – management principles such as 'hospitality' (Ciborra, 1996) and 'doing no harm' (Cohen and Prusak, 2000). Objectification through more attentive managers requires that they are more capable of absorbing what is learned within communities. This means the need to understand communities' history, their interpretive codes, their practices, and so on (Tsoukas and Chia, 2002: 579). Creating such absorptive capacity among dominant coalitions is extremely difficult as the knowledge shared by community is highly tacit. To become aware (focally) of this knowledge that is often subsidiary to the members, managers need to dwell into the communities' praxis. In addition, a lot of the learning of COP is 'heuristic', requiring active membership as well. Heuristic knowledge is gained through improvisations while carrying out tasks and often resides in the stories told by community members (Brown and Duguid, 1991).

Supporting objectification from inside instead of outside is also a strategy to support organizational learning. Objectification can take place for example via the intervention of 'domain experts', people who are considered to be the *primus inter pares* among the community members. Most communities informally select one individual or a group of people to be the *primus inter pares* of the community. This person plays an important role in objectifying the knowledge that is shared between the communities. His or her acknowledgement of the knowledge as being relevant, innovative, useful and so on to the community will stimulate other members to use it. This corresponds with the idea of reference groups and significant others, concepts that were introduced a century ago by symbolic interactionists (Shibutani, 1955; Thomas, 1914). It is important that managers recognize these key people and take their knowledge seriously. If not, knowledge will only remain relevant to the community itself.

These key community members also need to have a stake outside their community to support the acceptance of the value and usability of the knowledge by other organizational participants. Thus, in order for community knowledge to cross boundaries and become accepted by a larger audience, knowledge brokers who are seen as being 'significant others' are needed (Wenger, 1998).

Next to a more natural role of senior members or experts, experts can also take part in a jury of people who peer-review the knowledge of their community members. Brown (2000) provides an example taken from Xerox, that illustrates how peer reviewing can help objectify community knowledge. Photocopier and printer repairmen at Xerox ('reps') use a web-based system called 'Eureka' as a way of accelerating their learning and structuring the community knowledge on how to act as a successful repairman. The system is based on actionable expert knowledge concerning printers and copiers. To transform reps' opinions and experiences into 'warranted beliefs', contributors had to submit their ideas for peer review, a process facilitated by the web. The peers would vet and refine the story, and connect it to others. As such, these experts helped to make sure that knowledge contained by Eureka is perceived as valuable and reliable, while merely opinions and 'fantastic horror stories' were filtered out. Eureka is used as a tool to learn organizational knowledge and thus contributes to the process of organizational learning (Storck and Hill, 2000).

Highlighting the expert's role in COPs detracts the egalitarian image of COPs. However, when organizations are perceived as political arenas more than as friendly communities of communities, issues of power, structures and hierarchies cannot be ignored. Clearly, more research is needed to analyse the ambivalent role of COPs in supporting organizational learning and in specific in supporting the collective acceptance of shared knowledge.

CONCLUSIONS

A still-growing group of organizational practitioners and scholars perceive COPs to be the most promising vehicle to support organizational learning. Originally, this link between COPs and learning was introduced by ethnographic researchers who argued that during their day-to-day activity community members gradually learn the tacit knowledge that holds a community together. In general, the relationship is often perceived as positive, obvious and inherent. It is striking to note that the link between organizational learning and COPs is almost always taken for granted while the focus is on learning within organizations and not on learning by organizations, or 'organizational learning'. A social con-structivist perspective on the relationship between learning and COP provides a different view than we are used to. In this chapter, we have tried to critically analyse this optimistic relationship by introducing a model that perceives learning as the process of institutionalization. Communities have different roles during this process. We agree with the 'communitarian' view that during the process of externalizing and internalizing knowledge, COPs might serve as suitable structures to support learning. This learning is, however, limited to social learning within organizations. It does not inform us about the learning that occurs at a higher-level of abstraction: organizational learning. For this higher-level learning to take place, local tacit knowledge - which is often the outcome of community learning – needs to be collectively accepted by organizational members. We have argued that this process of objectification is often hindered by COP. In other words, although COPs are well suited to support learning within organizations, they have a tendency to obstruct learning by organizations. Clearly, empirical research is needed to analyse these and other possibilities for communities to support organizational learning. We believe that the social constructivist perspective on organizational learning as discussed in this chapter, provides an interesting framework to do so.

NOTE

1. The 'moments' of Berger and Luckmann correspond to a certain extent to Giddens' structuration theory (1984). Giddens is one of the most well-known contemporary sociologists who proposes a dialectical relationship between action and structure. Action and structure presuppose each other, instead of being mutually exclusive. Giddens is more explicit than Berger and Luckmann (1966) about the possible occurrence of the consequences of human action that are unknown or unintended.

REFERENCES

Abercrombie, N., Hill S., and Turner, B.S. (1984) *Dictionary of Sociology.* Harmondsworth: Penguin Books.

Argyris, C. and Schön, D. (1978) *Organizational Learning: a Theory of Action-Perspective.* Reading, MA: Addison-Wesley.

Barley, S. (1986) Technology as an occasion for structuring: evidence from observations of CT scanners and the social order of radiology departments, *Administrative Science Quarterly,* 31: 78–108.

Berger, P. and Luckmann, T. (1966) *The Social Construction of Knowledge.* London: Penguin Books.

Boland, R.J.J. and Tenkasi, R.V. (1995) Perspective making and perspective taking in communities of knowing, *Organization Science,* 6(4): 350–72.

Botkin, J. (1999) *Smart Business: How Knowledge Communities Can Revolutionize Your Company.* New York: Free Press.

Brown, J.S. (2000) Growing up digital: the web and the new learning ecology, *Change, the Magazine of Higher Learning,* March/April: 11–22.

Brown, J.S. and Duguid, P. (1991) Organizational learning and communities-of-practice: toward a unified view of working, leaning and innovation, *Organization Science,* 2(1): 40–57.

Ciborra, C.U. (ed.) (1996) *Groupware and Teamwork.* Chichester: John Wiley andSons.

Ciborra, C.U. and Lanzara, G.F. (1994) Formative contexts and information technology, understanding the dynamics of innovation in organizations, *Accounting, Management and Information Technology,* 4(2): 61–86.

Cohen, D. and Prusak, L. (2000) *In Good Company: How Social Capital Makes Organizations Work,* Boston, MA: Harvard Business School Press.

Cook, S.D.N. and Yanow, D. (1993) Culture and organizational learning, *Journal of Management Inquiry,* 2(4): 373–90.

Cyert, R.M and March, J.G. (1963) *A Behavioral Theory of the Firm,* Englewood Cliffs, NJ: Prentice Hall.

Davenport, T.H. and Prusak, L. (1998) *Working Knowledge: How Organizations Manage What They Know,* Boston: Harvard Business School Press.

Dixon, N.M. (2000) *Common Knowledge.* Cambridge MA: Harvard Business School Press.

Dodgson, M. (1993) Organizational learning: a review of some literatures, *Organization Studies,* 14(3), 375–94.

Dougherty, D. (2001) Reimagining the differentiation and integration of work for sustained product innovation, *Organization Science,* 12(5): 612–31.

Douglas, M. (1987) *How Institutions Think.* London: Routledge and Kegan Paul.

Duncan, R.B. and Weiss, A. (1979) *Organizational Learning: Implications for Organizational Design Research in Organizational Behavior.* Greenwich, CT: JAI Press.

Durkheim, E. (1978) *On Institutional Analysis.* Chicago: Chicago University Press.

Gherardi, S. (2000) Practice-based theorizing on learning and knowing in organizations, *Organization,* 7(2): 211–23.

Giddens, A. (1984) *The Constitution of Society.* Cambridge: Polity Press.

Hedberg, B.L.T. (1981) How organizations learn and unlearn. In P.C. Nystrom and W.H. Starbuck (eds), *Handbook of Organization Design,* vol. 1. New York: Oxford University Press.

Huber, G.P. (1991) Organizational learning: the contributing processes and the literatures, *Organizational Science,* 2(1): 88–115.

Huysman, M.H. (2000a) Rethinking organizational learning, *Accountancy Management and Information Technology,* 10: 81–99.

Huysman, M.H. (2000b) Organizational learning or learning organizations, *European Journal of Work and Organizational Psychology,* 9(2): 133–45.

Huysman, M.H. and de Wit, D. (2002) *Knowledge Sharing in Practice.* Boston: Kluwer Academic.

Jordan, B. (1989) Cosmopolitical obstetrics: some insights from the training of traditional midwives, *Social Science and Medicine,* 28(9): 52–65.

Lave, J. and Wenger, E. (1991) *Situated Learning: Legitimate Peripheral Participation.* Cambridge: Cambridge University Press.

Leonard, D. and Sensiper, S. (1998) The Role of Tacit Knowledge in Group Innovation, *California Management Review,* 40(2): 112–32.

Levitt, B. and March, J.G. (1988) Organizational learning, *Annual Review Sociology,* 14: 319–40.

March, J.G. and Olsen, J.P. (1976) *Ambiguity and Choice in Organizations,* Bergen, Norway: Universitetsforlaget.

Nicolini, D. and Meznar, M.B. (1995) The social construction of organizational learning: conceptual and practical issues in the field, *Human Relations,* 48(7): 727–46.

Nonaka, I. and Takeuchi, H. (1995) *The Knowledge Creating Company: How Japanese Companies Create the Dynamics of Innovation.* New York: Oxford University Press.

Orr, J. (1996) *Talking about Machines: an Ethnography of a Modern Job.* New York: IRL Press.

Parsons, T. (1960) *Structure and Process in Modern Societies.* Glencoe, IL: The Free Press.

Pentland, B.T. (1995) Information systems and organizational learning: the social epistemology of organizational knowledge systems, *Accounting, Management and Information Technology,* 5: 1–21.

Polanyi, M. (1966) *The Tacit Dimension.* London: Routledge & Kegan Paul.

Putnam, R.D. (1993) The prosperous community: social capital and public life, *American Prospect,* 13: 35–42.

Sandelands, L. and Drazin, R. (1989) On the language of organizational theory, *Organization Studies,* 10: 457–78.

Sandelands, L. and Srivatsan, V. (1993) The problem of experience in the study of organizations, *Organization Studies,* 14.

Schutz, A. (1971) *Collected Papers,* vols 1 and 2. The Hague: Martinus Nijhoff.

Scott, W.R. (1987) The adolescence of institutional theory, *Administrative Science Quarterly,* 32: 493–511.

Selznick, P. (1957) *Readership in Administration.* New York: Harper & Row.

Senge, P. (1992) *The Fifth Discipline: The Art and Practice of the Learning Organization.* London: Random House.

Shibutani, T. (1955) Reference groups as perspectives, *American Journal of Sociology,* 60: 562–9.

Simon, H. and March, J. (1958) *Organization.* Wiley: New York.

Sims, D. (2000), Organizational learning as the development of stories. In M. Easterby-Smith, L. Araujo and J. Burgoyne (eds), *Organizational Learning and the Learning Organization: Developments in Theory and Practice*. Thousand Oaks, CA: Sage.

Sole, D. and Huysman, M. (2001) Knowledge, practice and the role of location: a community of practice perspective, *Trends in Communication*, 8: 27–35.

Spender, J.C. (1996) Making knowledge the basis of a dynamic strategy of the firm, *Strategic Management Journal*, 17: 45–62.

Star, S.L. (1992) The trojan door: organizations, work and the 'open black box', *Systems Practice*, 5: 395–410.

Storck, J. and Hill, P.A. (2000) Knowledge diffusion through 'strategic communities', *Sloan Management Review*, Winter: 63–74.

Szulanski, G. (1996) Exploring internal stickiness: impediments to the transfer of best practice within the firm, *Strategic Management Journal*, 17: 27–43.

Teigland, R. and Wasko, M. McLure (2000) Creative ties and ties that bind. Proceedings of the 21st Annual International Conference on Information Systems, December, Brisbane, Australia.

Thatchenkery T.J. (1996) Organizational learning, language games and knowledge creation, Editorial note, *Journal of Organizational Change Management*, 9(1) 4–11.

Thomas, W.I. (1914) The Prussian–Polish Situation: an experiment in assimilation, *American Journal of Sociology*, 19: 624–39.

Tsoukas, H. and Chia, R. (2002) On organizational becoming: rethinking organizational change, *Organization Science*, 567–82.

Tsoukas, H. and Vladimirou, E. (2001) What is organizational knowledge?, *Journal of Management Studies*, 38: 973–93.

von Krogh, G., Ichijo, K. and Nonaka, I. (2000) *Enabling Knowledge Creation: How to Unlock the Mystery of Tacit Knowledge and Release the Power of Innovation*. Oxford and New York: Oxford University Press.

Walsh, J.P. and Ungson, G.R. (1991) Organizational memory, *Academy of Management Review*, 16(1): 57–91.

Weick, K. (1979) *The Social Psychology of Organizing*, 2nd edn. Reading, MA: Addison-Wesley.

Weick, K.E. and Roberts, K.H. (1993) Collective mind in organizations: heedful interrelating on flight desks, *Administrative Science Quarterly*, 38(3): 357–81.

Weick, K.E. and Westley F. (1996). Organizational learning: affirming an oxymoron. In S.R. Clegg, C. Hardy and W.R. Nord (eds), *Handbook of Organization Studies*. Thousand Oaks, CA: Sage Publications.

Wenger, E. (1998) *Communities of Practice*. New York: Cambridge University Press.

Wenger, E. (2000) Communities of practice: the key to knowledge strategy. In E. Lesser (ed.), *Knowledge and Communities*, Boston: Butterworth Heinemann.

Yanow, D. (2000) Seeing organizational learning: a cultural view, *Organization*, 7(2): 247–68.

IDENTITY AND IDENTITY WORK

Social organization is both means and bar to control. The concrete physical and biological settings in which actions occur are crucial. It is thus the outcomes and contentions among identities which is what cumulates into social organisation.

Harrison White, 1992: 16

In the first edition of Work Organisations, we sought to promote the study of identity and the 'identity work' of managers and employees for organisation analysis. At that time – the end of the 1980s – such issues were not prominent and certainly not much researched outside the realms of social psychology. Our goal was to bring some of the early critical thinking about identity that was emerging from labour process and other debates (Knights and Willmott, 1985) to what was known about issues such as roles, groups and stress in the OB literature. Picking up on themes in the rest of the book, identity was treated as a form of regulation. Shaping identities was important to employers because it was more likely to generate active consent to rules and controls than conventional bureaucratic methods. On the other hand, individuals and groups also seek to self-regulate their identities in search of stable, favourable outcomes. These negotiated transactions thus formed the basis of the 'identity work' described and discussed in the chapter.

Two decades later the situation is very different. Identity, in Europe at least, is arguably now the *most* written about topic in organisation and many other fields of study in the social sciences (Cornelissen, Haslam and Balmer, 2007). Given our original objectives, this is welcome, but it has come at a cost – identity tends to be over-sold as explanation and under-conceptualised as empirical object (Thompson and Marks, 2007). With respect to the former, this may be the fate of all fashionable concepts that become over-consumed and made to do too much work of explanation (Alvesson, 2007). As for its conceptualisation, this derives mainly in our view from its treatment by the dominant perspective – post-structuralism. Moving from the observation that identities are fluid and multiple social constructions rather than stable or enduring essences, post-structuralists assign to discourse the power to shape identities, whether they be individual or organisational (Collinson, 2003; Ainsworth and Hardy 2004). Organisational actors are not wholly passive, but their 'identity work' is limited primarily to positioning themselves within the interplay of discourses, choosing between 'subject positions'. The outcome is that the individual or other site of identity formation tends to be treated, in Thompson and Mark's term, as a blank slate to be textualised.

It is beyond our scope to give a detailed account and commentary on these new writings (see Webb, 2006). While we will make reference to ideas and debates, we want to remain close to our original objective of giving an account of identity work that reflects the assumptions about subjectivity at work – that employees are both subject to the actions of dominant power holders and subject of the pursuit of their own interests and identities. We want to restore a sense of the differences between the sources and sites of identity formation – self, group, organisation, occupation – and a sense of the tensions between them. In order to do this, we need to re-state and update a discussion of identity work, this time giving greater priority to perspectives from social psychology and other sources that, whatever their other flaws, facilitate a more rounded and complex picture than one which relies on discourse as medium and explanation.

The aims of this chapter are to:

◎ Give an account of identity and identity work that reflect the assumptions about subjectivity at work.
◎ Show how identity is used in producing images appropriate to our social, cultural and work context.
◎ Explore how issues of gender and ethnic identity have today become organisational issue of Diversity.
◎ Examine the notion of organisational identity and its relation to the individual involvement of identities in the workplace.
◎ Indicate how situational power is implicated in both 'perceived behavioural control' and individual and collective resistance.
◎ Explore how identity work uses the organisation and illustrate through the personal and group identity work done by managers.

EXPLANATIONS OF IDENTITY

The journey of an individual into and through the world of work is constituted by the mainstream agenda in organisational behaviour (OB) as a fairly discrete set of common and basic processes through which individuals develop identities and the behavioral and emotional repertoires which support them. Through these processes, notably learning, perception and socialisation, the individual is seen to develop distinctive patterns of personality, motivation and affiliation which can be factored and compared to give organisations performance-related data. There has been much of use to learn from examining that journey, but as an account of the development of subjectivity and identity within an organisational context, it still has distinct limitations. It fails to adequately understand individual identity as a social reality through which we transact with our environment. At a more macro-level of analysis, the sociological stream of organisation theory is much more comfortable with notions of groups acting according to economically determined interests. But objective reality is perceptually filtered through *subjective constructions* which interpret and shape our whole world in terms of what we value about ourselves. Our focus on subjective identity lies in this process, because as individuals we guide our actions according to what will in our view best defend, enhance or substantiate our identities. Identity is thus a tool that we use to present ourselves in, and possibly transform ourselves into, images appropriate to our social, cultural and work context.

Unless personality and identity are exclusively genetically-determined phenomena, there can be little doubt that social contexts and pressures shape an individual's identity. In researching differential socio-emotional development in male and female children, Lewis (1975) found that parallel to the earliest distinguishable biological influences, there are differences in the treatment of the two sexes by adults and other children. Thus, though biological influences undoubtedly have some effects on personality in the same way that they have an influence on hair colour and general bodily characteristics, these effects cannot easily be differentiated from social or environmental influences.

According to Weigert *et al.* (1986: 31), 'identity is a definition that transforms a mere biological individual into a human person. It is a definition that emerges from and is sustained by the cultural meanings of social relationships activated in interaction'. To extend the above example, if someone dyes or changes their hairstyle, they have taken steps to place a self-directed social construction on the body they were born with. Considering the myriad identifications we make with role models, reference groups, ideological contructs and symbols we are taking for ourselves, identities, both *personal* (who we think we are) and *social* (who we want others to think we are), are produced out of what we select as attractive or appropriate out of the social values, expectations and fashions of our time. The tradition of sociological social psychology represented by Weigert and others tried to avoid any contradictions between notions of personal and social identity, taking the view that identity is a *social product* both bestowed on the individual by others and appropriated by individuals for themselves. It takes the form of a *typified self*, any of a number of self-produced categorisations of what is available to the individual within the various situations in which they participate (see self-categorisation below).

Shifting the focus from personal to social identity, we can see that we constantly represent our subjective selves to others in our social environment. In the way we dress, speak and behave we present a changing image of who we are. Identity is in this sense a *negotiated* construction. Depending on who we are dealing with, we present images intended to appear appropriate to both the situation and the expectations of others. Using a symbolic interactionist framework, Erving Goffman (1971, see 'Impression management' below) explored this conception of self within a dramaturgical metaphor, representing social identity as a performance analogous to that of an actor.

The image presented is not necessarily the 'real' self of the person but a situationally appropriate image sustained by the 'actors' and those observing and/or interacting with them. The students in a lecture theatre, even though they may not consider themselves socially or intellectually inferior to the lecturer, collaborate to enable the lecturer to present a consistent performance. They thus maintain an image of authority for the lecturer and one of subordination for themselves, that is, social identities consistent within the situation. They exercise 'tact' in order to continue participating in the production of a performance that fits the perceived rules of the situation.

The interface between social and personal identity lies in this act of interpersonal negotiation. A social identity does not simply spring fully formed from the demands of the situation, but requires effort and practice from the individual and appropriate feedback from others. Thus the contexts from which we are able to construct unique subjective identities for ourselves consist mainly of 'rationalised' performances where we construct personal identity out of the strategies and responses we devise to deal with contingencies. The idea that we each possess a core identity relating to what we value about ourselves is examined in the *social learning* conception of identity (Miller, 1963). As a source of meaning, identity links us to others in the social structure through perceived similarities and processes of identification. As a definition or typification, identity sets us apart from others; it is the basis of social comparison, showing us the things and people which our particular personal meanings debar us from identifying with. Personal, subjective identity consists of the meanings and images we have found to represent us accurately in the past. Social identity, where it is different to the former, consists of the negotiated position between our personal identity and the meanings and images demanded of us in our current social context.

This leads us to a final aspect of identity as a linking concept between differing levels of explanation. We gain identities through interaction and association with the social and cultural groupings to which we belong. These groups provide us with points of reference and comparison out of which we can define ourselves, and through this route are in turn directly shaped by social structure. For this reason Miller (1963) saw identity as the foundation of the links between social structure and personality, and fundamental as such to the explanation of socialisation, motivation and psychological conflict. Likewise, the *social identity theory* of Tajfel and Turner (1979; 1986) links intergroup relations to social conflict and through *self-categorisation theory* (Turner, 1985) to the interpersonal dynamics of groups. Our personal transactions with social structures are conducted in the great part through the organisations we belong to, work for, and with which we have to deal. Organisations attempt to socialise people into their particular workplace cultures and management attempts to influence individual motivation to its advantage. The amelioration of the psychological, interpersonal and group conflicts engendered by these activities is a major rationale for the involvement of social and behavioural scientists in organisations.

REDEFINING THE AGENDA

To understand more adequately the individual's development towards an organisational participant who is active, yet acted upon, we need to further redefine some of the issues and agenda. For example, because so much of OB took the structures, workings and goals of organisational life for granted, it underestimated the degree to which the environment restricts sources of meaning for the securing of identities and imposes costs on individuals. The resources that individuals can bring to an identity project will depend on their *situational power* in the organisation (see below). Situational power does not depend simply on a person's place in an organisational hierarchy: a shop-floor worker can construct an identity just as, or even more, secure than that of someone with more position power. An individual's perception of his or her own situational power, whether at an interpersonal, group or organisational level, conditions how secure he or she feels, mediated by factors such as *self-monitoring*, *locus of control* and *self-efficacy*. These identities are not necessarily situation-specific, providing meaning and support outside the context they were constructed within, though there are of course limits. The 'organisation man', secure in his identification with organisational goals and objectives, may generalise associated attitudes and behaviours to situations where such an identity may be inappropriate.

The treatment of identity in mainstream psychology also neglected contextual issues in treating identity in an everyday fashion as being inherent in the person. Breakwell (1987: 95) argues that psychologists 'tend to treat identity as the origin of action'; they use it as a 'motivational variable', much as happened with emotions. In contrast, we see identity as the outcome of interaction within particular material contexts which act as constraints on available sources of meaning and on the process of identity construction and what is important here is how we use the organisation for our own purposes as opposed to how organisations and organisational discourses use us. The central limiting factor on available sources of meaning is the context of *intensified*, *fragmented* and *commodified* work. In an externally controlled environment, the most individuals can often hope for is to maintain or increase their situational power and material resources. Our relationships with, and our attribution of motives to, others are reduced to their instrumental function in the process of 'accumulation without regard to need' (Wexler, 1983: 122). Socio-psychological models of motivation continually reflect this, as in the rational calculations of personal advantage we are assumed to make in process models of motivation or in the mixed-models of emotional intelligence.

DIVERSE IDENTITIES

The instrumentality of relationships also extends into the definition of gender identities in the workplace. Writers such as Hearn and Parkin (1987) identify the *desexualised* nature of work organisations as reinforcing patriarchy and sexism. Instrumentality in the continuing forms of fragmented, Taylorised work relations defines masculinity and reproduces organisational work as a male concern:

> The workman is, potentially at least, nothing more than the doer of the task, without feelings and emotions. The ideal workman would appear to almost lose physical presence, or be a mere disembodied bearer of role, in effect part of a machine system. (Hearn and Parkin, 1987: 19)

Women workers have been and still are, excluded from the predominantly male culture of organisations, feminine gender identity being routinely suppressed or marginalised. Women managers especially are often required to adapt to masculine models of management, or risk being viewed as exceptions to women in general. Likewise domestic labour is not viewed as 'real' work in the fashion that paid work is; the identity construct of 'worker' is reserved for those carrying out the latter. Women's labour in organisations has often been an extension of domestic labour, as in the example of secretaries who act as 'office wives, protecting their charges from unnecessary interference and strain, making tea, buying presents, even cleaning their bosses' false teeth' (1987: 92). The expectations of and reactions to gender identities often appear contradictory or arbitrary, for example, why does it appear to be more acceptable to be a gay police chief than a gay footballer? In this case the contradiction can be understood in terms of formal support for and informal intolerance of gender identities, for example with a Police Service committed to eradicating institutional racism and gender discrimination as opposed to the casual vehemence of fans against players in a sport that does not yet allow women players in its top ranks.

Sexual, and racial, discrimination in labour markets was reinforced by stereotypical categorisations of women and black workers that portrayed them as 'naturally' inferior in various abilities or suited to only certain types of work. Notions such as women being better suited than men to boring, repetitive tasks served to legitimise restricted access to labour markets. Black workers in particular have been discriminated against in recruitment and selection processes on the basis of a stereotyped lack of acceptability in white workplace cultures. Jenkins (1986) notes that the causes of racism were often attributed to those who were discriminated against: 'managers do, in the main, see black workers as posing problems for their organisations. These problems were typically seen to be created by black workers, not by white racism' (1986: 114). Where institutions now attempt some amelioration of discrimination it is today carried out under the banner of *diversity training*; it is not so much social or business concerns that drive lower tolerance of discrimination but a fear of litigation and with public organisations a necessity to be seen to comply with legislation. *Diversity* itself is defined in terms of social identity theory by Nkomo and Cox (1999: 89) as, 'a mixture of people with different group identities within the same social system'. Nkomo and Cox (1999: 90) produce a useful conceptual map of approaches to identity and the effects of diversity in organisations, but they are focused on gender and minority (race in their terms) and as with subsequent institutional definitions (which generally add disability issues) do not take into account the diverse nature and skills of the disaffected, the maverick and the collectivist or even the 'Type B' personality. Diversity is thus for the 'deserving' minority and inextricably linked to organisational estimations of employee character and aspirations.

Where they are not simple compliance or even just lip service, attempts to 'manage' diversity appear to follow an HRM dominated, 'one size fits all' approach which fits with Giddens' (1990; 1991) *reflexive modernisation hypotheses* that managerial identity will become more gender-neutral and dominated by career-based concerns with self-marketing. In examining the 'career narratives' of managers, Wajcman and Martin (2002: 99) note that:

- What we have termed a market narrative was most commonly used by the managers in our study to understand and explain their career paths and to account for their likely future choices ... this narrative provided a flexible, sustaining framework for managers to understand their careers and make career choices.
- Men and women place themselves as apparently ungendered market actors in their career stories and can adopt much the same career strategies in dealing with the new labour market.
- While these findings accord with the reflexive modernization picture of largely ungendered career identities along with a strong sense of individual autonomy, our research also shows that 'choice' means quite different things in the private world for men and women.
- Because the available private identities remain so deeply gendered, women face a negotiation of employment and domestic responsibilities which is different from that of men.

Yet questions also need to be raised about possible disjunctures between managerial and worker identities. Wajcman and Martin contrast their findings with Sennett's (1998) notion of the *corrosion of character* where:

> He argues that the possibility of sustained, predictable, usually lifetime, engagement with a workplace has been the bedrock of people's identities – their 'character' – since the advent of industrial societies. With its principle of 'no long term', the new capitalism has torn away the basis for the formation of sustaining identities, resulting in a growing malaise as people search in vain for a place to anchor a meaning for their lives. (Wajcman and Martin, 2002: 987)

Since most workers only have the ability to be instrumental in extrinsic terms, the flexibility afforded to managers will be harder to come by, making Sennett's view possibly more appropriate in the employee context. This is supported by Webb (2004: 719) who argues that it is increased instrumentalism on the part of employers rather than short-termism which is the more damaging and results in 'the experience of increased responsibility without meaningful discretion and authority'.

It is important to recognise here that threats to job security do not inevitably produce organisational domination. Consent has to be mobilised, because domination by coercion is often 'inefficient', requiring constant reinforcement of such pressures and extensive monitoring of reactions to them. As with motivation earlier, domination of the individual through self-limitation and constraint is far more effective. This is engendered through individual assimilation of, and accommodation to, dominant workplace cultures and ideologies. At its most visible level, this process can be seen in the internalisation of norms and accepted standards of behaviour that occurs in organisational and group socialisation. If consent is not present, pressures to shape ourselves in appropriate images may not be perceived as legitimate, and could promote active resistance. In Westwood's (1984) 'Stitchco' study, women participated in a patriarchal labour process which management viewed as 'harmonious' in its appeals to common, progressive goals and paternalistic values. The women, however, had a 'clear understanding that there were sides in industry and that these sides maintained an uneasy truce which was easily broken' (1984: 25). Westwood argues that the 'deprivation, pain and waste that black and white working class women live with on a daily basis' can be 'a spur to action rather than defeat'. Domination can thus become the source of identity projects empowering creativity and resourcefulness, sisterhood being the focus of resistance that does more than enable survival in a hostile environment.

Of course the contextual issues raised above are not necessarily simply sources of constraint. They may for some be the very factors which allow them to secure identities. Workers with worries over job security may find meaning in defining themselves through nationalist or traditionalist sentiments, giving expression to their fears through hostility to 'immigrant' workers or women who should remain at home. Likewise, hostility and resistance to organisational goals and practices may arise out of the conditions of exploitation, domination and alienation which render others submissive. It would appear that identities are constructed out of whatever meanings and symbolic resources are readily available, and are constrained by the individual's ability to sustain them. Thus the construction of identity is a continuous process that has to be understood in the context of the workplace, where it is maintained and reproduced on a daily basis.

ORGANISATIONS AND IDENTITIES

If society is characterised by the involvement of individuals in organisational structures, then organisations are characterised by their attempts to *control the performance and behaviour* of the individuals of which they consist. It is this rule-bound control of individual behaviour that distinguishes organisational behaviour from other forms of social organisation. Home and family life, for example, are undoubtedly organised, and controls and sanctions are placed on the behaviour of family members. But this control is in no sense as systematic as that existing in even a small commercial organisation. On this basis, for work organisations of any type to maintain their present forms of authority, hierarchy and control, it becomes necessary to produce some kind of change in the types of regulation to which employees will consent.

However, organisations do not simply transform individual identities at work by some form of brainwashing. Neither do they simply depend on individuals' recognition of economic necessity to ensure their consent to the control of their performance in their work. The concept of 'economic man' is not adequate to explain workers' consent to change. Rules and procedures constraining work-related behaviour may conflict with attempts to secure stable and favourable identities. Alternatively, workers could construct viable identities out of the very rules which restrict them, becoming 'organisation men', or setting themselves up in opposition to their employers – or perhaps distancing themselves from the whole affair by concentrating on external interests. Whatever the survival and coping tactics employed by individuals, they may in time transform themselves into an image that functions in a way that is useful to the organisation they work for. Even the 'deviant' or militant worker may provide images of what the 'good' employee *should not be* (see Ackroyd and Thompson, 1999: 21–8, for a discussion), as well as providing a focus for the attribution of blame rather than the appreciation of diversity.

The claims made by Sennett (see above) have parallels with post-structuralist notions that there is no fixed, stable identity and that identity is constructed from dominant discourses, rather than actual and symbolic resources which vary in their availability. According to Thompson and Marks (2007: 1) this is to assume 'a congruence between the identity "needs" of the organisation and the individual'. This may wrongly conflate the notion of organisational identity in terms of public image with the actions of organisational members who construct organisational identities in order to survive their daily workplace experience. We can identify personal, social, collective identities and organisational identities in individuals, but organisations do not have mechanisms for securing identities, just as they cannot learn or have needs or tacit knowledge.

Identity is thus a key basis of individual involvement in organisations and the basis for manipulation achieved through negotiated transactions between organisational strategies of control and individual strategies for securing identity, but to deny agency to individuals in constructing identities is to ignore the choices and calculations inherent in many of the psychological processes people must go through to perceive and utilise the resources they produce identities from. The consequences of this are not always positive for the organisation, and we all have to cope in a creative fashion with the constraints of work or unemployment. Strategies used for survival can become powerful tools for extending our own abilities and capacities. Those who try manipulating our behaviour must face the fact that they are interfering with the self-perceptions and judgements that make us what we are. If manipulation goes too far, it may do no more than encourage employee identities more resistant to organisational control. Feelings of being manipulated could reduce feelings of situational power and lead people to rely on resources that they may have been reluctant to access earlier – union meetings are always better attended when management has pulled yet another stupid stunt.

IDENTITY WORK AND SITUATIONAL POWER

Subjective experience in organisations consists of *lived relationships* bounded by social, organisational and workgroup cultures in the context of structural and ideological constraints. These form the three basic contexts within which individual identity is continually reproduced. Lived relationships are the subjective arena of identity construction. Even though our subjective 'now' is informed by our past experience and moulded by the pressures brought to bear on us, we still act as if we are independent and self-directed entities. Thus our everyday existence can continue as if it largely by-passes the influence of cultural and structural constraints on our behaviour. Thus *situational power* is central to the explanation of organisational behaviour. This is recognised in what Azjen and Madden (1986) term 'perceived behavioural control', which, according to Augoustinos and Walker (1995: 25), links behavioural attitudes and norms in the 'actor's perception of the ease or difficulty of performing the behaviours'. The extent to which we can control our behaviour and estimate our ability to act will determine the kind of strategies available for achieving our personal agendas or identity projects.

Social, organisational and workgroup cultures are, then, the arenas in which 'fitting behaviour' is moulded and regulated and in which we perform *identity work* (Goffman,

1971; Cohen and Taylor, 1978). Just as our perceptions of the world are simplified by the use of stereotypical categories, the activities we carry out in the workplace are simplified by the use of stereotyped categories of behaviour. These various cultural contexts also represent the medium of communication and translation of structural contexts to everyday existence. These are the limiting factors on identity construction in work and social life. They act to define possible sources of meaning and activity in hierarchical organisations and also provide the contextual limitations on what is acceptable practice for those who study, design and intervene in organisations. The element of self- and other regulation in identity work is acknowledged in post-structuralist accounts but is often accompanied by a caveat such as in Alvesson and Willmott (2002, cited in Sturdy et al., 2006: 845) that identity work must also be conceptualised as interpretive activity, which 'refers to people being engaged in forming, repairing, maintaining, strengthening or revising' their personal constructions or narratives (Sveningsson and Alvesson, 2003: 1165)'.

From a social identity theory perspective the main context of identity formation and the enactment of situational power is the group, but it is not simply by declaring oneself a member that a group identity is secured. Kaufman's study of How Working-Class Individuals Construct Middle-Class Identities (2003: 481) notes that, 'Self-avowals are not enough to achieve a desired social identity; rather, individuals must engage in the requisite identity-work activities in order to be successful in social transformation'. Neither is the strength of identification to be taken for granted, as may often be the case in post-structuralist accounts. Reflecting on social identity theory, Thompson and Marks (2007: 8) note that factors such as small group size and group heterogeneity increase identification. From this perspective, the act of self-categorisation itself is evidence that, 'individuals are more than inert receptors of organizational narratives'. Deaux and Martin, 2003) argue that social identification is driven mainly by status but mediated by identification with large-scale categorisations (e.g. race or religion), whereas interpersonal networks are more important drivers of collective identity.

Other factors mediating situational power such as individual and group concerns with job security, status, promotion, conflict and satisfaction, can be characterised under a number of related categories:

- the prediction and control of reality
- coping with uncertainty
- retaining autonomy and discretion
- maintaining or enhancing situational power.

The concern with uncertainty here returns us to the views of Knights and Willmott (1989) and Collinson (2003) which see insecurity and anxiety as the driving force behind an ultimately fruitless search for a secure and stable sense of self. Overall, these concerns represent the tensions created by trying to maintain and monitor the strategies through which we enact behaviours. An identity secure in the ability to control these tensions both forms a bulwark against threats and provides personal standards for social comparison and action. The strategies utilised by individuals and groups to secure or appropriate identity will thus seek to control sources of power and meaning. As a consequence, identity construction may threaten the organisation of work (Knights and Willmott, 1985; Weigert, 1986; Breakwell, 1987). At the same time we must recognise that in focusing on individual insecurity and threat, post-structuralist approaches neglect vital mediating factors, such as unions and professions, of an agency role in securing identities through offering collective resources; it is not after all for nothing that unions and professions are known as identity groups.

Organisational strategy, in trying to reduce uncertainty, is willing to allow room for the maintenance of worker identities insofar as they make the control of behaviour and production processes more effective. In implementing the introduction of computer numerically controlled (CNC) machine tools, firms such as Westland Helicopters allowed an element of manual input from operators on the basis that human intervention is necessary in automated processes because they are not absolutely error-free (Corbett, 1985a). The ubiquity of the modern systems analysts and the all-too-familiar IT help-line attests to the fact that in maintaining computer systems human skill and decision-making is still paramount. Such decisions allow operators to exert some levels of skill and discretion within labour processes that were once seen as increasing tendencies towards deskilling. Thus alongside gains in the reduction of uncertainty in the production process, there may also be benefits to organisations in reducing the level of threat to skilled identities implied by automation of processes and skills.

The greater the effort put into attempts to define employees' work lives, the greater the use of undefined areas by workers to develop 'informal work group cultures'. Cultures of this type can provide workers with a degree of autonomy and a basis for active resistance. By the same token, membership of sub-cultural groups in organisations may provide the same benefits to threatened identities as they do for sub-cultures in wider society: 'the threatened can regain self-esteem, generate positive distinctiveness and promote continuity' (Breakwell, 1986: 141). Although Breakwell argues that societal sub-cultures have virtually no impact on power structures, they are, she maintains, the focus of possible social concerns and the associated 'moral panics' (Cohen, 1973) that identify them as being 'scheduled for control'.

This is not to say that managers never recognise this tendency and take steps to short-circuit the development of informal groups that may become hostile to organisational goals. Drago and McDonough (1984: 67) quote from a management planning document that was part of a 'controlled participation experiment' at the General Food's Topeka plant: 'No power groups will exist within the organisation that create an anti-management posture.' In trying to predict and control reality, it is our subjective concepts and values that are most amenable to change, as we cannot on our own hope to change the structural framework of the organisations within which we work. Even for those with the power to effect change, there is still no absolute security of position or certainty that their actions will produce results fully in line with their projects. Thus, in coping with the uncertainties of organisational life most individuals are forced either into a strategy of accommodation which necessitates a gradual redefinition of self and subjective reality, or a strategy of assimilation which requires these to be subjected to the superordinate identity of the group.

Situational power is likewise implicated in individual and collective resistance to organisational controls. Resistance can be both a source of meaning and a pressure on the security of identity, founded on the perception by individuals of contradictions between the goals, ideologies, approved identities and required behaviours manifested in organisational settings. Leonard (1984: 116–18) identifies four sources of pressures leading to resistance, avoidance and dissent (see Thompson and McHugh 2002, for a wider discussion):

- Contradictory consciousness – results in reactions from deviance or theft to industrial sabotage or 'destructive' actions
- Unconscious resistance – results in reactions from anxiety and frustration to neurosis and psychosis

- The development of individual capacities – reducing alienation through personal activities either within or outside work
- Participation in collective action – enhancing situational power through collective strength and raising of consciousness.

The first two sources are about having one's self redefined by situational and structural pressures, that is, the condition of being subject to. The second two concern redefinitions of self that can counter subordination and are about being an active subject. All four reflect to various extents the forms of coping with stress noted by Moos and Billings (1982). What such pressures do *not* mean is that resistance is inevitable, even though it may be structured into the forms and processes of organisations. Where there are no overt conflicts, it is possibly easier for individuals to accept managerial definitions of reality; to become 'organisation people' and to gain meaning from their appointed roles. It must be remembered, however, that these responses are interdependent processes, which can be conceptually separated, but which are all part of the cycle of organisational control and resistance. In securing and maintaining a stable and meaningful identity, individuals are faced with the difficulty of presenting consistent images to the other people with whom they must deal. When threats arise, they are left with the choice to accommodate or resist. Both involve possibly substantial redefinitions of the identities they have secured. However, just as in the world of fashion or popular music, where people's creative and autonomous control over their own image and expression are eventually incorporated into commercial products, the smart company will incorporate the efforts of individuals to indulge in non-alienated activity into the organisation of the labour process. In the world of the work organisation, the 'revolt into style' may be transformed into the instrumental rewards of the suggestion box as we have already seen with the practices of Knowledge Management.

Impression management and scripting

Before discourse became the dominant explanatory framework, the management of identities had been explored in the tradition of Goffman's (1959) work on *impression management* (IM). Goffman focuses on the presentation of self and coping strategies within identity work, where meaning and status are sought by individuals in the ordering of interaction. The individual, like an actor on stage, attempts to maintain a consistent and believable performance for the audience: those who have a significant influence over the role they play. When used in this sense, identity is malleable and instrumentally defined. However active and manipulative such identities are, they are still dependent on the collaboration of others not to interfere with the performance. We know that the performance of an actor is not real. But according to Goffman we exercise 'tact' to allow the performance to proceed, as in the case of a management 'pep-talk'.

Goffman's *dramaturgical* model (1959, especially chaps 3 and 7) established the basics of informal rules for interaction and the relations between personal and social identity. It makes the distinction between *frontstage* (the arena where the performance is carried out and interaction is primarily with the 'audience' or 'client') and *backstage* where the interaction is primarily with other 'actors' and the 'resources' for performance are created. Goffman essentially sees IM as a form of self-presentation and ongoing self-definition of what he called the *personal front*. It is this personal front which enables us to maintain *inauthentic social relations* with others in order to advance our personal interests while still appearing to exercise normative self-control in both formal and informal groups. A similar notion to personal front used by

Harré is that of *persona*, though this implies more of a conscious choice in selecting appropriate persona than Goffman would admit to. Thompson and Marks (2007: 10) contextualise the personal front within organisational identity by claiming that:

> The front acts as the vehicle of standardisation, allowing others to understand the individual on the basis of projected character traits with normative meanings. As a 'collective representation', the front establishes a proper 'setting,' 'appearance,' and 'manner' for the social role assumed by the actor, uniting interactive behaviour with the personal front. (Goffman, 1959: 27)

Schlenker (1980) had previously tried to reconcile the purposive and passive or reactive aspects of IM when he defined it as 'the conscious or unconscious attempt to control images that are presented in real or imagined social interactions' (cited in Russ, 1991: 220). We should, however, note the caveat that regardless of agency, in using IM, we do not necessarily use it as well as others or rely on it to the same extent; based apparently on our skill at self-monitoring: More recent developments of Goffman's work are noted by Thompson and Marks who argue they:

> have recently emerged in the form of role identity theory (e.g. Thoits and Virshup, 1997) and identity theory (Burke, 1980; Burke and Stets, 2001). Again, role identity theory acknowledges the function of individual interests, in that individuals are perceived as different to other group members with their own duties and resources, when transposed onto the group level, however, there is still the assumption that interests compete, so a negotiation processes is undertaken throughout which the maintenance of the group identity is seen of greater importance than the individual (or indeed, group) interests. (Thompson and Marks, 2007: 11; see also Deaux and Martin, 2003, for a discussion of integrating developments in identity theories)

Thoits and Virshup, 1997 claim that psychological theories of identity cope better than sociological ones with 'conflict between social structures and individuals, and attempts to explain social change' (cited in Deaux and Martin, 2003: 102). Thoits and Virshup refer to identity work as *identity performances*, linking such efforts more closely to IM than is generally the rule in social identity theory. In terms of more traditional OB approaches to IM Giacalone and Rosenfeld's excellent set of readings on *Applied Impression Management* (1991) discusses the widespread and significant implications of IM in areas such as organisational development, careers, appraisal, negotiation and conflict, gender and culture. They also provide useful summaries of the major models of IM. Leary and Kowalski (1991: 87–8) focus on the concepts of *impression motivation*, 'the desire of individuals to generate specific impressions in others' minds in order to maximise social and material outcomes, self-esteem, and/ or cultivate a particular public identity', and of *impression construction*, 'the process of choosing the kind of impression to create and deciding exactly what behaviours would be effective in transmitting such an image'.

Tedeschi and Norman (1991: 105) conceptualise the IM process as a reward exchange where, 'each party is providing reinforcements to the other for his or her ultimate gain'. Baumeister (1991: 197) similarly views the goals of impression management as audience pleasing and constructing the ideal self, particular practices being mediated by normative and cultural pressures. Martinko (1995: 259–77) provides a detailed applied model that, while recognising 'many IM behaviours may be unconscious and unintentional', views IM 'as a systematic and purposive process of behaviour self-management that is both conscious and intentional'. The specific issues Martinko sees as being of future interest to IM are the extent to which IM behaviour is *plastic* or malleable or is conversely located in traits, and thus to what extent we can be trained in IM. Martinko also raises questions of ethics and credibility, individual, group and cultural differences and, perhaps most important of all, raises the relation of IM to self-monitoring as conceptualised by Snyder and Copeland (1985). The Martinko model is essentially prescriptive, but like many such models it acts better as a description of the processes involved than as practical guidance because of the multitude of variables involved.

The extent to which IM works in a practical sense is documented by Baron and Byrne (1997: 67–9), citing experimental studies which stress the importance of other-enhancement (for example, ingratiation; see below) as a key factor in gaining higher performance ratings at work. They also cite evidence (1997: 503–6) pertaining to IM in job interviews, especially with reference to effects of appearance, gender and the role of expectations in interviewer style and behaviour. Arnold and colleagues note the importance of IM as a set of skills in their commentary on Goffman's work (1998: 243–4). Examples of the type of skills and associated contexts involved are in interviewing, testing, communication and presentation. Such techniques are discussed in more detail by Feldman and Klich (1991: 69) who summarise them as:

- Ingratiation: flattery, agreement, doing favours
- Intimidation: veiled threats, appearing dangerous
- Self-promotion: embellishing accomplishments, overstating capabilities
- Exemplification: appearance of dedication or self-sacrifice
- Accounting: denying responsibility, assuaging problems
- Supplication: promoting sympathy, nurturance or allegiance from superiors.

Such *protective* impression management including excuses, apologies and damage control is seen as important by Rosenfeld, Giacolone and Riordan (1995), who cover its measurement and relations to HRM in some detail.

Kunda's study of 'Tech' (1992, chap. 5) also provides numerous and excellent examples of related forms of identity work. These include routine *identity displays* of behaviours which either embrace or distance the worker from organisational roles, and *artefactual displays*, for example, of signs and posters, in personal workspaces which supply the image of 'a strong individual surviving in a hard, competitive, often irrational world' (1992: 196). Artefactual displays are a particular form of *non verbal communication*, which itself is a specific aspect of IM and includes Goffman's notion of *signing* in relation to the tactics and techniques we use to register impressions on others. Both types of display are seen as dramatic performances balancing the display of the successful organisational self with an image of ability to meet organisational concerns, giving oneself some space for manoeuvre.

Such performance may break down in the context of threats and constraints in the work environment, and we may be forced to respond with impressions and performances which are 'out of character' for the expected role. Kunda characterises these as *enlargement dramas*, where in formal or informal circumstances the routine order of role-playing is allowed temporarily to break down, and individuals are allowed to enlarge upon the selves they generally present, exhibiting attitudes or capabilities beyond their required roles. Such dramas are often associated with temporary or marginal members of organisations. Similarly, individuals may experience difficulty in coping with situations where their projected images are not adequate to achieving some measure of control or meaning. For example, Hochschild, in examining the supervision of emotional labour, cites the reaction of a flight attendant whose pay cheque had been mishandled: 'I can't take this all day and then come back here and take it from you! You know I get paid to take it from the passengers, but I don't get paid to take it from you' (1983: 18).

The IM element of Kunda's identity displays is analogous to the *display rules* noted by Mann (1999, see below). These rules are generally organisation-specific, but they can be related to the scripted cultures such as the 'have a nice day' (HAND) culture which, she argues, are spreading out from the service sector. The HAND culture is characterised by the *fast-food server* script which is used by waitresses, shop assistants, receptionists and flight attendants to guide IM and emotional labour to encourage customers to come back. The rules are not, however, homogenous across cultures, the rule about smiling, for example, being contrary to expectations in Japan and some Muslim cultures, though in some Mediterranean cultures such as Greece they are even stronger than in the US/UK (1999: 24–6). The 'have a rotten day' culture, on the other hand, though again familiar from Hochschild's conception of emotional labour, is characterised by the *debt collector* script, where people such as bouncers, security staff and police use displays of anger, irritation or disapproval 'to discourage re-use of the service' (1999: 45). The final script Mann notes is the *lawyer* script characteristic of the 'have a cool day' culture used in many professional and social settings to mask emotions. Doctors, managers and politicians might use this script, which emphasises lack of warmth and emotion, in order to maintain an image of 'detached concern' (1999: 43). The importance of these scripted cultures is both in their integration of IM and emotional labour, and in the extent to which learning them is crucial to the development of careers and the professional identities associated with them. This reaches its zenith in the notion of *personal branding* (Peters, 1997) where the commodification of the self is recommended as the route to career success and requires the careful packaging of identity in IM terms (see Lair, Sullivan and Cheney, 2005 for a further discussion). However, career development is in effect a misnomer for many undertaking routine work in modern occupations. Scripted impression management effectively is the job and the employees are often carrying out *dramaturgical labour* (McHugh, 1997), involving both regulation of their impressions and advocacy for the organisation. Within such strictures, identity work in contexts such as call centres must be carried out in whatever spaces a scripted culture leaves to them. (Callaghan and Thompson, 2002).

Identity working: strategies for organisational survival

With the capacity to redefine meanings and manage impressions, human beings are capable of creating their own self-fulfilling prophecies and self-attributed judgements, shifting the ground on which they stand to justify both success and failure. Indeed strategies of this kind could in one sense be said never to fail entirely. In counterpoint to strategies which lead to negative consequences for the individual, there are forms of making out which can lead more unambiguously to social recognition, approval and self-justified identities. For example, pressure to define identity in line with assumed leadership qualities can lead to subjectively supportive behaviours and self-perceptions. The failure of others to recognise an individual as a leader, or attempts to undermine their leadership, might lead to perceived contradictions with the leader's self-justified role. These could be handled by more autocratic attempts at control, justified by attributions of deviant characteristics to those causing the disturbance. Conversely, if strategies to cope with the situation fail and put the identity of the ostensible leader at risk, he or she could distance him or herself from the role on the basis that dealing with such people was impossible or not worth the effort.

Such strategies are by no means restricted to leadership roles, nor are they simply abstract categories of identity work, but basic strategies of *domination* and *distancing* (Knights and Willmott, 1985) which allow managers or others to ignore the fact that their power is dependent on the compliance of their colleagues or subordinates. Compliance in this sense is related to Rotter's (1972) notion of internal and external *loci of control*. People who feel that they are externally controlled may also put themselves into a state of *learned helplessness*, where the tendency to comply becomes part of the way individuals define themselves (Seligman, 1975).

At the same time, distancing is also one of the main patterns of identity work identified by Cohen and Taylor (1978), whose focus is not on power and interdependence, but rather on 'escape attempts'. Escape from, or resistance to, the mundanity and unpleasantness of everyday life is in this sense crucial to our subjectively 'making out'. However, the strategies they see as employed in identity work can still have relevance to the understanding of how making out is incorporated into the social relations of production. Cohen and Taylor start out at the level of the 'regularities which we happily accept as part of life' (1978: 26). These regularities are not necessarily tedious behavioural repetition, but are scripts to which we *unreflexively accommodate* as a method of managing the 'paramount reality' of our objective world. Scripts in this sense are more than the 'mindless' behaviour posited by Langer or the 'sensorimotor' activity posited by Hacker and Volpert.

The habitual dependence on scripts referred to by Cohen and Taylor can be a defence against uncertainty, as well as providing meaning through their very regularity. However, our capacity for self-reflection allows us to create a *zone for self* or *identity domain* (1978: 32), which enables us to distance ourselves from those who appear to be committed to the scripts by which they live. The capacity to be self-reflexive can effectively remove the need actually to do anything about the conditions of our existence, because we critically separate ourselves from them in our thoughts. At the same time we often deprecate those we see as not having our own level of critical self-awareness, defining them as something less than ourselves. The paradox here is our fellow workers are likely to have the same thoughts about ourselves, since they do not see our thoughts, only our regulated actions and routine behavioural displays.

A concomitant capacity with which self-reflexiveness endows us is the release of the *escape into fantasy* where we can alter the conditions of our life to our own satisfaction. This form of escape is akin to the strategy of unconscious resistance identified by Leonard. Leonard's identification of these escapes with position in the organisational hierarchy can now be understood, in that fantasy is free. Cohen and Taylor also note socially institutionalised routes of escape which are seen as legitimate self-expression, where 'assertions of meaninglessness of the activity are virtually taboo' (1978: 95). These *activity enclaves* give us free areas in our lives, where, in the terminology of Seve and Leonard, we can develop 'personal concrete capacities'. Such socially approved escapes from work or the lack of it include hobbies, games, sports, holidays and the attractions of mass culture.

On the other hand, there are less socially approved activity enclaves which are often viewed as self-obsessive or destructive. 'Preoccupations' with sex, gambling, drugs and even dependence on therapy are examples of this form of escape. They are, however, only different to other forms in terms of the social, legal and historical contexts in which they are carried out. Again self-reflexiveness carries its own internal contradictions. Distancing ourselves from the roles we play is, in the end, another limited and passive strategy which tends to confirm existing organisational structures, separating the individual from the possibilities inherent in social relations.

Finally, to escape from this vicious spiral of making out through reconstruction of identity concerns, Cohen and Taylor identify the strategy of *self-conscious reinvestment*. Individuals become recommitted to aspects of the very regularities – language, rituals, clothing – from which they are escaping. Within work organisations this represents the return to the fold, making something of one's life, or the rescue of career. All of these means of psychic escape can be utilised to further managerial control, either by employees' dependence on the financial and social supports necessary to pursue them or, in the case of reinvestment, the cleaving-back to the very structures of control themselves. For those who run organisations, the problem is to monitor and control the identity work of employees to ensure that they do not overstep the bounds of the acceptable. For the employee, the problem is to discover the appropriate mode of escape, enjoyment and making out for the subjective and objective conditions pertaining at the time. Indeed in the introduction to the second edition of *Escape Attempts* Cohen and Taylor, after trying manfully to come to terms with the post-structuralist appropriation of individual agency and rejection of any paramount reality, conclude that:

> We think now that we should have shown more appreciation of the comic/heroic diversity of people's search for something outside of paramount reality, more recognition of folk wisdom, more sensitivity to the idea that the very activity of 'attempting' to escape is an imaginative way to understand more about the limitations of our world. We would feel less constrained now to explain away the resultant diversity, inventiveness and messiness by appealing to what Rorty calls the 'aesthetic priesthood's' attempt to escape from time and chance. (Cohen and Taylor, 1992: 28)

This recalls our earlier comments that what is important in identity work is how we use the organisation as much as how organisations use us and nowhere is this better exemplified than in the area of managerial identity work.

MANAGERIAL LABOUR AND IDENTITY WORK

Managerial education outside organisations is based on reinforcing the ideological identity work required of managers. The content of managerial education is effectively directed at making concrete the notion that systematic control over complex and variable processes is possible. For managers, the expected rewards in financial and career mobility terms are bought through a process of personal and group identity work. This increases self-perceived competence at handling the contingent uncertainties of organisational life, with the concomitant organisational gains of increased effort and commitment in overcoming goal barriers. Management education can be a means of reinforcing self-image and confidence. In Sturdy and colleagues' terms, the MBA thus becomes: 'a means for acquiring appropriate language fluency in management and the self-confidence to gain legitimacy and social privilege in senior management' (2006: 841), a form of, 'therapeutic language training' (2006, 855).

The form and content of control processes are influenced by the responses of managerial groups to pressures on the identities produced in their role as agents of capital. Mobilising their consent to expose themselves to the threats and pressures of management roles has its own particular place in the labour process. It also underpins the mobilisation of consent of production workers to comply with that supervision:

> Managers, though suffering from frustration and a perceived lack of strategic control, provide operational and systemic flexibility in organisations through

their labour...it is the buffering provided by managerial labour between strategic policies and productive labour itself that is necessary to provide the continuance of structured forms of organising work. (McHugh, 1997: 2)

That changes in the managerial labour process have often fragmented and diminished the power of individual managers (Tuelings, 1986). This will depend, of course, on the position and situational power of the managers involved, but it does point to the fact that managerial work has its own levels of alienation and fragmentation. If this is so, then dominant organisational groups will also expend effort and devise strategies to secure and defend their identities. Hochschild (1993: xi), for example, notes that managers are involved in emotional labour in regulating both their own feelings and those of others. This dual responsibility can have mixed effects, Sturdy and colleagues (2006: 845) noting that:

Sennett (1998) for example, has highlighted the fragility and fragmentation of management identities in conditions of flexibility, downsizing and changing management culture – 'How can a human being develop a narrative of identity and life history in a society composed of episodes and fragments'. (1998: 26; see also Heery and Salmon, 2000; Webb, 2004)

In delineating forms of managerial work, McHugh (1997) argues that managers, as well as being involved in operational, emotional, intellectual and dramaturgical practices, perform attributional labour in regulating and ascribing intent and commitment to themselves and their subordinates. Causal judgement in attributional terms is thus claimed to be a significant factor in managerial versions of impression management and identity work, especially in processes such as performance appraisal and locating the pathology of organisational problems. The implication here is that managerial activity may be derived more from attributions about causes of events than from simple responses to circumstances. As such, there may be a managerial bias to dispositional attributions in defining performance objectives for employees, and an environmental bias in defining such objectives for themselves. At the same time McHugh (1997: 8) cites Leavitt and Bahrami (1988: 65) to the extent that 'managers are both blessed and cursed by that tendency to ascribe causality, because the causality – either way – is often ascribed to them rather than to other aspects of the situation'.

Effective managerial identity work can thus utilise worker resistance and associated damage to productivity and profitability as an ideological justification for managers' own strategies to enhance identity. At the same time, managerial responsibility for shaping the identities and emotions of employees can threaten managers' own identities and emotions. Managers make considerable emotional investments in the design and outcomes of culture change programmes. Yet those programmes tend to be predicated on unrealistic expectations that employees will 'buy into' or 'take ownership' of the objectives and practices. When that does not happen, it is managers who have to carry the 'culture burden' (Thompson and Findlay, 1999). They are caught in the middle between selling the message to the troops and explaining why it is not working to the board. Their identity as effective change agents can be secured only by taking responsibility for redoubling efforts to 'communicate effectively', or alternatively becoming cynical about and partially disengaging from the change process itself.

Managers, may then misbehave in ways that serve their interests at the expense of the organisation, Ackroyd and Thompson (1999) present an analysis of how acting contrary to organisational interests through various categories of misbehaviour produces managerial practice. They look at the factors influencing managerial decisions about and responses to misbehaviour (1999: 81) and the kinds of managerial strategy these are typically related to (1999: 88). Especially important here is the concept of 'controlled autonomy', which is what HRM policies pursue but seldom achieve because of the barriers placed on change, including those of managerial identity. Ackroyd and Thompson offer a useful account of how the dynamics of control act to produce and amplify misbehaviour, adding detail to classic concepts such as the 'vicious spirals' associated with McGregor's Theory X and Y. Though this is schematic and stylised, it does offer insights into the process of control, rather than using control as an abstract determinant concept like authority or power. It also raises the notion of two effects that intensify the 'impulse to control' (1999: 95–6). The first, the measurement effect, is the area in which classic organisational psychology serves managerial strategy in producing technologies of regulation. The second, the innovation effect, where 'increased managerial attention will cause behavioural innovation' (1999: 95). Thus processes of surveillance, environmental scanning and self-monitoring produce new behaviours and practices to identify, subvert and constrain them. Ackroyd and Thompson thus provide linkages from managerial labour and identity work to specific psychological processes such as learning, group dynamics and attribution.

SUMMARY AND KEY POINTS

Identity work is conscious and unconscious, individual and collective, competitive and collaborative. It is the vehicle of self-expression and enactment, and at the same time binds us to systems of ideological self-legitimation through which we accede to systems of control, both internal and external. The networks we access and the roles we are expected to take on in the workplace provide the scripts, our interactions and negotiations with others the arena in which we act them out. It appears that what we strive towards in producing consistent role performances and in maintaining a secure identity is a situation where we do not have to negotiate who and what we are with others, where our concerns, actions and status are automatically legitimate. In this sense, identity work is the medium through which we express power over ourselves, others and situations.

We buy into systems of control in order to increase our situational power, and at the same time we resist pressures to make us completely controlled by our role and the demands of others. In many ways identity work is the primary work of organising, if not of organisations themselves. As such, it must also be the primary work of those who structure the processes of organising towards corporate ends. One appeal of management, beyond the extrinsic rewards, is that just being a manager automatically affirms and protects identity, at the expense of diminishing the manager's capacity to resist the role demands the position confers. The manager as a communicator of role demands has in effect committed him- or herself to controlling the identity work of others, which in turn commits him or her to one or another form of response to such pressures.

It is through identity work that the conditions of being a subject and of being subject gain substance for managers and workers alike. The negotiation and pursuit of identity concerns and projects make up the drama of everyday organisational experience. As we have seen, the psychological processes underwriting that drama cannot give an adequate account of it in purely mechanistic terms. Neither, though, can interpretative or structural accounts afford to ignore the influence those processes have on us in our journey to becoming fully-fledged participants in the modern work organisation.

FURTHER READING

Ostensibly there should be a myriad of further readings on this topic, the problem being that the very amount of work now extant on identity tends to confuse the issue, especially in terms of the alternative readings available in post-structuralist accounts. For example, the collection by Pullen, Beech and Sims (2007) has the worthy and the obfuscating in equal measure in Part 1, though Part 2 on methods is a very good resource for anyone interested in researching identity. The approach we have taken in this edition is informed in detail by Thompson and Marks' (2007) ILPC paper on the 'Blank Slate'; to follow up on the issues raised there see Webb's (2006) sociological text and Leidner's (2006) paper. Knippenberg and Schie's (2000) paper provides a useful psychological perspective though in socio-psychological terms it is still worthwhile to go back to Breakwell's (1992) text, which is still available. If you want a rewarding read in the area then go back to Goffman's *Presentation of Self* which is still a staple for social psychology students. And last but not least, Cohen and Taylor's *Escape Attempts* is a much more wide-ranging exposition than the narrow focus we have portrayed here.

Breakwell, G.M. (1992) *Social Psychology of Identity and the Self Concept*, Guildford: Surrey University Press in association with Academic Press.

Cohen, S. and Taylor, L. (1992) *Escape Attempts: The Theory and Practice of Resistance to Everyday Life* (2nd edn), London and New York: Routledge.

Goffman, E. (1959) *The Presentation of Self in Everyday Life*, Garden City, NY: Doubleday.

Knippenberg, D.V. and Schie, E.C.M.V. (2000) 'Foci and Correlates of Organisational Identification', *Journal of Occupational and Organisational Psychology*, 73: 137–47.

Leidner, R. (2006) 'Identity and Work', in M. Korczynski, R. Hodson and P. Edwards (eds.), *Social Theory at Work*, Oxford: Oxford University Press, 424–63.

Pullen, A., Beech, N. and Sims, D. (2007) *Exploring Identity: Concepts and Methods*, London: Palgrave Macmillan.

Thompson, P. and Marks, A. (2007) 'Beyond the Blank Slate: Towards an Understanding of the Formation of Identities and Interests in the Employment Relationship', International Labour Process Conference.

Webb, J. (2006) *Organisations, Identities and the Self*, London: Palgrave Macmillan.

REFERENCES

Ackroyd, S. and Thompson, P. (1999) *Organisational Misbehaviour*, London: Sage.

Ainsworth, S. and Hardy, C. (2004) 'Discourse and Identities', in D. Grant, C. Hardy, C. Oswick and L. Putnam (eds), *Handbook of Organizational Discourse*, London: Sage.

Alvesson, M. (2007) Shakers, Strugglers, Story-tellers, Surfers and Others, Paper presented to Research Workshop, University of New South Wales, March.

Alvesson, M. and Willmott, H. (2002) 'Identity Regulation as Organizational Control – Producing the Appropriate Individual', *Journal of Management Studies*, 39(5): 619–44.

Augoustinos, M. and Walker, I. (1995) *Social Cognition: An Integrated Approach*, London: Sage.

Azjen, I. and Madden, T. J. (1986) 'Prediction of Goal-Related Behaviour: Attitudes, Intentions, and Perceived Behavioural Control', *Journal of Experimental Social Psychology*, 22: 453–74.

Baron, R. A. and Byrne, D. (1997) *Social Psychology* (8th edn), Needham Heights, MA: Allyn & Bacon.

Breakwell, G. M. (1986) *Coping with Threatened Identities*, London: Methuen.

Breakwell, G. M. (1987) 'Identity', in H. Beloff and A. M. Colman (eds), *Psychology Survey 1987*, Leicester: British Psychological Society.

Callaghan, G. and Thompson, P. (2002) 'We Recruit Attitude: The Selection and Shaping of Call Centre Labour', *Journal of Management Studies*, 39. 2: 233–254.

Cohen, S. (1973) *Folk Devils and Moral Panics*, London: Paladin.

Cohen, S. and Taylor, L. (1978) *Escape Attempts : The Theory and Practice of Resistance to Everyday Life*, Harmondsworth: Pelican.

Cohen, S. and Taylor, L. (1992) *Escape Attempts: The Theory and Practice of Resistance to Everyday Life* (2nd edn), London and New York: Routledge.

Collinson, D. (2003) 'Identities and Insecurities: Selves at Work', *Organization*, 10. 3: 385–409.

Corbett, J. M. (1985a) 'The Design of Machine-Tool Technology and Work: Technical Science and Technical Choice', unpublished draft, Sheffield: MRC/ESRC Social and Applied Psychology Unit.

Deaux, K. and Martin, D. (2003) 'Interpersonal Networks and Social Categories: Specifying Levels of Context in Identity Processes', *Social Psychology Quarterly*, 66. 2: 101–117.

Drago, R. and McDonough, T. (1984) 'Capitalist Shopfloor Initiatives, Restructuring and Organising in the '80s', *Review of Radical Political Economics*, 716. 4: 52–77.

Feldman, D. C. and Klich, N. R. (1991) 'Impression Management and Career Strategies', in R. A. Giacolone and P. Rosenfeld (eds), *Applied Impression Management: How Image-Making Affects Managerial Decisions*, Newbury Park, CA: Sage.

Giddens, A. (1990) *The Consequences of Modernity*, Cambridge: Polity Press.

Goffmann, E. (1959) *The Presentation of Self in Everyday Life*, New York: Doubleday Anchor.

Goffman, E. (1971) *The Presentation of Self in Everyday Life*, Harmondsworth: Pelican.

Hearn, J. and Parkin, W. (1987) *Sex at Work: The Power and Paradox of Organisation Sexuality*, Brighton: Wheatsheaf.

Heery, E. and Salmon, J. (eds) (2000) *The Insecure Workforce*, London: Routledge.

Hochschild, A. R. (1993) 'Preface' to S. Fineman (ed.), *Emotion in Organizations*, London: Sage.

Jenkins, R. (1986) *Racism and Recruitment: Managers, Organisations and Equal Opportunities in the Labour Market*, Cambridge: Cambridge University Press.

Knights, D. and Willmott, H. (1985) 'Power and Identity in Theory and Practice', *Sociological Review*, 33. 1: 22–46.

Knights, D. and Willmott, H. (1989) 'Power and Subjectivity at Work: From Degradation to Subjugation in Social Relations', *Sociology*, 23. 4: 535–58.

Lair, D. J., Sullivan, K. and Cheney, G. (2005) 'Marketization and the Recasting of the Professional Self: The Rhetoric and Ethics of Personal Branding', *Management Communication Quarterly*, 18. 3: 307–43.

Leavitt, H. J. and Bahrami, H. (1988) *Managerial Psychology: Managing Behaviour in Organizations* (5th edn), Chicago: University of Chicago Press.

Leidner, R. (2006) 'Identity and Work', in M. Korczynski, R. Hodson and P. Edwards (eds), *Social Theory at Work*, Oxford: Oxford University Press.

Leonard, P. (1984) *Personality and Ideology: Towards a Materialist Understanding of the Individual*, London: Macmillan.

Lewis, M. (1975) 'Early Sex Differences in the Human: Studies of Socioemotional Development', *Archives of Sexual Behaviour*, 4. 4: 329–35.

McHugh, D. (1997) 'Self-Serving Bias: The Attribution of Cause as a Significant Form of Managerial Labour', paper presented to the 15th International Labour Process Conference, Edinburgh University, March.

Martinko, M. J. (ed.) (1995) *Attribution Theory: An Organisational Perspective*, Delray Beach, FL: St Lucie.

Miller, D. R. (1963) 'The Study of Social Relationships: Situations, Identities and Social Interaction', in S. Koch (ed.), *Psychology: A Study of a Science*, vol. 5, New York: McGraw-Hill.

Moos, R. H. and Billings, A. G. (1982) 'Conceptualizing and Measuring Coping Resources and Processes', in L. Goldberger and S. Bresnitz (eds), *Handbook of Stress: Theoretical and Clinical Aspects*, New York: The Free Press, pp. 212–30.

Nkomo, S. M. and Cox, T. Jr (1999) 'Diverse Identities in Organisations', in S. Clegg, C. Hardy and W. R. Nord (eds), *Managing Organizations: Current Issues*, Sage, London, pp. 88–103.

Peters, T. (1997) *The Brand Called You*, available at http://www.transformingmlm.com/resources/Brandcalledyou.pdf.

Rosenfeld, P., Giacolone, R. A. and Riordan, C. A. (1995) *Impression Management in Organizations*, London: Routledge.

Rotter, J. B. (1972) 'Generalised Expectancies for Internal versus External Control of Reinforcement', in J. B. Rotter, J. E. Chance and E. J. Phare (eds), *Applications of a Social Learning Theory of Personality*, New York: Holt, Rinehart & Winston.

Russ, G. S. (1991) 'Symbolic Communication and Image Management in Organizations', in R. A. Giacolone and P. Rosenfeld (eds), *Applied Impression Management: How Image-Making Affects Managerial Decisions*, CA: Sage.

Schlenker, B. R. (1980) *Impression Management*, Monterey: Brooks/Cole.

Seligman, M. E. P. (1975) *Helplessness*, San Francisco: Freeman.

Sennett, R. (1998) *The Corrosion of Character: The Personal Consequences of Work in the New Capitalism*, London: W. W. Norton.

Sturdy, A., Brocklehurst, M., Winstanley, D. and Littlejohns, M. (2006) 'Management as a (Self) Confidence Trick: Management Ideas, Education and Identity Work', *Organization*, 13. 6, 1 November: 841–60.

Sveningsson, S. and Alvesson, M. (2003) 'Managing Managerial Identities: Organizational Fragmentation, Discourse and Identity Struggle', *Human Relations*, 56. 10: 1163–94.

Tajfel, H. and Turner, J. C. (1979) 'An Integrative Theory of Intergroup Conflict', in W. G. Austin and S. Worschel (eds), *The Social Psychology of Intergroup Relations*, Monterey, CA. Brooks-Cole.

Teulings, A. (1986) 'Managerial Labour Processes in Organised Capitalism: The Power of Corporate Management and the Powerlessness of the Manager', in D. Knights and H. Willmott (eds), *Managing the Labour Process*, Aldershot: Gower.

Thompson, P. and Findlay, T. (1999) 'Changing the People: Social Engineering in the Contemporary Workplace', in A. Sayer and L. Ray (eds), *Culture and Economy after the Cultural Turn*, London: Sage.

Thompson, P. and McHugh, D. (2002) *Work Organisations* (3rd edn), Basingstoke: Palgrave Macmillan.

Thompson, P. and Marks, A. (2007) 'Beyond the Blank Slate: Towards an Understanding of the Formation of Identities and Interests in the Employment Relationship', International Labour Process Conference.

Turner, J. C. (1985) 'Social Categorization and the Self-Concept: A Social-Cognitive Theory of Group Behaviour', in E. J. Lawler (ed.), *Advances in Group Process: Theory and Research,* vol. 2, Greenwich, C T: JAI.

Webb, J. (2004) 'Organizations, Self-Identities and the New Economy', *Sociology*, 38. 4: 719–38.

Webb, J. (2006) *Organisations, Identities and the Self*, Basingstoke: Palgrave Macmillan.

Weigert, A. J., Smith Teitge, J. and Teitge, D. W. (1986) *Society and Identity: Towards a Sociological Psychology*, New York: Cambridge University Press.

Westwood, S. (1984) *All Day, Every Day: Factory and Family in the Making of Women's Lives*, London: Pluto.

Wexler, P. (1983) *Critical Social Psychology*, Boston, MA: Routledge & Kegan Paul.

INDEX